Scheherazade's Feasts

Scheherazade's Feasts

Foods of the Medieval Arab World

Habeeb Salloum
Muna Salloum
Leila Salloum Elias

PENN
University of Pennsylvania Press
Philadelphia

Book designed by Elizabeth M. Glover

Published by
UNIVERSITY OF PENNSYLVANIA PRESS
Philadelphia, Pennsylvania 19104-4112
www.upenn.edu/pennpress

Printed in the United States of America on acid-free paper

10 9 8 7 6 5 4 3 2 1

Library of Congress Cataloging-in-Publication Data
Salloum, Habeeb.
Scheherazade's Feasts : Foods of the Medieval Arab World / Habeeb Salloum, Muna Salloum, and Leila Salloum Elias. — 1st ed.
p. cm.
Includes bibiographical references and index.
ISBN 978-0-8122-4477-9 (hardcover : alk. paper)
1. Cooking, Arab. 2. Food habits—Arab countries. 3. Cooking, Medieval. I. Elias, Leila Salloum. II. Salloum, Muna. III. Title.
TX725.A65S25 2013
641.5917'4927dc23 201233431

We dedicate this book to Freda Abu Rizk (Bourzk) Salloum.

Wife of Habeeb and mother of Muna and Leila, she was the inspiration behind our drive to write about and re-create recipes from the medieval Arab past. Freda believed in continuing the traditions of old Damascus, who learned from her mother the continuing traditions of cooking, its techniques, its secrets, and its flavors. It was a rich culinary heritage that Freda firmly believed should be presented and recorded for the future. Unexpectedly, she left, but within each page, each recipe, and each ingredient, she remains, for it was Freda who taught us that love is the most important ingredient of life and whose life and traditions inspired this writing. And it was she who urged us to dedicate this book to her most precious grandchildren, Laith, Mazin, Jinaan, and Shaadi, and to her great-grandsons, Bilal and Tamer, who were to be born after her passing. For it was Freda who said, for the love of their heritage and with our past, we give you our future to pass on.

Contents

Note on Translation

We decided to translate rather rigidly from the Arabic to the English to show the reader the many instances of difficult interpretation regarding amounts, cooking methods, and ambiguous instructions. Many times pronouns proved to be the problem when trying to distinguish the ingredient to which the author was referring. We felt that the reader should experience the same situation the authors initially came across when translating and redacting.

Of course, we could have provided a much clearer translation, but this would take away from the flavor of the original.

Concerning the recipes from al-Baghdādī's *Kitāb al-Ṭabīkh*, although we used the 1934 Arabic text edited by al-Jalabī as the base of our translations, we did incorporate those corrections made by Perry in his *A Baghdad Cookery Book*.

Introduction

Muḥammad ibn al-Ḥasan al-Baghdādī, author of the thirteenth-century cookbook *Kitāb al-Ṭabīkh*, determined the classes of pleasure in life to be wit, drink, food, clothes, sex, scent, and sound. But it was the pleasure of food that al-Baghdādī found foremost, without which none of the others could be enjoyed.

The love of gastronomy in the medieval Arabic world gave rise to a mass of prose and verse by writers infatuated with the beauty, sensual appearance, and perfumed aura of certain dishes. At the hands of a poet, a dessert becomes an object of desire. Al-Rūmī's passion for almond fingers (*lawzīnaj*) resonates as he notes "the mere sight of them excites admiration and delight," while Aḥmad ibn Yaḥyà declares that the pleasure of eating the filled pancakes known as *qaṭā'if* may be compared to the joy of ʿAbbās when he became Caliph. With rhythmic wonder, these writers extol the virtues of their preferred edible delights. If they are among the most articulate commentators on the food and foodways of the medieval Arabic world, they are far from idiosyncratic in their passion.

From the seventh to the thirteenth centuries, the Muslims developed an opulent cuisine in their lands, from the borders of China in the east to the Iberian Peninsula in the west. For the common folk who ate their rice, lentils, wheat, and chickpeas daily at home, there was no need to record recipes; their foodways were based on oral tradition, passed on from generation to generation according to time and environment. Elaborate culinary preparations were left to those who had the time and means for them. Proud of their creativity and adventurous in their borrowing of foods and dishes from the societies they encountered and with which they lived, the Arabs set their culinary delights down in writing and wrote books glorifying the art of cooking and the use of a multitude of ingredients. The sources that have come down to us, then, overwhelmingly reflect the eating habits of the royal courts and urban upper classes. It is primarily from four centers—Baghdad and Aleppo under the Abbasids (750–1258), Cairo under the Fatimids (909–1170), Córdoba under the Umayyads (756–1031), and *Mulūk al-Ṭawāʾif* (the Petty Kingdoms) of al-Andalus of the later eleventh century—that the culinary literature reaches us today.

By the ninth century, Baghdad, the capital of the Abbasid era, drew in masses of peoples involved in various trades, professions, academic pursuits, and artistic fields. All brought with them the techniques of their own local or regional cooking traditions. The city to which they came was described as a "paradise on earth," replete with orchards and gardens, lush vegetation, palatial edifices, and learning centers. Over the course of the coming centuries, the population would grow to somewhere between a half million and a million persons, all naturally needing to be fed. With its multitude of inhabitants of various ethnicities, the food culture of Baghdad evolved richly and rapidly.

The availability of edible goods will always affect a culture's cuisine, and the greater the variety of products within reach, the greater the impetus to create and experiment. The cooks of Baghdad, wanting to impress, would compete with others to see who could make which dish better. There were, however, critics of such heightened culinary activity. The Arab historian Ibn Khaldūn (d. 1406) wrote that too much food and the moisture in it instigate the production of excessive destructive substances that eventually "produce a disproportionate widening of the body, as well as many corrupt, putrid humours," resulting in "a pale complexion and an ugly figure" (65). Furthermore, persons living in fertile areas where agricultural products are many, animal husbandry prolific, and herbs, spices, and fruits abundant, are inclined to being "stupid in mind and coarse in body" (66). Ibn Khaldūn also believed that the effect of abundance on the body even influences matters of religion and divine worship. Those who inhabit the desert live frugally, having adapted themselves to hunger and abstinence. They are the people who are more religious and more prepared for worship of God, completely contrary to those who live in settled areas accustomed to luxury and abundance (66–67). One Arab, ʿAwf ibn al-Qaʿqāʿ, looked upon a *mawlà* (a non-Arab Muslim) of Persian origin with disdain because this client preferred his own Persian food to that of the Arabs. So it was that the Persian issued a warning to his own people that the Arab "soft life of affluence would turn them lax and corrupt, and to open a door to a life of luxury would do them more harm than locking a door to excess of pleasures" (*al-Bukhalāʾ* 74–75).

But luxury, or at least abundance, was at hand.

In the medieval period vegetable and fruit stands in the many Arab cities and towns would have provided both fresh and processed ingredients for preparing meals. In the *Kanz al-Fawāʾid fī Tanwīʿ al-Mawāʾid* (*The Treasure of the Benefits in the Varieties of the Dining Table*), an early culinary compendium, we read of the availability of ground or crushed chickpeas in the souk; the author advises that it is better to choose, shell, and crush them one's self, and to rub them with good oil and add saffron as needed (10). But eating-places that offered ready-to-eat or made-to-order fare also filled the souks. It would have been no more unusual for a ninth-century Baghdadi to purchase take-out nut- or cheese-filled *qaṭāʾif,* simmering in a hot and sweet rosewater or orange blossom water-based syrup, than it is for the modern consumer in any Arab city of the East. Similarly, the description in early medieval literature of the aroma of freshly grilled meats dripping in fat emanating from the souks resonates in our own time: the succulent smells of lamb, beef, and chicken shawarma, kebabs, kaftas, and shish kebab enhanced with pomegranate syrup and a multitude of spices have become recognized as the fast foods of the Arab world.

By the fourteenth century, there were a great number of souks on the eastern side of Baghdad, the largest and most organized being the *Sūq al-Thulathāʾ,* in which, the chronicler Ibn Baṭṭūṭah tells us, everything was available (225). Many found the souks' places to eat highly attractive. The service was quick and the food tasty. Thus, the choice made in the literary work of Hamadhānī (967–1007), in his tale of the *Maqāmah* of Baghdad, is not surprising: when ʿĪsà ibn Hishām invites a friend to eat and offers him either a home-cooked meal or food from the souk, the two end up opting for the latter.

Food that was popular among the working classes or peasants would be reintroduced on the tables of middle-class merchants or at the opulent feasts of rulers, the latters' version altered by the addition of more expensive ingredients. The common sweet *hays*, for example, originally made with bread crumbs and dates, is described in the elite culinary sources as requiring pistachios, almonds, and spices as well. Most often, however, it was from the court of the caliph that gastronomic fashion emanated. Baghdad was in many respects an agricultural city, attached to a verdant hinterland in which the basic staples and much of gastronomic refinement could grow. Yet commercial ties with urban centers and countries throughout and beyond the Caliphate were increasingly cultivated in order to bring in the new and additional foodstuffs necessary to satisfy aristocratic tastes and desires. Baghdad would serve as the key site for their diffusion.

It was during the time of Abbasid Iraq that various food and fiber crops, especially from India, first arrived and settled in the eastern part of the Arab world before spreading west to al-Andalus. Contractual agreements between merchants and their agents proliferated. In Baghdad's food markets, stocked with local and imported fruits and vegetables, one would find apples, pomegranates, apricots, and a pure and very sought-after olive oil from Syria. From Kufa came oils made from the essence of violets and roses; Yemen and Isfahan provided saffron; honey arrived from Mosul; Tabaristan's juicy citrus fruits were in demand; currants from Herat arrived in loads; cane sugar, an important commodity for Baghdad's delectable sweets, came in from Ahwaz, salted fish and buttermilk from Khwarizm; India provided cloves, spikenard, and nutmeg; Nishapur sent quinces; figs were the main import from Hulwan; and succulent pears arrived in boxed bundles from Nahavand. Stories from the eleventh-century *One Thousand and One Arabian Nights* describe the bounty of Baghdad's souks: Shāmi (Syrian) apples, Osmani (Turkish or Ottoman) quinces, peaches from Oman, cucumbers grown in the Nile, Egyptian limes, Sultani oranges and citrons, and jasmine grown in Aleppo.

As is the case today, however, weather conditions, natural disasters, or a lack of laborers could affect the availability and price of goods. One writer laments of prices on the road to Mecca so high that a *raṭl* of bread cost one *dirham* when normally it would have cost only a half (al-Ṭabarī XXXIV 6). Another tells of a great famine in 915 occurring in al-Andalus, the likes of which had never been recorded. In that year, the price for a *cafiz* (a dry measure) of wheat had risen in the souk of Córdoba to 3 *dīnār*s; by the time of the famine of 1113, the price of wheat would reach 15 *dīnārs* a bushel (Ibn Ḥayyān 383; ʿIdhārī II 167–68).

As the eastern Arabs moved west to settle in North Africa and the Iberian Peninsula, they brought with them the qualities and features that made civilization flourish in Damascus and Baghdad. From the eighth century on, the Arabs of Iberia lived in a kind of place not found north of the Pyrenees. By the tenth century, when fewer than 40,000 people lived in Paris, the Córdoba of the Moors is said to have boasted a population of half a million. We also read that it had lighted streets, libraries with hundreds of thousands of volumes, some seven hundred mosques, and nine hundred public baths. The homes of the wealthy had fountains, plumbing, and running water. Learning in the fields of the life and physical sciences, mathematics, literature, philosophy, music, architecture, and cuisine flourished. And of course, this large and sophisticated population needed to be fed.

Many of the dishes and ingredients that traveled with the Arabs to al-Andalus remained much as they had been at home. Others were transformed using the ingredients available in the regions where they now became popular, and when the Andalusian Arabs wrote their cookbooks, they identified the foods that originated in the eastern part of the Arab world and those that developed in the West. The irrigation projects of the Arabs transformed the Iberian countryside, and many crops—beans of several kinds, endives, spinach, chard, radishes, leeks, carrots, celery, onions, eggplant, and artichokes—grew abundantly. Wheat fields and olive groves were expanded; lemon trees were cultivated under improved watering systems and care; and bitter oranges, cherries, apples, pears, and figs were grown. Vineyards proliferated, and a variety of a seedless grape known as *corinto* was used to produce the Arab syrup called *rubb,* employed in the same way as honey, or, when mixed with water, made into a drink still found today in Spain under the name *arrope.* Grapes, consumed popularly as fresh fruit, were also turned to raisins, wine, and vinegar and were dried for use in cooking. Indeed, these Moors of al-Andalus introduced culinary practices that were to change the eating habits of the rest of Europe.

Abū al-Ḥasan ʿAlī ibn Nāfiʿ, a famous and extremely talented musician from Baghdad and better known by his nickname Ziryāb, Arabic for "blackbird," arrived in Córdoba under the patronage of the Andalusian *Amīr* ʿAbd al-Raḥmān II (r. 822–852). The musician and poet became a minister of culture, an arbiter of fashion and taste; it is said that Ziryāb's influence is felt to this day, especially in music and food. One might say that prior to his arrival in al-Andalus in 822, there had been no style in food presentation since the days of the Roman Empire. Ziryāb changed that. He brought with him dishes from his native Baghdad and introduced fine tablecloths and glassware, eating utensils, and kitchen gadgets. It is reported that he brought, too, a new order of serving food for the table: the Arab elite now sat to dine beginning with soups or broths, followed by cold dishes and entrées, and then, finally, fruits, desserts, and mixtures of nuts. A century before, the physician Jibrāʾīl ibn Bukhtīshūʿ had advised that sweets be taken after a meal (al-Rāghib al-Aṣbahānī II 619). Now, the order by which dishes were presented according to their classification became established in Andalusia and spread across the Pyrenees. It remains the standard order of the meal that we follow today.

The fabulous monuments left by the Arabs in Andalusia—the Alhambra in Granada, the *Mezquita* in Córdoba—remain for the eye to behold, but the strength of their presence also remains in the food of Spain and the language used to describe it. Witness the hundreds of Spanish words of Arabic origin related to agriculture, fruits, vegetables, and spices: *azúcar*, sugar, directly from the Arabic, *al-sukkar*; *azahar*, orange blossom, from *al-zahar*; *azafrán,* saffron, from *al-zaʿfarān*. But it is perhaps in its sweets that the Iberian Peninsula especially retains its seven centuries of Arab culinary heritage. The legacy of the Arabs continues to be revealed in sumptuous desserts flavored with rose water, anise seed, cinnamon, sesame, and ground almonds and soaked in honey. The famous marzipan cookies of Spain, formed in various shapes and made only from almond paste and sugar, are perhaps the most important contribution of the Arabs. Marzipan has been made in Toledo since the eighth century, stuffed with pine nuts or egg yolks crystallized in sugar. In Rioja, one adds lemon, while in Andalusia, marzipan comes in the shape of bars stuffed with crystallized fruits and iced with sugar.

The Arabs occupied Sicily from 827 to 1091, and enjoyed there the citrus fruits they cultivated on a wide scale. Orchards of lemon (Italian *limone* and Arabic *līmūn* or *laymūn*) and orange (Italian *arancia*, Arabic *al-nāranj*) were to be found in all parts of the island. Today, they are so widespread that the aroma of their flowers, which still carry an Arabic name, *zagara*, from *zahr,* hovers over every path and road.

The Arab domination of Malta (870–1060) left its mark on that island's cuisine too. Many of Malta's food and cooking terms continue to carry their Arabic names: eggs are *bajd*, from Arabic *bayḍ*; *ftira*, a type of bread, goes back to Arabic *faṭīrah*; *gbejniet*, cheese, to Arabic *jubn*.

The creation of food cannot be confined to the kitchen, and from the tenth century on a flurry of agricultural manuals and botanical and geographical works appeared all over the Muslim world. These texts[1] detail methods for cultivating fruit trees. They describe the effects of temperature and winds on crops; controls against pests and diseases; how to fertilize the soil; plowing methods; preparations for harvesting and threshing; and studies of rice, corn, and pulses.

Herbs and spices became the subjects of industrious experimentation. The Umayyads, the first Muslim dynasty (661–750), had made use of robust spices to render their dishes more appetizing, and in later eras the Abbasids became known for their extensive use of mixed spices and seasonings. Expertise in the use of the correct spices is, as the thirteenth-century *Anonymous Andalusian Cookbook* (*Kitāb al-Ṭabīkh fī al-Maghrib wa al-Andalus fī ʿAṣr al-Muwaḥḥidīn*) explains, the foundation on which cuisine is built, distinguishing good food both for flavor and for the benefits to the body. The influx of new edibles and the introduction of new dishes were major factors in developing more studies on dietetics and health and in what and how one ate or drank.

Specialists wrote medical treatises on diet, and dietetic manuals on healthy living, such as the great works of the eleventh-century Ibn Jazlah (known in Latin as Gege), could also be read as cookbooks. If it was the physician who would diagnose the illness, it was the cook who must understand humoral theory, since hygiene and dietary regimen were considered the sources of good health. Reasons were given why specific foods or dishes should be eaten in summer or winter, or to alleviate an illness. *Lawzīnaj* was good for loosening phlegm. Beef was to be avoided because of its heaviness on the digestive system, lamb being the more salubrious meat.

Keeping nutrition and health in mind, the Abbasids were creative in their meals. Most of their caliphs were known for continuing the tradition of maintaining personal physicians at their table as they ate, heeding their advice and supervision in consuming certain prepared dishes. Hārūn al-Rashīd (r. 786–809), for example, would not take his meals unless in the presence of his personal physician, Jibrāʾīl ibn Bukhtīshūʿ (Ibn Abī Uṣaybiʿah 475–76). It is said that once the caliph was sitting at his dining table, ready to begin his meal, and called for his physician. When Ibn Bukhtīshūʿ could not be found, Hārūn al-Rashīd immediately ordered a house-to-house search, and only when the physician arrived could the meal begin.

Accounts proliferate of caliphs, emirs, and governors who would not take a meal unless a doctor was beside them. It is said that the tenth-century Buwayhid emir ʿAḍud al-Dawlah would not eat unless a doctor was next to him to answer queries as to what was nutritious and what was not. The governor of North Africa in the early ninth century, Ziyādah Allāh ibn al-Aghlab, would follow his physician's advice to a tee, abiding by all his instructions. Isḥāq ibn ʿUmrān, the physician, would tell the governor, "Eat this, don't eat that," and al-Aghlab would obey (Ibn Abī Uṣaybiʿah 478).

Thus, it is not completely implausible that the tenth-century *Amīr* Sayf al-Dawlah al-Ḥamadhāni, ruler of Aleppo, would gather 24 physicians at his dining table, among them his personal physician, ʿĪsà al-Raqqī. If the number is an exaggerated one, it nevertheless confirms the importance of medical advice in choosing what to consume and what to avoid in the medieval Arab world. A proverbial saying concluded that the best medicine was to take the hand away from the food while still craving it (Ibn ʿAbd Rabbih VI 304).

A culture that values refined cuisine concerns itself with matters of etiquette as well, and instructions or descriptive essays on the manners at the table expected of upper gentry appear in culinary, travel, and historical texts of the Golden Era of the Arab-Muslim world. So, for example, in one book on misers, the author lambasts those who lack etiquette and offers specific epithets for those who do wrong with kitchen and table manners. Another book on misers and avarice includes an attack on those who snatch food off a table like a falcon seizing and an eagle swooping, without any friendly familiarity and pleasantries beforehand (*al-Bukhalāʾ* 58). It was the custom of Hārūn al-Rashīd, we read, to send for companions and for a number of cultured men so as to pass the evening in conversation and repast (al-Ṭabarī XXXIV 14). The practice of conversing at the dining table in Abbasid courts, however, was in complete contrast to the scene in the Persian Sassanid court, where no one would speak until the food was removed from the table (*Tāj* 18).

Hygiene, food ornamentation, and table manners were all considered matters of basic necessity in medieval Arab culinary and medical treatises. Chapters are devoted to how pots, casseroles, and other vessels and cooking utensils need to be completely cleaned; the various pots and pans required for cooking specific dishes; the color scheme to make a serving table appeal to its guests; and various specifics on how to eat or decorate certain foods. One caliph's banquet, it is said, included attractive women forming themselves into a fountain from which wine flowed into a basin below for the service of the guests (Berriedale-Johnson 22).

The tenth-century writer al-Warrāq tells the story of a sultan's chef who prepared a dish of the stew known as *sikbāj* for a group of men who regularly met to play chess. The meal was a great success, but the taste was different from that to which they were accustomed. They asked the cook what the secret was to making such a tasty and succulent variety of *sikbāj*. The cook explained that there is no difference between what is served on a royal table and what is served on other tables except for the cleanliness of the food and the cleanliness of the cooking pots, washed before and immediately after use (al-Warrāq 9).

Manuals are explicit in their descriptions of the great range of kitchen utensils required for cooking and the science and art of their care. Al-Warrāq, for example, expounds on the necessity of using new pots for the preparation of dishes in order to attain the purity of flavors. Al-Baghdādī advises that previously used cooking vessels should be washed and then beaten with brick dust, then with potash and dried rose petals, perfuming them then with mastic and galangal (8). The *Kanz* recommends that a washed pot be rubbed with citron and orange leaves (5).

Such is the importance of clean cooking utensils that it pervades the texts of many of the medieval cookbooks, but instructions are equally clear about the importance of the cleanliness of the cook: the person responsible in any kitchen should have short nails, and hands should be washed frequently before and after the meal (this rule applying to the diner as well). Some caliphs and kings even ordered that their foods be cooked in their presence to ensure cleanliness; others felt the need to cook their meals themselves (Chabbouh 39).

The personal hygiene of the guests at the table did not escape scrutiny. Chapters in manuals describe the various types of soaps and toothpicks diners should use to clean their hands and mouths before eating and the perfumes they should apply before sitting down at the table. When dining with the caliph, one was well advised to use a *siwāk*, a small stick for polishing and cleaning the teeth and keeping the breath fresh, still used today in the Arabian Peninsula. Court protocol prescribed that in the presence of the caliph, one must wear an undergarment made of cotton in order to avoid perspiring (al-Ṣābīʾ 33). The Andalusian cookbook author al-Tujībī offers a recipe for a common kind of soap, made only from chickpeas (279–280).

One tale in *The Thousand and One Nights* tells of a guest sitting at a table spread with food but refusing to eat until he could wash his hands forty times with soap, forty times with potash, and forty times with galangal (279). Although a fable, this shows that unclean hands that smelled of food were an offense; thus the basin of water was always ready to cleanse the diner's hands before the meal. The *ibrīq* or water pitcher served the same purpose as it does now in the contemporary Arab world.

In medieval sources, as in modern cookbooks, attention is paid to the types of utensils required to prepare specific appetizers, entrées, and desserts. When making pastry, for example, yeast doughs should rise in a container called the *miʿjanah*; candy is poured onto the *ṣalāyah*, a marble slab, and allowed to cool; the *miḥrāk* is a stirring poker for cooking; the *qaṣabah* a wooden (or sometimes metal) cane used for shaping dough for frying or just for stirring. Al-Warrāq specifies the pots, knives, cutting boards, spoons, and other utensils required in the kitchen, including a pestle for pounding dried spices and a stone mortar for pounding meat and greens. According to the *Kanz*, it is necessary that the same ladle not be used for different types of dishes, for each dish requires its own (8). Ovens had to be built to a certain specification so that their smoke would not affect the taste of the cooking dish (al-Warrāq 12).

Under the Umayyads, spoons were made of wood or clay, the latter imported from China. By the fourteenth century Baalbek, in modern Lebanon, was known for its wooden spoons and bowls, especially those made in nesting sets of ten each. Craftsmen complemented their spoons by fabricating leather carrying cases, to be worn attached to a belt; someone invited to a meal with friends would thus have his own spoons ready for use (Ibn Baṭṭūṭah 83–84).

The medieval Arab kitchen called for the use of a different spoon for each dish prepared and served. At times, the meticulous care in using clean utensils while eating might seem to border on the obsessive. The tenth-century vizier al-Muhallibī would sit down to eat with two servants standing beside him, one on the left, empty-handed, and the other on the right holding about 30 smooth (*majrūdān*) glass spoons. If the vizier had a dish of rice and yogurt, for example, he would take a spoon from his servant on the right, eat one mouthful of the rice and then hand the used utensil to the servant on the left. Every bite taken required a new spoon; he would continue doing this until he was finished eating (al-Kutubī I 354; Yāqūt al-Ḥamawī *Muʿjam al-Udabāʾ* IV 1710).

Under the Abbasids, napkins of knitted or embroidered fabric would have been used. In the palaces, the caliphs and princes ate from plates of silver and gold and from embellished bowls and platters from China. And many such were needed if Hārūn al-Rashīd is at all representative; he would spend 10,000 *dirham*s on the thirty different dishes his cook would prepare for him each day (Maḥjūb/Khaṭīb 224).

The cleanliness of food products and their prices were regulated by a special category of officials known as *muḥtasibūn* or market inspectors. These officials maintained records of every detail concerning the way food was prepared and sold in public marketplaces. They determined the taxes due, but also regularly patrolled the souks to ensure that sellers and cooks were adhering to government hygiene policies, and that the foods being sold were clean and fresh. It was bad news for a *qaṭāʾif*-maker if the *muḥtasib* found these sweets being sold in the noonday sun, as market regulations permitted their sale only in the early morning or during the coolness of the evening. The *muḥtasib* would also check scales to make sure that proper weights and measures were given and that the customer was receiving the right value for the money.

From pre-Islamic times to the present, Arab custom holds the virtues of generous hospitality in the highest honor and esteem. For centuries, hosts have offered their guests foodstuffs of quantity and quality. During the early Umayyad era, caliphs and princes were even known to invite the masses from cities, towns, and villages to meals as their guests, perhaps a legacy from their desert pasts. We find that in al-Andalus ʿAbd al-Raḥmān I (r. 756–788) would partake of meals with those members of the general public who had come to present petitions or grievances to the *Amīr*, sitting at the same table with them and discussing their needs (al-Maqqarī I 214). It was only natural on the part of rulers, perhaps, to assume that a content populace would be a peaceful and stable one as well. Sometimes such acts of hospitality could backfire, however. That seems to have been the case when a disgruntled Arab Bedouin swore he would never again eat with a stingy ruler who watched his every bite. In actuality, Caliph Muʿāwiyah had noticed a hair on a piece of food the Arab was eating and called his attention to it. The caliph's warning was taken as a slap in the face by the guest, who believed the ruler was watching the amount of food being consumed (Ibn Quṭaybah III 221).[2]

To win over the hearts of the people, tables were spread so that, it is said, thousands could sit with princes and emirs and eat together in the morning and evening. The first to be given credit for doing this is ʿUbayd Allāh Ibn ʿAbbās, known for his attempt to reconcile the

Umayyads and the followers of ʿAlī. It is said that he would spend 500 *dīnār*s daily for meals (al-Rāghib al-Aṣbahānī II 649). The generosity of Umayyad governor al-Ḥajjāj ibn Yūsuf is also recounted, but on a much grander scale. Each day during Ramadan he would have 1,000 dining tables set up; when the holy month had passed, the number would be cut back to 500. Each table sat ten, and was replenished with ten varieties of food, tender grilled fish, and rice with sugar. So important was this to al-Ḥajjāj that he would go about personally inspecting and examining each plate placed on the tables. If he found the rice dish lacking the sugar, he would order that sugar be brought. Woe to whoever had forgotten to add the condiment; he would be beaten 100 times (al-ʿAskarī *al-Awāʾil* II 63; Ibn ʿAbd Rabbih V 14–15).

There are many anecdotes about hosts and their fabulous tables laden with varieties of sumptuous dishes and drinks. Take, as an example, the gourmet taste of a host in the Abbasid era. Abū al-ʿAtāhiyah arrived for a visit to the home of the singer Mukharriq. He found, placed before him and the other guests, the most delicious food and drink: bread made from semolina, vinegar, greens, salt, and grilled kid meat. After this, the guests were served grilled fish, of which they ate until full. Next, the sweets were brought out, and the assembled company washed their hands. This done, the guests were then served fruit and sweet basil and, finally, wine. Mukharriq invited his guests to choose whatever they wanted from the table. Abū al-ʿAtāhiyah did so and drank until his host passed out (Maḥjūb/Khaṭīb 229).

In both the eastern and western parts of the Arab world, the pursuits of gastronomic delights led to not only the compilation of recipes and the table manners associated with good food and good etiquette, but even to new forms of literature. One of these appeared in the late fifteenth century, a type of debate known as *munāẓarah*. A good example is Ibn al-Ḥajjār's tale *Kitāb al-Ḥarb al-Maʿshūq bayn Laḥm al-Ḍaʾn was Ḥawāḍir al-Sūq* (*The Book of the Loving War Between Mutton and the Ingredients of the Market-Place*) that describes the battle waged by King Mutton and his men against King Honey and his army; among the forces of King Mutton are various types of meat, among those of King Honey are vegetables, fruit, milk products, and fish.

More conventional culinary treatises had been produced throughout the Islamic world for centuries.

Thanks to the *Kitāb al-Fihrist* of Ibn al-Nadīm (d. 995), we know that Ibn Quṭaybah (d. 883) wrote a book entitled *Nutrition*; Abū Ḥasan ibn Khālid ibn Barmak (d. 937) penned *The Delightful Book of Cooked Food* and *Excellencies of Sikbāj*; ʿUbayd Allāh ibn Aḥmad ibn Abī Ṭāhir (d. early tenth century) contributed *Al-Sikbāj and Its Excellencies* to the tradition; and Ibn Khurdādhbih (d.ca. 896), court companion of the Abbasid caliph al-Muʿtamid (r. 870–892), was author of *Cooked Food*. There is even a cookbook attributed to a caliph, Ibrāhīm ibn al-Mahdī (r. 817–819), also called simply *Cooked Food*.

Though many of these texts are no longer extant, some of their recipes, and the poetry and anecdotes that frequently accompany them, were recorded by others. There are recipes credited to the caliphs al-Maʾmūn, al-Wāthiq, and al-Muʿtaṣim, the physician Yūḥannā ibn Māsawayh, the courtier Yaḥyà ibn Khālid al-Barmakī (d. 806), the ninth-century astronomer Yaḥyà ibn Abī Manṣūr al-Mawṣilī, and Abū Samīn, presumably either a chef in the court of the caliph al-Wāthiq or just a table companion who enjoyed cooking.

Most food historians specializing in the history of Arab and Muslim cuisines recall the notable gourmet and man of culture Ibrāhīm ibn al-Mahdī as the author of the first functional and thorough cookbook in the Arabic language. The son of the caliph al-Mahdī and the younger half-brother of the caliphs Hārūn al-Rashīd and al-Wāthiq, he wrote from inside the caliph's court. A century later, the redactor al-Warrāq suggests that one of the great influences on Ibrāhīm was his servant-girl Bidʿah, who was "the most skilful of people" in the art of cooking (133).

Together they collaborated as "the gourmand and the cook," creating in Arabic *Kitāb al-Ṭabīkh* (*The Book of Cooking*). The book contained not only recipes but also poetry about food, with certain recipes or their ingredients written in rhythmic meter. In all, some forty recipes have survived from Ibrāhīm ibn al-Mahdī's cookbook, preserved in later culinary manuals. One perfect example of rhyme and recipe is cited in al-Warrāq in which Ibrāhīm describes the preparation of a summer *bāridah* (pl. *bawārid*, appetizers) (72).

The Baghdadi physician Yaḥyà ibn ʿĪsà ibn Jazlah (d. 1100) instructed his readers in his *Risālah fī al-Sukkar* (*A Treatise on Sugar*) how to prepare honey, milk, musk, vinegar, ambergris, and camphor for medical purposes (the last two ingredients used for their scents). His other work on food, the *Minhāj al-Bayān fī mā Yastaʿmiluhu al-Insān* (*A Systematic Exposition of What Is Used by Man*), is a lexicon that lists medicaments, drinks, and nutriments both compound and simple. Of great importance is that the recipes provided are written from the perspective of a medical professional, each ending with a description of its health merits. There are more than a hundred of these, more than two hundred definitions of gastronomic ingredients, and about sixty characterizations of recipes, the majority of which represent dishes known in the Abbasid culinary inventory (Garbutt 44). Both books were dedicated to the caliph al-Muqtadī (r. 1075–1094) and shed light on the period between the earliest extant culinary text of al-Warrāq and that of Muḥammad ibn al-Ḥasan al-Baghdādī (d. 1239), the *Kitāb al-Tabīkh* completed in 1226.

The history of structured culinary writing among the Arabs really began in Baghdad during the Abbasid era and continued in al-Andalus. The earliest known cookbooks in Arabic, according to the recipe book of the tenth-century Baghdad author, Abū Muḥammad al-Muẓaffar ibn Naṣr ibn Sayyār al-Warrāq, appeared as compendiums in the early ninth century.

The name "al-Warrāq" indicates that he or his family owned a bookstore, a mark of education. He was part of that extraordinary society of the Abbasid era and chose to delve into the world of cuisine for his literary contribution to world literature. In his *Kitāb al-Ṭabīkh wa Islāḥ al-Aghdhiyah al-Maʾkūlāt*, al-Warrāq preserved about a hundred of these ninth-century recipes and added more of his own, in 132 chapters. Privy to what the Abbasid caliphs served on their magnificent tables, he had access to the actual recipe books of their households and often cited his sources.

Al-Warrāq's manual reveals the level of creativity in the Baghdad of his time. He recommends the use of ingredients such as eggs, rue, celery, cucumber, and pomegranate seeds as garnishes; these enhance the taste of the dish, but more than anything, are applied for the pleasure of the eye. One meat dish he offers is decorated with sausages, eggs, cheese, olives, and vegetables, while in the case of pastries, al-Warrāq speaks of almonds dyed red or yellow (the yellow deriving from saffron) used to decorate sweets such as *khabīṣ*, a type of pudding. To further enhance the sensory appeal of foods, he advises adding perfumes and spices such as musk, amber, aloe, camphor, saffron, cloves, spikenard, nutmeg, cubeb pepper, and rosewater. These were expensive commodities, underlining the fact that the recipes were intended for the upper classes of society.

In 1226, Muḥammad ibn al-Ḥasan ibn Muḥammad ibn al-Karīm al-Kātib al-Baghdādī (d. 1239) wrote his compendium titled *Kitāb al-Ṭabīkh*, containing 160 recipes. His purpose, he explains, was for his own use and for others who might wish to use it. The work is the outcome of a life spent consulting many sources and encountering many strange and unfamiliar things in other cooking manuals. A. J. Arberry was the first historian to translate the work into English, in 1939, based on the first edited version of the original manuscript by Dāwūd al-Jalabī (Chelabi); it was updated by Charles Perry in 2005.

The *Kanz al-Fawāʾid fī Tanwīʿ al-Mawāʾid* (*The Treasure of the Benefits in the Varieties of the Dining Table*) has neither date nor author identified in any of its manuscript copies. Modern scholars have postulated, however, that it probably predated the *Kitāb al-Ṭabīkh* and may have served as one of al-Baghdādī's main sources (Marín/Waines 4). Of possible Egyptian origin and circulated in the same milieu as the works of al-Warrāq and al-Baghdādī, the book offers about 750 recipes for food and drinks, instructions on how to preserve edibles in vinegar, and even a section on household cleaning. It discusses the cooking of Syria, Baghdad and Mosul, North Africa (al-Maghrib) and Andalusia, Yemen, Greece, Georgia, Assiut, Nubia, Alexandria, Nablus, Turkey, and Cairo and the cooking habits of the Kurds, laying down for the record the story of interaction of various cultures in the Arab world. There are numerous health references associated with certain recipes, making it obvious that the author had a great concern for health matters, even more than the other eastern Arabic texts (Marín/Waines 6).

Another thirteenth-century work is the *Kitāb al-Wuṣlah ilà al-Ḥabīb fī Waṣf al-Ṭayyibāt wa al-Ṭīb,* generally attributed to the Aleppo historian Kamāl al-Dīn ibn al-ʿAdīm (d. 1262), a connoisseur of cuisine and etiquette. What we know of him is that he lived during the

Ayyubid period and that he was a member of or frequent visitor to the courts of the Ayyubid princes. The importance of this book is that it details the foods and manners of the highest levels of thirteenth-century Syrian society. The *Wuṣlah* contains numerous recipes for drinks, omelets, stews, roasted and fried meat, vegetables, rice, wheat, fruit and yogurt dishes, breads, pastries, sauces, and syrups. There are 74 recipes for cooking chicken alone. The book lists recipes from myriad places and designates them as such: Maghribī foods such as couscous; a dessert called "Turkoman hats"; Arab- or Egyptian-style fish fillets; *Faranjī* , or European, grills; *ʿamal al-Rūm*, or dishes made by the Byzantines. Ibn al-ʿAdīm also offers little insights into some of his personal favorites, such as *judhābah*, rice with yogurt and saffron that is placed beneath grilled meat and more delicious for him than the barbecue itself (556).

A fourteenth-century cookbook entitled *Kitāb Zahr al-Ḥadīqah* (*The Book of the Garden's Flowers*) by Aḥmad ibn Mubārakshah Shihāb al-Dīn, is, according to Charles Perry, an indiscriminate collection of recipes from al-Baghdādī's cookery book and the *Kitāb al-Wuṣlah* (Perry, "Medieval Arab Fish," 480). It, too, describes in detail the culinary offerings of its time and offers a separate section on fish dishes. The *Kitāb Waṣf al-Aṭʿimah al-Muʿtādah* (*The Book of the Description of Familiar Foods*) dates from the fourteenth-century Mamluk period; its anonymous author is an Egyptian. It includes 160 recipes, all similar to those found in al-Baghdādī's earlier cookery book. Damascus's fifteenth-century Ibn al-Mabrad (or Ibn al-Mubarrad), a legal scholar who wrote on various topics, was also the author of *Kitāb al-Ṭibākhah* (*The Book of Cookery*). The work includes 44 recipes.

Among the culinary works of al-Andalus is Ibn Razīn al-Tujībī's extraordinary thirteenth-century book of recipes, *Faḍālah al-Khiwān fī Ṭayyibāt al-Ṭaʿām wa al-Alwān* (*The Delights of the Table and the Best Types of Prepared Foods*), providing an incredible overview of the culinary art of the Muslim West, from Spain to Tunisia. Al-Tujībī records the local methods involved in creating the Arab and Berber cuisines of al-Andalus and North Africa at the beginning of the Banū Marīn (Marinids) dynasty. Written sometime between 1239 and 1265, it contains 441 recipes, some of them so detailed that the reader is able to envision the processes of a complicated preparation such as *mujabbanah al-miqlah*, a deep-fried dough stuffed with cheese. *Kitāb al-Ṭabīkh fī al-Maghrib wa al-Andalus fī ʿAṣr al-Muwaḥḥidīn li-Muʿallif Majhūl* (*An Anonymous Andalusian Cookbook of the Thirteenth Century*) also survives, a culinary text describing food at the time of the al-Muwaḥḥidūn (Almohad) dynasty in Andalusia. The author seems quite concerned about whether various food types should be served on separate dishes or all together on one platter. In addition to providing insight into the life and culture of thirteenth-century Andalusia, the manual moves beyond that region's boundaries to describe edible preparations attributed to other places where they were created: dishes from Africa and Egypt; chicken and eggplant dishes created by the Abbasid Ibrāhīm ibn al-Mahdī; a sweetmeat accredited to a certain Abū ʿAlī from Baghdad; a Sicilian entrée; recipes from Toledo; and cakes from Tunisia, Africa, and Sicily. What emerges in both these works is the influence of the culinary arts practiced in the eastern Muslim Empire, with Baghdad as the pivotal capital of not only the empire but of high culture in every respect. These two books provide evidence of Baghdad's culture moving west, reaching North Africa and the Iberian Peninsula, and thereafter affecting the tables of Europe.

Those who cooked or initially wrote down the recipes that follow were actors in the theater of the culinary arts, using their talents, intuition, ingenuity, and taste to contribute to the history of the world's cuisine. They were not necessarily concerned with the minute details or measurements.

We have attempted here to recreate their medieval dishes for the modern cook, reviving as best we can those dishes prepared by the Arabs of history that seem most likely to please the contemporary palate. Each recipe is given first in a close translation of its original source, and next in our modernized redaction. To prepare and taste these foods is to enter the world of a magnificent and cosmopolitan past, where far-flung cultures met in the kitchens and on the dining tables of the affluent, be they caliphs, kings, princes, or nobles, intellectuals or merchants. Their foodways were recorded for future generations by those who saw the importance of continuing and adding to the traditions of their forefathers. As credit to these writers, we have tried to preserve a part of the glorious history they have handed down to us.

Our selection of recipes has taken into consideration the mixture of ingredients offered, the interesting spice and herbal combinations involved, and the methods employed to produce a dish. What we chose represents only a minuscule array of the vast number of culinary creations fashioned in the kitchens of the medieval Arab world. Although we have attempted to adhere as closely as possible to the source recipes, in some cases, revisions were necessary. Instead of the wooden or brass mortar, we choose to recommend the food processor; certain aromatics and herbs that are not readily available we have replaced with others that seem to us close enough in flavor and aroma; egg whites are much easier to beat into a firm meringue with an electric mixer than without; and a kitchen counter top readily serves as a makeshift marble slab.

Whether by conquest, trade, or political or educational exchange, medieval Arab food and foodstuffs had a major impact on non-Arab societies of Europe, Asia, and North Africa. Yet today, of all the great cuisines in the world, the medieval Arab kitchen is perhaps the least known in the West.

In recording his recipes, al-Baghdādī proposed that food was among the foremost of life's pleasures, and we think it incumbent on the reader to test his proposition. For our part, having tried and tasted more than a hundred recipes, we find him to be right.

Appetizers

Green Olive Spread

(*Zaytūn Akhḍar Marṣūṣ*: Pressed Green Olives)

Serves 4–6
Vegetarian

> *Remove their pits. Pound for them peeled, roasted walnuts and dissolve in lemon juice. Add to it* aṭrāf al-ṭīb, *tahini, salted lemon pieces chopped small, parsley leaves stripped from their stem, mint, and rue. Knead together in order that it can be removed to be put on bread. Add to it dried coriander, caraway, and a little pepper.*
>
> —Ibn al-ʿAdīm, *Kitāb al-Wuṣlah ilà al-Ḥabīb fī Waṣf al-Ṭayyibāt wa al-Ṭīb*

Realizing that the olive pickers were shaking the trees to release their fruit, the Umayyad caliph Hishām (723–743) instructed that the olives be picked properly. To do so otherwise would allow the fruit to burst open and the branches of the tree to break (al-Ṭabarī XXVI 80). For the ruler of the caliphate to show his concern as to how olives were to be harvested correctly was a sign of their value. The olive tree is native to the Mediterranean region and has been cultivated there for millennia, and olives have always been considered a staple in the Mediterranean diet.

Today in the Arab world olives are served at breakfast, lunch, or dinner and eaten as between-meal snacks.

This spread is crunchy, nutty, and tangy, ideal when served on Arabic bread, toast, or even a good piece of crusty French bread.

1/2 lb. green olives, pickled in salt, washed, pitted, and ground in food processor
4 tbsp. ground walnuts
1 tbsp. lemon juice
1/8 tsp. aṭrāf al-ṭīb
2 tbsp. tahini, dissolved in 3 tbsp. water
1/4 lemon with peel, finely chopped and sprinkled with 1/4 tsp. salt
2 tbsp. finely chopped parsley
1 tbsp. finely chopped fresh mint leaves
1 tsp. finely chopped fresh rue
1/4 tsp. ground coriander seeds
1/4 tsp. ground caraway seeds
1/4 tsp. black pepper

Thoroughly combine all the ingredients and serve as a dip or a spread.

Labnah with Chopped Greens and Walnuts

(*Shīrāz bi Buqūl*: Dried Curds with Vegetables)

Serves 4–6
Vegetarian

It is a tasty relish that is appetizing and wholesome. Its method of preparation is to take mint, celery, and vegetable leeks. Strip off the leaves of the celery and the mint. Cut everything in small pieces with a knife and pound in the mortar. Then mix well with dried curds. Sprinkle with a little salt, as much as is needed, and finely pounded mustard. Sprinkle over it coarsely pounded walnut hearts and use it. If dried curds are not available, replace it with māst laban, *yogurt thickened with rennet from which its water has been drained, and mix with it a little sour yogurt and use.*

—al-Baghdādi, *Kitāb al-Ṭabīkh*

Al-Baghdādi recommends that when *shīrāz* (dried curds) are not available, the cook should use yogurt that has been strained through a cloth, and we echo his suggestion. *Labnah*, popular with eastern Arabs, is nothing more than yogurt that has been strained in a cheesecloth bag for 24 hours, allowing the excess water to drain. The result is a thickened, creamy cheese product with many uses.

Enjoy this easy-to-prepare thick and creamy spread as an appetizer or for breakfast on toasted Arabic bread. The combination of the nuts and greens with the slightly tart taste of the yogurt makes for a good start for any day or any meal.

---

32 oz. (2 lb.) labnah, *purchased or made by straining plain yogurt in cheesecloth for 24 hours*
1/2 cup fresh mint leaves, finely chopped
1/2 cup celery leaves, finely chopped
1/2 cup finely chopped green stalks of leeks
1/2 tsp. salt
1/2 tsp. ground mustard
1/2 cup walnuts, coarsely chopped

Place *labnah*, mint, celery, and leeks in a bowl and mix well. Stir in salt and mustard, then sprinkle the walnuts over the mixture or stir them in. Transfer to a serving bowl. Refrigerate for 2 hours and serve.

Fried Eggs with Vinegar and Spices

(*Bayḍ Maṣūṣ*: Soaked Eggs)

> *Throw sesame oil in a pot. Remove the celery leaves from its stalk and throw them on top of it. When they are cooked, sprinkle them with cinnamon, mastic, and caraway. Then pour over it a sufficient amount of vinegar and color it with a little saffron and enough salt. Break the eggs over it and then cover the pot. Once cooked, remove.*
>
> *—Kanz al-Fawā'id fī Tanwīʿ al-Mawā'id*

Get ready for the unique taste of eggs flavored with vinegar. It is light and a good opening to any meal. This dish should be served immediately, scooped up with tortillas (our favorites) or toast. It goes well served alongside Green Olive Spread (*Zaytūn Akhḍar Marṣūṣ*; see page 15).

1/3 cup light sesame oil
1/2 cup celery leaves, finely chopped
1/2 tsp. cinnamon
1/8 tsp. mastic
1/2 tsp. whole caraway seeds
2 tbsp. white vinegar
pinch of saffron
1/2 tsp. salt
6 eggs

Heat the oil in a saucepan over medium-low heat. Sprinkle celery leaves over oil and allow to cook for 1 minute. Sprinkle cinnamon, mastic, and caraway over leaves.

Mix vinegar, saffron, and salt. Stir gently into saucepan, and bring contents to a boil.

Break eggs into the saucepan, leaving the yolks intact. Cover and allow to cook until eggs are set, approximately 3 minutes.

Serve immediately.

Fava Bean Salad

(*Bāqillà bi Khall*: Fava Beans in Vinegar)

Serves 4–6
Vegetarian

> *Take fresh green fava beans as soon as they are fully mature. Remove their outer pods, then boil them in water and salt until well cooked. Dry them off, then sprinkle (a little caraway and finely pounded cinnamon on them). Pour a bit of sesame oil on them. Then put good vinegar to cover them, and it is used.*[1]
>
> —al-Baghdādi, *Kitāb al-Ṭabīkh*

Tradition has it that the Prophet Muḥammad considered vinegar the best condiment, believing that a house without vinegar was an empty one (al-Rāghib al-Aṣbahānī II). It is used in meat-based dishes such as Sweet and Sour Lamb and Vegetable Stew (*Sikbāj*; see page 66), Lamb and Prune Tajine (*Murūzīyah*; see page 49), Lamb and Vegetables with Spiced Onion Sauce (*Dīkabrīkāt*); see page 77), and vegetable recipes such as *Bāqillà bi Khall*, which remains a popular appetizer today. Throughout the Arab East, broad beans or fava beans preserved in vinegar and garlic serve as one of the multitude of *mazzah* (appetizer) dishes. This salad-like bean appetizer is lightly spiced and tangy. Make sure it has been chilled enough before serving.

1 tsp. salt
1 lb. fresh green fava beans, pods removed, or 1 lb. frozen green fava or baby lima beans
1/2 tsp. ground caraway seeds
1/2 tsp. cinnamon
1/4 cup light sesame oil
1/4 cup vinegar

Bring lightly salted water to a boil in a saucepan. Add beans, making sure there is enough water to cover, and bring again to a boil. Boil over medium-high heat for 10 minutes. Drain beans and allow to cool.

Place beans in serving bowl and gently stir in caraway and cinnamon.

Mix oil and vinegar, pour the mixture over beans, and toss.

Refrigerate for about 2 hours and serve cold.

Fava Beans with Yogurt and Garlic

(*Bāqillà*: Fava Beans)

Serves 4–6
Vegetarian

> *Take fava beans and remove outer shells and boil. Place upon them yogurt and garlic and good oil on its surface and dried thyme. Vinegar can be substituted for the yogurt but it will not taste as good.*
>
> —Ibn al-ʿAdīm, *Kitāb al-Wuṣlah ilà al-Ḥabīb fī Waṣf al-Ṭayyibāt wa al-Ṭīb*

In the Arab East today, where fava beans are known as *fūl* and are quite often eaten fresh, it is the rare table at which some variety of *fūl* is not served as an appetizer with garlic, cumin, pepper, salt, and lemon juice.

The modern dish *Fūl Mutabbil bi Laban* is a common appetizer and almost a replica of the medieval recipe we present here. We sometimes serve it as a meal in itself or as a side dish with any type of grilled meat. To add more zest to the dish, try adding a few more cloves of garlic.

---

1 lb. fresh green fava beans, pods removed, or 1 lb. frozen green fava or baby lima beans
1 1/2 cups yogurt
2 cloves garlic, crushed
3/4 tsp. salt
1/4 tsp. black pepper
2 tbsp. olive oil
1/2 tsp. dried thyme

Bring water to a boil in a saucepan, add beans, making sure there is enough water to cover, and bring again to a boil. Boil over medium-high heat for 10 minutes. Drain and allow to cool.

Place beans, yogurt, garlic, salt, and pepper in a bowl, then gently stir. Spread on a flat serving dish, and sprinkle with oil and thyme. Refrigerate until ready to serve.

Spicy Chard and Fava Bean Dip

(*Bāridah min Bāqillà li-Ibn Abī Nūḥ al-Kātib*: a Bāridah made of Fava Beans of Ibn Abū Nūḥ al-Kātib)

Serves 4–6
Vegetarian

> *Snip off (the ends of) fresh fava beans. Boil them. Peel them. Pound in a mortar with chard leaves that have also been boiled. Pound with them shelled pistachios, walnuts, and almonds. Then, remove them from the mortar and fry them in a frying pan with sesame oil and olive oil mixed together*

with the white part of onions. Then throw into it black pepper, cloves, spikenard, cassia, coriander, cumin, and murrī *while in the pan. Then remove it and put it in a serving dish. Then arrange skinned almonds over the top in the shape of stars, having colored some of them yellow with saffron. Take mustard foam and serve it with it, God willing.*

—al-Warrāq, Abū Muḥammad al-Muẓaffar ibn Naṣr ibn Sayyār, *Kitāb al-Ṭabīkh wa Iṣlāḥ al-Aghdhiyah al-Maʾkūlāt wa Ṭayyibah al-Aṭʿimah al-Maṣnūʿāt*

Bawārid (plural of *Bāridah*), literally "cold things," were made with various meats, poultry, and fish, and with different vegetables. There are even *Bawārid* designated as special dishes for Christians during Lent (al-Warrāq 119–20). A combination would be served, followed by the hot entrées, much like today's *mazzah* of Lebanon and Syria.

Mazzah are served in small dishes, their number usually reflecting the generosity of the host and the importance of the meal to follow. Such was also the case with the medieval *Bawārid*.

This appetizer is best scooped up with Arab bread or toasted French bread. It is spicy and nutty in flavor, a very tasty opener for any dinner.

We have omitted the hard-to-come-by spikenard and suspect that you won't miss it at all from this aromatic and spicy dish.

---

1 lb. frozen green fava beans, thawed
2 cups packed chopped Swiss chard leaves, cooked in boiling water for 1 minute and drained
2 tbsp. pistachios
2 tbsp. walnuts
4 tbsp. almonds
2 tbsp. finely chopped onions
1/2 tsp. black pepper
1/8 tsp. ground cloves
1/4 tsp. chopped fresh rue
1/2 tsp. cinnamon
1/8 tsp. ground coriander seeds
1/2 tsp. cumin
1 tsp. salt
1/4 tsp. red miso

1/4 cup light sesame oil
1/4 cup olive oil
1/8 tsp. saffron dissolved in 2 tbsp. water

Boil beans in a saucepan over medium-high heat for 10 minutes in enough water to cover. Drain and allow to cool.

Place the beans, Swiss chard, pistachios, walnuts, and 2 tbsp. almonds in a food processor and process into thick paste.

Transfer to a mixing bowl, add the remaining ingredients, except for remaining almonds, sesame oil, olive oil, and saffron-water mixture, and mix well.

Heat the sesame and olive oil in a frying pan over medium heat, then add the bean mixture and stir constantly for 6 minutes. Remove from the heat and place on a serving platter.

Place the remaining almonds in the dissolved saffron until they turn yellow (a few minutes). Decorate serving platter contents with the almonds in a star shape.

Fava Bean Dip with Fennel and Cumin

(*Lawn min al-Baysār*: a Dish Made of Fava Beans)

Serves 4–6
Vegetarian

> *Pick out fava beans and wash in hot water a number of times. Then coat with oil and place in a pot coated with oil. Then throw fresh water over them to cover them, a chopped onion, a whole head of garlic, cumin, coriander, and fennel. Cook over the fire and stir with a spoon until it becomes like marrow. After removing the garlic and onion from the pot and seasoning it with salt, then empty it into a dish and sprinkle cumin and oil over it. Whoever wants to eat it with small radishes and onions or with olives, do so.*
>
> —al-Tujībī, *Faḍālah al-Khiwān fī Ṭayyibāt al-Ṭaʿām wa al-Alwān*

This is a heavy dip, well spiced with an unusual taste, and best scooped up with Arab bread. Fava beans tend to be bland, but with the addition of cumin and ground fennel seeds there is a good robust flavor.

The recipe is found in the section of al-Tujībī's cookbook for dishes made with fresh and dried fava beans. Our assumption is that dried beans were used in this particular dish. That, at least, is how we have prepared it with success!

1 1/2 cups dried fava beans, soaked overnight and drained
6 tbsp. olive oil
1 large onion, chopped
1 head garlic, peeled
1 tsp. ground coriander seeds
1/2 tsp. ground fennel seeds
1 1/2 tsp. cumin
1 tsp. salt

Place the beans in a saucepan, add 4 tbsp. oil, and stir until beans are coated. Set aside.

Tie the onion and garlic in a small cotton bag and place in the saucepan with the beans. Add enough water to cover the beans plus 4 inches, the coriander, fennel, and 1 tsp. cumin, and bring to a boil. Cover and cook over medium heat for 2 hours or until the beans soften, adding more water if necessary. Remove the saucepan from the heat and discard the onion and garlic.

Place the beans with the remaining liquid in a food processor and process until well mashed. Stir in the salt. Spoon onto a serving platter and sprinkle with the remaining oil and cumin.

Serve with radishes, green onions, and olives or other accompaniments.

Tangy Eggplant Stir-Fry

(*Bādhinjān*: Eggplant)

Serves 4–6
Vegetarian

> *Cut into small pieces and boil. Squeeze out its water. Take enough sesame oil and fry chopped onions, and cook the eggplants with them, until they are done. Pour over it chopped parsley, rue, mint, dried coriander, caraway,* aṭrāf al-ṭīb, *garlic, a little oil and vinegar and then use.*
>
> —*Kanz al-Fawā'id fī Tanwīʿ al-Mawā'id*

Eggplant's initial introduction to the Arabic-speaking world was not a welcome one. For example, one man, Abū Ḥārith, refused to eat it because its color resembled that of a scorpion and its appearance that of the long-necked bottle used in blood-letting. Yet he was accused one day of eating the same vegetable. In response to his hypocritical action, Abū Ḥārith quickly defended himself, explaining that since death comes to all, eating eggplant is part of the process leading to it (Ibn Quṭaybah III 288).

What eventually caused the changing taste for eggplant for the Arabs and made it popular on the courtly tables was, as some say, the marriage of the caliph al-Maʾmūn to Burān. The new bride, it is said, was the one whom the dish of lamb and eggplant, *Burāniyah* (see page 74), was named after.

Today much has changed, and it is impossible to imagine Arabic cuisine without eggplant. Cooks of the Arab world even create a dessert made with it, *Bādhinjān Maʿaqqad*, tender small boiled eggplants immersed in an orange blossom sugar-based syrup and dipped in sugar.

We recommend scooping this tangy eggplant dip with bread or serving it as a side dish.

---

1 small eggplant, about 1 lb.
1 tsp. salt
3 tbsp. light sesame oil
1 medium onion, finely chopped
4 tbsp. finely chopped parsley
1 tbsp. finely chopped fresh mint leaves
1 tsp. finely chopped fresh rue
1/4 tsp. ground coriander seeds
1/4 tsp. ground caraway seeds
1/4 tsp. aṭrāf al-ṭīb
2 cloves garlic, crushed
1 tbsp. olive oil
2 tbsp. vinegar

Peel the eggplant, dice into 1-inch cubes, place in a saucepan, and cover with water. Stir in salt. Bring to a boil, then simmer over medium heat for 15 minutes. Drain in a sieve, allowing to sit for 10 minutes.

While the eggplant is draining, sauté the onion in the sesame oil over medium heat for 5 minutes. Add the eggplant and sauté over medium heat, stirring occasionally until eggplant is well-cooked, about 5 minutes. Stir in the remaining ingredients and stir-fry for 1 minute more. Remove from heat, spoon onto a platter and serve.

Seared Eggplant with Walnuts

(*Bādhinjān Maḥshī li-Ibn al-Mahdī*: Ibn al-Mahdī's Stuffed Eggplant)

Serves 4–6
Vegetarian

> *Take eggplant, boil and chop into small pieces. Take walnuts, pound them and put them in a vessel (with the eggplant). Throw salt on them. Knead with vinegar and press into a large, deep bowl. To smoke it, pour oil over a fire until it smokes. Pull it out from the bowl like a patty and (flip it) searing it until both sides are smoked. Add to it some vinegar and caraway. If you would like to put onion on it, then do so. Drizzle olive oil over it and present it, God willing!*
>
> —al-Warrāq, Abū Muḥammad al-Muẓaffar ibn Naṣr ibn Sayyār, *Kitāb al-Ṭabīkh wa Iṣlāḥ al-Aghdhiyah al-Maʾkūlāt wa Ṭayyibah al-Aṭʿimah al-Maṣnūʿāt*[2]

This dish, attributed to Ibrāhīm, son of the caliph al-Mahdī, is one of three of his *Bawārid* recipes that appear in al-Warrāq. The association of eggplant with members of the courtly class appears to have marked its rise in status after having been considered a bitter and non-appealing vegetable, compared in taste to the bitter fruit of the zaqqum tree (al-Rāghib al-Aṣbahānī II 617).

This recipe may be a precursor to the modern *Bābā Ghannūj*, a popular eggplant purée dish served as a dip throughout the eastern Arab world. In the modern preparation, the original walnut, vinegar, salt, and oil paste is replaced by tahini, a sesame seed paste.

We garnish the dish with finely chopped onions fried in olive oil, which we prefer here to the taste of raw.

Use as a dip and serve with Arab bread.

---

1 large eggplant, about 2 lb., peeled
2 tsp. salt
1 cup finely ground walnuts
3 tbsp. vinegar
3 tbsp. olive oil
1 tsp. ground caraway seeds
1 large onion, finely chopped or julienned and fried in olive oil (optional)

Place the eggplant in a large saucepan and cover with water. Add 1 tsp. salt, then bring to boil. Cover and cook over medium heat for 10 minutes or until cooked, and drain. Chop into small pieces and place in a strainer for 30 minutes, gently pressing down with a ladle to force out the excess water.

In a bowl, mix together the eggplant, walnuts, remaining salt, and 2 tbsp. of the vinegar. Knead well.

Heat the oil in a frying pan over medium-high heat until it begins to smoke. Add the eggplant-walnut mixture to the pan, flattening it with a wide metal spatula to form a patty. Allow to sear on both sides, turning over once. Remove with the spatula and place on a chopping board. Chop into small pieces and spread on a serving dish

Sprinkle the remaining 1 tbsp. vinegar, 1 tbsp. olive oil, and caraway over the eggplant mixture. If desired, spread onions over the dish, then serve.

Pickled Onions

(*Baṣal Mukhallal*: Vinegared Onions)

Serves 4–6
Vegetarian

> *Cut onions into large pieces and wash in water and salt. Pour over them vinegar, lemon juice, olive oil, chopped parsley, mint, coriander, caraway, and* aṭrāf al-ṭīb. *This can be eaten after one day.*
>
> *—Kanz al-Fawāʾid fī Tanwīʿ al-Mawāʾid*

Medieval Arab doctors generally agreed that eating either grilled or raw onions increased the appetite and sexual desire. Mixing onions with water and honey and applying the mixture to the eyes could improve sight. Onions mixed with rue would heal a dog bite. But eating too many onions could impair the mind. When boiled onions are eaten, they cause a high flow of urine and tears; while birds prepared with ginger and onions cause an increase in sexual desire and semen (Ibn Quṭaybah III 283).

With or without their medical benefits, vegetables pickled in vinegar were part of the menu of luxury foods. Pickled vegetables and fruits such as eggplants, turnips, onions, cucumbers, olives, and even grapes and raisins were offered before the main meal; with their inclusion in the Arabic medieval recipe books, they held an elevated status.

2 tsp. salt
4 medium Spanish onions, peeled and cut into large pieces
1 cup vinegar
1/4 cup lemon juice
1/4 cup olive oil
1/2 cup finely chopped parsley
2 tbsp. finely chopped fresh mint leaves
2 tbsp. finely chopped coriander leaves
1 tsp. caraway seeds
1 tsp. aṭrāf al-ṭīb

Mix the water and salt in a large bowl, then add the onions, making sure that there is enough water to cover them. Allow to sit for 1 hour, then drain.

In another bowl mix together the remaining ingredients. Gently stir the liquid mixture into the onions. Cover tightly and refrigerate for 24 hours.

Serve as a side dish as you would serve pickles.

Honeyed Carrots in Rosewater

(*Jazar*: Carrots)

Serves 4–6
Vegetarian

> *Take good fresh carrots and peel them. Chop into small pieces. Throw out their cores. And take bee's honey, wine vinegar, ginger, and* aṭrāf al-ṭīb *and put them on the fire, allowing them to boil well. Add the carrots to it. Cook on low heat until it thickens like* ḥalāwah. *Put it in a salted vessel. And add to it a little saffron and musk.*
>
> —Ibn al-ʿAdīm, *Kitāb al-Wuṣlah ilà al-Ḥabīb fī Waṣf al-Ṭayyibāt wa al-Ṭīb*

When Muḥammad ibn Abī al-Mūʾammal stated that he would choose a dish of carrots cooked in vinegar, olive oil, and *murrī* over a costly dish of truffles cooked with butter and pepper, he had a reason for it. It was not because carrots were cheaper, but because they were tastier and better for the health (*al-Bukhalāʾ* 98). From his statement it appears that carrots were common and inexpensive in medieval Iraq. So common were they that in his guide to elegant living the ninth-century al-Washshā' makes it clear that Baghdad's aristocracy preferred not to handle carrots or even look at them except when intent on eating them.

The eastern Arabs referred to carrots as *jazar*, while in *al-Andalus* they were known as *isfannarīyah*, the latter term giving way to the Spanish *zanahoria*.

Since musk is not easily available, we have substituted rosewater as a replacement for this aromatic. Also, the original recipe instructs the cook to remove the hearts of the carrots, but we found this to be unnecessary when the carrots are fresh and tender.

This is a slightly sweet appetizer that would go well with any vinegar-based stew such as Sweet and Sour Lamb and Vegetable Stew (*Sikbāj*; see page 66).

---

6 tbsp. honey
2 tbsp. wine vinegar
1 tbsp. grated ginger
1 tsp. aṭrāf al-ṭīb
1 lb. carrots, peeled and chopped into small pieces
1/2 tsp. salt
pinch of saffron
1 tsp. rosewater

Cook the honey, vinegar, ginger, and *aṭrāf al-ṭīb* in a saucepan over medium-low heat, stirring constantly until the mixture comes to a boil, about 10 minutes. Lower heat and allow to simmer for about 2 minutes.

Add the carrots and cover. Continue cooking, stirring occasionally, until the liquid thickens, about 25 minutes. Remove from heat and pour onto a serving platter.

Stir the salt and saffron into the rosewater, then sprinkle over the carrots.

Serve immediately.

Cauliflower with Tahini-Walnut Sauce

(*Tatbīl al-Qanbīṭ*: Seasoned Cauliflower)

Serves 4–6
Vegetarian

> *Take boiled cauliflower and cut in small pieces. Strain. Then take oil, tahini, walnut hearts, vinegar, mustard, mint, caraway, and* aṭrāf al-ṭīb. *Then season the cauliflower with this and (serve) it with the rest of the* bawārid.
>
> *—Kanz al-Fawā'id fī Tanwī' al-Mawā'id*

In the Middle Ages, as today, a vegetable dish served with tangy sauce added an appealing touch to the dining table, and we suspect that this cauliflower with a tahini-based sauce would have been a real crowd-pleaser.

There is a very similar and popular appetizer in the modern Arab East made of cauliflower florets deep-fried golden brown with a sauce made of tahini, lemon juice, water, and garlic drizzled over them.

It is not clear in the source recipe whether water should be mixed with the tahini. We find that a better and smoother sauce results with the addition of water. Without it, the sauce is too thick and dry.

4 cups cauliflower florets
1 tsp. salt
2 tbsp. olive oil
4 tbsp. tahini mixed with 4 tbsp. water
1/4 cup vinegar
1/2 cup chopped walnuts
1 tsp. ground mustard
1 tbsp. fresh mint leaves finely chopped or 1 tsp. finely ground dried mint
1/2 tsp. caraway seeds
1/2 tsp. aṭrāf al-ṭīb
1/2 tsp. salt

Boil cauliflower in salted water for 5 minutes. Drain, chop into small pieces, and place in a serving dish.

To make the sauce, mix together the olive oil, tahini-water mixture, and vinegar until smooth, then stir in the remaining ingredients.

Sprinkle the sauce evenly over the cauliflower. Refrigerate before serving.

Hummus with Ground Nuts

(*Ḥummuṣ Kasā*: A Cover of Chickpeas)

Serves 4–6
Vegetarian

> *Take boiled chickpeas and pound finely. Take vinegar, good oil, tahini, pepper,* aṭrāf ṭīb, *mint, parsley, thyme, a little of walnuts, almonds, pistachios,*

hazelnuts, cinnamon, caraway, dried coriander, salt, salted lemons, and olives. Spread. Leave one day and one night and serve.

—Kanz al-Fawā'id fī Tanwī' al-Mawā'id

As they were in the Middle Ages, chickpeas remain one of the most popular pulses in the Arab world. The mature pods, when still green, can be roasted, peeled, and served as appetizers or stripped and used raw in cooking in the same manner as green peas. In most cases they are harvested when fully matured and then dried. Like other dried beans and peas, they make an excellent ingredient in all types of soups and stews, even serving as a substitute for meat.

The medieval Arabs enjoyed chickpeas. These were a near standard ingredient in *Bawārid*s, soups, and entrées in medieval times. Yet, leave it to al-Washshā' to find fault when he advises that they should not be eaten because they cause flatulence (192).

Ḥummuṣ Kasā was considered a *Bāridah*, prepared with various ingredients and with chickpeas as the base (the *Kanz* includes 10 such varieties of the dish). We very much like the recipe below, for a dish similar to modern hummus, but crunchier, nuttier, and spicier than what you have probably encountered.

---

1 cup dried chickpeas, soaked overnight in enough water to cover well, then drained
2 tbsp. vinegar
3 tbsp. olive oil
4 tbsp. tahini dissolved in 3/4 cup water
1/2 tsp. black pepper
pinch of aṭrāf al-ṭīb
2 tbsp. fresh mint leaves, finely chopped
2 tbsp. fresh parsley, finely chopped
1/4 tsp. ground thyme
1 tbsp. ground walnuts
1 tbsp. ground hazelnuts
1 tbsp. ground almonds
1 tbsp. ground pistachios
1/8 tsp. cinnamon
1/8 tsp. ground caraway seeds
1/8 tsp. ground coriander seeds
3/4 tsp. salt
4 tbsp. fresh lemon juice
1/2 cup chopped olives

Place the chickpeas in a saucepan with water to cover, plus 4 inches more. Bring to a boil, cover, and simmer over medium-low heat for approximately 1 1/2 hours or until well cooked, adding water as needed. Drain and allow to cool. Place the chickpeas in a food processor and grind well. Stir in the remaining ingredients, then process for another minute until well blended.

Spoon the mixture evenly onto a flat serving platter, cover, and refrigerate overnight. When ready to serve, each diner can scoop this dip up with Arab bread or crackers.

Sautéed Spinach with Garlic and Coriander

(*Isfānākh Muṭajjan*: Spinach Cooked in a Saucepan)

Serves 4–6
Vegetarian

> *Take spinach and cut off the roots at the bottom and wash. Then boil lightly in water and salt and dry it from the water. Then, refine sesame oil and throw it (the spinach) in it stirring it until its aroma emerges. Then pound a little garlic and put it in it. Sprinkle cumin, dried coriander, finely pounded cinnamon and serve.*
>
> —al-Baghdādi, *Kitāb al-Ṭabīkh*

The Arabs introduced spinach to Spain and then to Sicily in the early ninth century. By 1074 Ibn Ḥajjāj wrote a treatise on spinach, and Ibn Baṣṣāl, gardener to the sultan of Toledo, included it in his *Book of Agriculture* in 1085. The twelfth-century agriculturalist Ibn al-ʿAwwām called this green the "Queen of the Vegetables," while others rhapsodized it in verse and stories lauding its countless attributes (Watson 62). Such is the case of the famous poet Abū Nuwās (756–814), who proclaimed, "a dining table without greens is like a wise man without brains" (al-Rāghib al-Aṣbahānī II 612).

From Spain its cultivation spread to the remainder of Europe. Almost all the European languages derive their names for this leafy green from the Spanish *espinaca*, which originated from the Arabic *isfānākh*.

In the Arab East today, spinach is often used interchangeably with other greens such as dandelion, endive, and Swiss chard. Dishes made in this manner are referred to as *ʿAṣṣūrah*.

Isfānākh Muṭajjan's garlicky flavor goes well as an accompaniment to any type of roasted poultry or meat dish.

2 bunches fresh spinach, stemmed and washed thoroughly
2 tsp. salt
1/4 cup light sesame oil
3 cloves garlic, crushed
1/2 tsp. cumin
1/2 tsp. dried coriander leaves
1/4 tsp. cinnamon

Bring water to boil in a large saucepan with 1 tsp. salt. Add the spinach and bring to a boil again, boiling for a further minute. Remove spinach and place in a strainer, shaking to remove as much excess water as possible. Drain for 20 minutes.

Heat the sesame oil in a frying pan over medium heat. Stir in the spinach and sauté for 3 minutes, stirring constantly.

Stir in the remaining salt and other ingredients, sautéing for a further minute.

Serve either hot or cold.

Cold Roasted Chicken with Almonds and Pomegranate Seeds

(*Bāridah Mujarrabah*: A Bāridah That Has Been Tried)

Serves 4–6

> *Take a chicken or pullet and grill it. Place it on a platter. Take almonds, peel them and pound them finely. Add to it sugar or sweet rosewater syrup and pour it over the platter (contents) adding chopped rue over it. Pour over it good-tasting sweet olive oil. Decorate it with egg yolk and pomegranate seeds, God willing!*
>
> —al-Warrāq, Abū Muḥammad al-Muẓaffar ibn Naṣr ibn Sayyār, *Kitāb al-Ṭabīkh wa Iṣlāḥ al-Aghdhiyah al-Ma'kūlāt wa Ṭayyibah al-Aṭ'imah al-Maṣnū'āt*

The medieval Arab culinary books provide a number of recipes for chicken mixed with pomegranate seeds or juice. In this *Bāridah*, the seeds, the only edible part of the pomegranate, are used for decorative purposes but do enhance the taste of the dish.

A single seed of a pomegranate is said to have caused the tragic end of a love affair between Caliph Yazīd ibn ʿAbd al-Malik (r. 720–724) and his songstress and servant girl Ḥabābah. One day, in Damascus, the caliph decided to spend time alone with her and instructed his servants that he not be disturbed for any reason.

In the privacy of their quarters, while enjoying each other's company, the caliph playfully threw his mistress pomegranate seeds to catch in her mouth. Suddenly, she began to choke and he rushed to save her. It was too late. She died in his arms, and he was inconsolable. The young caliph, in his distress, isolated himself and died shortly thereafter (*al-Aghānī* XV 111–113).

We promise a happier outcome here, where the pomegranate garnish adds a surprisingly delicious tang and crunch while serving as a most colorful and elegant decoration. We assume that the egg yolk mentioned in the source recipe is hard-boiled.

---

3 lb. cold roasted chicken, whole or disjointed, with skin or with skin removed
3 tbsp. olive oil
1/2 cup finely ground almonds mixed with 2 tbsp. sugar
2 tbsp. finely chopped fresh rue
1 boiled egg yolk, chopped
seeds from 1 medium pomegranate

Place chicken on a serving dish and rub all over with the oil. Sprinkle the almond and sugar mixture evenly over the chicken, then sprinkle the rue evenly over the top.

Decorate with the yolk and pomegranate seeds, then serve.

Cold Roasted Chicken with Lime and Cucumber

(*Bāridah li-Abī Jaʿfar al-Barmakī*: A *Bāridah* of Abū Jaʿfar al-Barmakī)

Serves 4–6

> *Take pullets and grill them. Disjoint them and place them in a platter. Throw in it coriander, black pepper, cumin, and cassia. Add in it the juice of unripe sour grapes. Chop over it mint, tarragon, and fresh thyme. Drizzle over it*

good-tasting olive oil and chopped fresh herbs. Decorate by putting chopped small cucumbers all around it, God willing.

—al-Warrāq, Abū Muḥammad al-Muẓaffar ibn Naṣr ibn Sayyār, *Kitāb al-Ṭabīkh wa Iṣlāḥ al-Aghdhiyah al-Maʾkūlāt wa Ṭayyibah al-Aṭʿimah al-Maṣnūʿāt*

When Caliph Muʿāwiyah's guest al-Ḥasan grabbed the cooked chicken placed before him, broke it into pieces, and very quickly ate it all, the caliph, in awe, asked his guest, "Is there any animosity between you and the chicken?" Al-Ḥasan responded to the apparently concerned caliph, "Why? Was there any relationship between you and the chicken's mother?" (*Tāj* 14).

This cold dish is named after Abū Jaʿfar al-Barmakī, a member of the powerful Persian Barmakid family during the reigns of Caliph al-Mahdī and his son Caliph Hārūn al-Rashīd. Learned and well-versed in political etiquette, Abū Jaʿfar has also come down in history as a connoisseur of good food.

The flavors of the herbs in combination with the chicken, spices, lime juice, and crunchy cucumber make this colorful dish a welcome presence at any table. It is best served with any type of crusty bread on the side.

Note: Verjuice, the juice of sour grapes, *ḥiṣrim* in Arabic, is available in Middle Eastern supermarkets. One can use *ḥiṣrim* or substitute lemon or lime juice, as has been done in the following redaction.

1 small roasted chicken, about 3 pounds, disjointed
1/4 cup finely chopped fresh coriander or 1/2 tsp. ground coriander seeds
1/2 tsp. black pepper
1/2 tsp. cumin
1/4 tsp. cinnamon
1/2 cup lime juice
1 tbsp. finely chopped fresh mint leaves
1 tbsp. finely chopped fresh tarragon
1 tbsp. finely chopped thyme
1/4 cup light sesame oil
3/4 tsp. salt
1 tsp. finely chopped rosemary
1 tsp. finely chopped basil
1/2 tsp. sumac

1/2 tsp. grated ginger
2 small cucumbers, finely chopped

Place the chicken in a large bowl.

In a separate bowl, combine coriander, pepper, cumin, cinnamon, and lime juice, then add mint, tarragon, thyme, and oil. Mix well, pour over chicken, and coat thoroughly. Place coated chicken in a serving dish.

Sprinkle the remaining spices evenly over the chicken. Distribute the chopped cucumbers evenly around the chicken and refrigerate until ready to serve.

Herbed Chicken Salad

(*Bāridah Maʿjūnah*: A *Bāridah* Paste)

Serves 4–6

> *Chop cold grilled chicken into very small pieces and chop in the same way, elecampane, fresh coriander, parsley, rue, mint, tarragon, fresh thyme, small cucumbers, preserved ginger, and crumble into it date buds and a boiled egg yolk. Knead this with wine vinegar,* murrī, *dried coriander, black pepper, caraway seeds, and cassia. Form it like* al-furnīyah *[round cake]. It is decorated with the white chopped part of onion and chopped black olives and finger-length cut turnip[3] pieces.*
>
> —al-Warrāq, Abū Muḥammad al-Muẓaffar ibn Naṣr ibn Sayyār, *Kitāb al Ṭabīkh wa Iṣlāḥ al-Aghdhiyah al-Ma'kūlāt wa Ṭayyibah al-Aṭʿimah al-Maṣnūʿāt*

Even though many *Bawārids* are vegetable-based, fish, red meat, and poultry were also used as ingredients in these cold appetizers, and chicken roasted until it was golden like a dinar was a favorite (al-Masʿūdī VIII 239).

Bāridah Maʿjūnah is similar to a modern chicken salad in texture, though very different in taste. It is a medley of herbs and spices, crunchy and refreshing.

Since elecampane is not an easy herb to find, we have replaced it with fresh dandelion leaves. For cucumber, it is best to use the small pickling type, especially if you choose not to peel it. Date buds called for in the recipe (*ṭalʿ*) are the first dates appearing inside the spathe, obviously a difficult ingredient to find for the modern kitchen. We have omitted them. As for the turnips, we recommend using the pickled variety found in any Middle Eastern grocery for the extra tangy taste they give to this appetizer.

---

5 cups finely chopped roasted chicken
2 tbsp. finely chopped dandelion leaves
2 tbsp. finely chopped fresh coriander leaves
2 tbsp. finely chopped parsley
1 tsp. finely chopped fresh rue
1 tbsp. finely chopped fresh mint leaves
1 tbsp. finely chopped fresh tarragon
1 tbsp. finely chopped fresh thyme
1 cup finely chopped cucumbers
1 tbsp. finely chopped preserved ginger
2 boiled egg yolks, chopped
2 tbsp. wine vinegar
1 tsp. red miso
1 tsp. ground coriander seeds
1 tsp. black pepper
1/2 tsp. caraway seeds
1/2 tsp. cinnamon
1 small white onion, finely chopped
1/2 cup pitted black olives, finely chopped
6 pickled turnip slices, cut into thin strips

Place the chicken in a mixing bowl, add dandelion, fresh coriander, parsley, rue, mint, tarragon, fresh thyme, cucumbers, ginger, and egg yolk, and mix well.

Add the wine vinegar, miso, dried coriander, pepper, caraway, and cinnamon. Knead the ingredients together to form a paste. Place in a round serving dish. Decorate with the onions, olives, and pickles. Refrigerate before serving.

An Almond-Mustard Condiment

(*Khall wa Khardal*: Vinegar and Mustard)

Serves 4–6
Vegetarian

> *Take sweet almonds, peel and finely pound. Then let them marinate in sharp-tasting vinegar until they become soft. Finely pound mustard and mix the amount desired with it with a little mixed spices and use it.*
>
> —al-Baghdādī, *Kitāb al-Ṭabīkh*

Vinegar was widely used in the medieval Arab kitchen to tone down the sharp and bitter taste of certain foodstuffs, but also as a sour flavoring agent, especially in *Bawārids*. And while other spices were worth their weight in gold during the Middle Ages, mustard was inexpensive. Arab doctors prescribed it for certain ailments, whether applying it to a shaven head or inhaling it for stuffiness, mixing it with milk as a diuretic, or eating it with Swiss chard for those with epilepsy (Ibn Quṭaybah III 293).

Khall wa Khardal combines these two ingredients with almonds in a condiment that was said to aid the digestion when partaking of heavy meals. It is strong-flavored, but we find that it goes well with chicken, fish, or grilled meat. Spoon only a little onto your plate.

2 cups blanched whole almonds, finely ground
1/4 cup vinegar
2 tbsp. ground mustard seed
1 1/2 tsp. aṭrāf al-ṭīb

Place the almonds in mixing bowl and stir in vinegar. Cover and refrigerate for 1 hour. Add the mustard and *aṭrāf al-ṭīb,* and mix well. Transfer to a serving dish.

Herb Sauce for Fish

(*Ṣalṣ*: Sauce)

Makes about 1 1/2 cups sauce
Vegetarian

> *Take what is needed of herbs and chop finely. Then take almonds that you pound finely with the herbs. Then pound a head of garlic with them. Then add on them pepper, caraway, thyme, cinnamon, and saffron in the amount needed. Then add fresh vinegar to it, enough to cover it. Then place over a fire until the vinegar decreases. Squeeze over it enough lemon, then cut over it in pieces salted lemon. Remove and eat it with fish.*
>
> *—Kanz al-Fawāʾid fī Tanwīʿ al-Mawāʾid*

Though the Arabic term *ṣalṣ*, according to Perry ("The Ṣalṣ" 499–502), is of Romance origin, this particular sauce does not reflect any European roots. In the tenth century *ṣibāgh* was the term used for unfermented sauces that would be served as condiments beside the prepared dishes. Food could be dipped into these sauces, or the sauces could be poured over it.

There is a tale told of sauce and the beloved folkloric figure Juha. One day Juha is visited by a man who brings him a rabbit as a gift. Grateful, Juha receives him well. A few days later, two more individuals visit Juha and tell him that they are neighbors of the man who brought the rabbit. Hospitable Juha invites them to dinner. A week later, another knock comes to the door. This time four men arrive at Juha's home and introduce themselves as neighbors of the neighbors of the man who had initially brought the rabbit. Juha invites them in and feels as host he must prepare dinner for them. He goes to the kitchen and brings back a large bowl filled with hot water. He hands a spoon to each one and bids them to help themselves. The visitors dip in and exchange puzzled looks. "O! Virtuous man! What type of soup is this?" Juha replies, "Oh virtuous neighbors of the neighbors of the owner of the rabbit, this is the sauce of the sauce of the rabbit!" (Cattan 124–25).

We made the *Ṣalṣ* by hand but found that it was too thick. We then tried making it in a food processor, which smoothed out the texture—and made it more of a sauce.

The author of the *Kanz* suggests eating this with fried salt-water fish. We suggest it as a sauce for grilled, baked, or fried fish.

6 tbsp. finely chopped parsley
6 tbsp. finely chopped coriander

6 tbsp. finely chopped basil
3 tbsp. finely chopped fresh mint leaves
3 tbsp. finely chopped mustard leaves
1/2 cup finely ground almonds
1 head garlic, peeled and pounded
1 tsp. black pepper
1/2 tsp. ground caraway seeds
1/2 tsp. dried thyme
1/4 tsp. cinnamon
pinch of saffron
1/2 cup vinegar
1 lemon
3/4 tsp. salt

Place all the ingredients except vinegar, lemon, and salt in a food processor. Process for 1 minute.

Place the mixture in a small saucepan and add vinegar. Warm over medium heat for 5 minutes, stirring occasionally.

Squeeze the lemon, reserving the rind, and add 2 tbsp. juice to the saucepan. Stir well. Finely chop the lemon rind, sprinkle with salt, stir into the saucepan, and remove from heat.

Place in a serving bowl and cover. Refrigerate until ready to use.

Soups

Cold Yogurt and Cucumber Soup

(*Khulāṭ Baysānī*: A Mixture from Baysan)

Serves 4–6
Vegetarian

> *Take yogurt made of goat's milk and add to it salt as needed. Add it to water. Break into it mint leaves, tarragon leaves, sweet fennel cut in the size of a finger, fresh thyme, and powdered dried thyme. Add cucumber to it at the right time. Leave it for one day, then eat it seasoned with oil, garlic, and lemon juice.*
>
> —Ibn al-ʿAdīm, *Kitāb al-Wuṣlah ilà al-Ḥabīb fī Waṣf al-Ṭayyibāt wa al-Ṭīb*

It is said by some that yogurt has its roots in the Arabian Peninsula. Nomadic peoples setting off for a new location put their milk in goat-stomach bags and began their long trek under the hot sun. When they finally stopped, they discovered that their milk had curdled. The heat combined with the up-and-down motion of the camels and the bacteria from the stomachs had yielded a surprising result: the fermented dairy product that came to be one of the staples of the Bedouin diet. And from the nomadic Bedouin to the tables of the caliphs, yogurt has never stopped being part of the Arab diet, regardless of its common origin.

Most of the soups in the Arabic medieval cookbooks are hot broths, used for curative purposes. *Khulāṭ Baysānī*, however, falls under the category of pickled and salty foods. It is a cold soup, similar in consistency to a thick gazpacho.

In the contemporary Arab East, there is a popular dish enjoyed, especially during the hot summer days, called *Khiyār wa Laban* (cucumber and yogurt) similar to this soup. One can also compare it to Greek *Tzatziki*, a yogurt dish made of skinned and diced cucumber, diced dill, mint, and plain yogurt.

Goat's milk yogurt will give a richer flavor.

2 cups plain yogurt, from goat or cow's milk
2 tsp. salt
2 cups cold water
2 tbsp. finely chopped fresh mint leaves
1 tsp. finely chopped tarragon leaves or 1/4 tsp. ground tarragon
1/2 cup fresh fennel greens, chopped in 1/2-inch pieces
1 tsp. finely chopped fresh thyme
1/2 tsp. dried thyme
1 medium English cucumber, diced in 1/2-inch cubes
2 tbsp. olive oil
4 cloves garlic, crushed
1 tbsp. lemon juice

Mix the yogurt and salt in a serving bowl. Stir in herbs and cucumber and refrigerate overnight.

When ready to serve, add the oil, garlic, and lemon juice, mixing well.

Spiced Lamb and Fava Bean Soup

(*Māʾ al-Bāqillà*: Water of Fava Beans)

Serves 4–6

> *It is made like that [Hearty Lamb and Chickpea Soup; see page 42] using in place of chickpeas, peeled fava beans that have been soaked and split in two halves. When you ladle it out, put a little lemon juice on it, or finely pounded sumac from which the seeds have been cleaned.*
>
> —al-Baghdādi, *Kitāb al-Ṭabīkh*

A Bedouin, when asked what name was given to soup by his people, responded, "the hot one" (*al-sakhīn*). Consequently, the next question followed, "Then what do you call it if it gets cold?" Without flinching, the Bedouin responded, "We don't allow it to get cold!" (Ibn Quṭaybah III 226)

There is a recipe similar to the one below in the fourteenth-century *Description of Familiar Foods*, but with broken pieces of thin bread as an optional ingredient. This soup is delicious either way.

---

3 tbsp. olive oil
1 lb. lamb, lean breast or leg, cut into 1/2-inch cubes
1 1/2 tsp. salt
1 1/2 tsp. ground coriander seeds
2 tsp. cumin
1 tsp. cinnamon
8 cups water
1 cup fava beans soaked overnight, drained, skin removed, and split
1/2 to 1 cup finely chopped dill
1 large onion, finely chopped
6 tbsp. sumac

Heat the oil in a large saucepan and sauté the meat cubes over medium heat for 5 minutes, stirring constantly. Add the salt, coriander, cumin, and cinnamon and continue sautéing for another 3–5 minutes or until the meat browns. Add the remaining ingredients except the sumac and bring to a boil. Lower the heat to medium, cover, and simmer for 1 hour.

Ladle into a serving bowl and sprinkle the sumac evenly over the top. Serve immediately.

Hearty Lamb and Chickpea Soup

(*Māʾ wa Ḥummuṣ*: Water with Chickpeas)

Serves 4–6

> *Its method is to stew the meat in the usual way as has been described. Add to it salt, coriander, and cumin in the amount needed, cinnamon, peeled chickpeas, dill, and an onion, chopped. Then, cover with water and keep it*

on the fire until it is cooked. Discard its fat. Allow it to settle over the fire and then remove.

—al-Baghdādi, *Kitāb al-Ṭabīkh*

An earlier version of this recipe appears in the *Minhāj al Bayān* as *Mā' al-Ḥummuṣ* (Chickpea Water), with a slight variation that includes the addition of sesame oil, fava beans, and milk, if so desired.

This is a good, slightly spicy, and hearty soup and very easy to prepare.

---

3 tbsp. olive oil
1 lb. lean lamb, cut into 1/2-inch cubes
1 1/2 tsp. salt
2 tsp. ground coriander seeds
2 tsp. cumin
1 tsp. cinnamon
8 cups water
1 cup dried chickpeas, soaked overnight, drained, and skin removed
1/2–1 cup finely chopped dill
1 large onion, finely chopped

Heat the oil in a large saucepan and fry the meat cubes over medium heat for 5 minutes, stirring constantly. Add the salt, coriander, cumin, and cinnamon and continue stirring for another 3–5 minutes or until the meat browns. Add the remaining ingredients and bring to a boil. Lower heat to medium, cover, and simmer for 1 hour, adding a little more water as needed.

Serve immediately.

Tart Chickpea Soup

(*Nawʿ al-Ḥummuṣ al-Yābis*: A Type of Dried Chickpeas)

Serves 4–6
Vegetarian

Pick out dried chickpeas, wash them, then soak them covering them with fresh water. Then cook them in a pot on the fire in the same water in which they were soaking with chopped onions, pepper, coriander, and a little saffron. When they are cooked, add a little murrī *and vinegar. Leave it to sit for a while then pour into a bowl. Or squeeze on it lime juice instead of the onions and vinegar.*

—al-Tujībī, *Faḍālah al-Khiwān fī Ṭayyibāt al-Ṭaʿām wa al-Alwān*

So versatile and inexpensive were chickpeas during the tenth century that a traveler to Egypt noted that in the souk of al-Fustāt alone he counted 90 places where one could eat boiled chickpeas (al-Qalashandī 449 alwarraq.net). This versatile pulse is just as ubiquitous today.

There is a soup in Tunisia today called *Lablabī* whose origin could well have been this recipe. Dried rather than canned chickpeas should be used for this soup for better tasting results.

1 cup dried chickpeas, soaked overnight in enough water to cover by 4 inches
1 large onion, finely chopped
3/4 tsp. salt
1 1/2 tsp. black pepper
1 1/2 tsp. ground coriander seeds
pinch of saffron
2 tbsp. red miso
2 tbsp. vinegar
few drops of lime juice (optional)
1/4 cup fresh coriander leaves, chopped (for decoration)

Place the chickpeas and water in a saucepan, adding more water if necessary to about 4 inches above the chickpeas. Stir in the salt, pepper, coriander, and saffron.

Bring to a boil, then lower to medium-low heat and cover, stirring occasionally. Cook until chickpeas are tender, about 2 hours. Remove from heat.

Stir in the miso and vinegar. Cover and allow to sit for about 10 minutes before serving.

If desired, sprinkle lime juice and coriander over the soup.

Aromatic Soup with Pomegranate Seeds and Rice

(*Marqah Ḥabb al-Rummān wa al-Aruzz al-Maqlū*: A Broth of Pomegranate Seeds and Toasted Rice)

Serves 4–6
Vegetarian

> *Take pomegranate seeds, dry toasted husked rice, sesame seeds, long pepper, ginger, cumin, and salt. Place them all in a pot and cook with water until the broth is thin enough to drink from. This is good for the liver, fever, the gall, wind in the ureters and the sides. It clears any organ attached to the oesophagus, strengthens the body, and settles the stomach making it strong. This is beneficial having been tested.*
>
> —al-Warrāq, Abū Muḥammad al-Muẓaffar ibn Naṣr ibn Sayyār, *Kitāb al-Ṭabīkh wa Iṣlāḥ al- Aghdhiyah al-Ma'kūlāt wa Ṭayyibah al-Aṭʿimah al-Maṣnūʿāt*

It was recognized as early as the sixth century in Arabia that a diet too heavy in meat could cause medical problems. Caliph ʿUmar al-Khaṭṭāb (r. 634–644) warned that gluttony for meat is like gluttony for wine (*al-Bukhalā'* 108). The seventh- to eighth-century theologian al-Ḥasan al-Baṣrī of Medina explained that he had reached the age of ninety without having any loose teeth, any bone out of place, or muscle swollen; no buzzing in the ear, no watering of the eye, and no incontinence of urine—all because he had eaten lightly all his life (*al-Bukhalā'* 110–111).

It is no surprise, then, that many of the "healing" or curative soups from the medieval culinary texts are without meat. And to be sure, with the abundance of meat, fish, and poultry on the dining tables of the elite and the diversity of their preparation, a return to the simple, safe, and light could be a remedy in itself.

The original recipe for this soup calls for husked rice. This involves dry-roasting the rice in a skillet on low heat until the grains are toasted. To save time we suggest skipping this stage and using long grain rice. And, as the soup is somewhat bland, we have replaced the long pepper (*dār fulful*) with chili flakes.

3 large fresh pomegranates
1/2 cup long grain rice, rinsed
1/4 cup sesame seeds

1 tsp. chili flakes
2 1/2 tsp. powdered ginger
2 tsp. cumin
2 1/2 tsp. salt
8 cups water

Cut the pomegranates into quarters from top to bottom. Bend each fleshy piece back to loosen the seeds. Invert the quarters over a bowl and tap them to release the seeds, using fingers or a fork as necessary. Discard any membrane attached to the seeds.

Place all the ingredients in a saucepan and stir. Bring to a boil, then lower heat to medium-low and cover, stirring occasionally, for about 30 minutes.

Serve hot.

Squash and Lentil Soup

(*Marqah Nāfiʿah li al-Saʿāl*: A Broth That Is Beneficial for Cough)

Serves 4–6
Vegetarian

> *Take a gourd, onion, lentils, water,* murrī, *and cumin and cook together. One should eat it and sip it [without salt for indeed it is beneficial, God willing].*[1]
>
> —al-Warrāq, Abū Muḥammad al-Muẓaffar ibn Naṣr ibn Sayyār, *Kitāb al-Ṭabīkh wa Iṣlāḥ al-Aghdhiyah al-Maʾkūlāt wa Ṭayyibah al-Aṭʿimah al-Maṣnūʿāt*

According to al-Washshā's guide to elegant living, *Maraq/Marqah* (broth) should never be sipped so eagerly as to produce uncouth sounds (191). We are not at all sure that he would approve of our behavior when we consume this mellow tasting soup.

1 cup peeled, seeded, and diced acorn squash
1 large onion, finely chopped
1/2 cup split red lentils
8 cups water
1 1/2 tbsp. red miso
2 tsp. cumin

Combine all ingredients in a saucepan and bring to a boil. Cover and cook over medium-low heat, stirring occasionally, until lentils and vegetables are tender, about 30 minutes.

Serve hot.

Note: For those who prefer a smoother broth, the *Marqah* can be puréed immediately before serving.

Meat and Chickpea Soup

(*Shūrbā Khaḍrā'*: Soup of Greens)

Serves 4–6

> *Its procedure is to cut fatty meat into medium-sized pieces and slightly fry in sheep tail's fat. Once it has browned, add to it as much salt as is needed, finely ground dried coriander, pieces of cinnamon, and a handful of peeled chickpeas. Cover with water, then kindle a fire under it. As it is boiling, throw away its scum. Take two bunches of the greens of fresh leeks and cut them with a knife into small pieces. Then pound them in the mortar, and add them to the pot. Then take a portion of red meat and pound finely with spices, along with a handful of chickpeas, washed rice, and a little bit of the pounded leeks. Make from it kebabs and add them to the pot. Once everything is cooked, add more water as needed. Then, take rice being a quarter of the amount of the water, and wash (the rice) a number of times and then put it in the pot. Then, let it continue to boil until it is fully cooked, but not overcooked. Then leave it on the fire until it settles and then remove.*
>
> —al-Baghdādi, *Kitāb al-Ṭabīkh*

Fava beans, chickpeas, and lentils, along with vegetable greens, have formed the bases of many Arab soups and broths since the days of the Babylonians and ancient Egyptians.

Such is the case with the medieval *Shūrbā Khaḍrā'*, a vegetable soup to which two types of meat are added. Although a little time-consuming to prepare, the soup is flavorful. The "greens" specified in this recipe are leeks; though spinach or Swiss chard can be substituted, the leeks give this soup its special taste.

1 cup ground lamb or beef
1/2 cup dried chickpeas, soaked overnight and drained, then divided into 2 portions of which 1 portion is finely ground
1/2 tsp. black pepper
1/4 tsp. aṭrāf al-ṭīb
1/4 cup long grain rice, rinsed
3 cups very finely chopped green stalks of leeks
2 tbsp. olive oil
1/2 lb. lamb shoulder or stewing beef, cut into 1-inch cubes
2 tsp. salt
2 tsp. ground coriander seeds
2 small cinnamon sticks
8 cups water

Combine the ground meat, ground chickpeas, pepper, *aṭrāf al-ṭīb*, 2 tbsp. rice, and 2 tbsp. leeks and form into small balls double the size of marbles. Set aside.

Heat the oil in a saucepan and fry meat cubes over medium heat for 10 minutes or until they begin to brown, stirring occasionally. Add salt, coriander, cinnamon sticks, and whole chickpeas, stirring constantly for 1 minute. Add the water, then bring to a boil, removing any scum as it forms. Stir in the remaining leeks, then gently stir in the meatballs and the remaining rice. Turn the heat to medium-low, cover, and cook for 1 hour, or until the meat is tender and the chickpeas are soft.

Serve immediately.

Entrées

LAMB

Lamb and Prune Tajine

(*Murūzīyah*: A Sweet Prune Tajine)

Serves 4–6

One and half raṭls *of meat, four* ūqīyahs *of prunes, a half* raṭl *of onions, the weight of half and a quarter [3/4]* dirhams *of saffron, and two and half* ūqīyahs *of raisins, and four* ūqīyahs *of good quality wine vinegar in a pot large enough. Boil the meat without spices. When it is done, add the measure of a* raṭl *and a half of water. When the water boils, wash the onions, cut them, then wash them in salt water, then in water. Add them to this meat and leave to boil, letting the onions cook part way. Then add to the pot the prunes which were soaked in water; raisins and jubjubes done in the same manner. Leave to cook until the prunes and raisins sweeten. If you wish, add three* ūqīyahs *of sugar to the mixture after it comes to a boil. Dilute the saffron and add it. When it comes to a hard boil, throw mint in it and* aṭrāf al-ṭīb *and lower the heat.*

—Kanz al-Fawā'id fī Tanwīʿ al-Mawā'id

The Arabs in Granada called this dish *al-ʿĀṣimīy*, but in Morocco, where it remains popular to this day, it was and is still known as *Murūzīyah*. In the recipe in the *Anonymous Andalusian Cookbook* it is identified as one of the foods of Africa and Egypt (130). No matter what the spelling, pronunciation, or provenance, the typical ingredients are meat or poultry and fruit, sweetened with honey or sugar.

An amazing taste of "sweet and meat" with a touch of fresh coriander, *Murūzīyah* is a tajine with a little bit of thick sauce, ideally served with white rice or plain couscous.

---

1 1/2 lb. lamb, cut into 1-inch cubes
2 medium onions, finely chopped
1 1/2 tsp. salt
1 cup pitted prunes, soaked overnight and drained
2/3 cup raisins
1/4 cup wine vinegar
2 tbsp. sugar or honey
1 pinch saffron diluted in 2 tbsp. water
1 1/2 tsp. dried mint or 2 tbsp. finely chopped fresh mint leaves
1 tsp. aṭrāf al-ṭīb
1/4 cup chopped fresh coriander leaves

Place the meat and enough water to cover in a saucepan and bring to a boil. Cover and cook, stirring occasionally, over medium heat for 40 minutes or until the meat is cooked, skimming off the scum.

Add the onions and bring to a boil, then cover and cook for 10 minutes.

Stir in the salt, prunes, raisins, vinegar, sugar or honey, and saffron and bring to a boil again.

Add the mint and *aṭrāf al-ṭīb*; then lower heat to medium-low and cook for 10 minutes, covered. Gently stir in the coriander.

Serve hot.

Spiced Lamb with Walnuts

(*Shawī*: Grilled Meat)

Serves 4–6

> *Take fatty good grilling meat and sheep's tail. Chop finely. Put in a shallow earthenware pot. Put it over the fire. Take for it roasted walnut hearts and*

throw over roasted and pounded coriander and caraway, parsley, mint and lime. Put in the middle a little aṭrāf al-ṭīb. *Put in a dish and eat hot. It is tasty.*

—Kanz al-Fawā'id fī Tanwīʿ al-Mawā'id

According to the geographer Ibn Ḥawqal, Baghdad's tenth-century Sūq al-ʿAẓīm was the city's principal bazaar/marketplace. Amid the hustle and bustle of people coming and going, and with a medley of food and trade activity, one would be drawn to the aroma of barbecued lamb and kebabs and order on the spot what was being grilled.

Even though the recipe below is titled *Shawī* (grilled), the process for cooking the meat does not involve grilling at all. The meat is cooked in a pot and, yet, surprisingly, it takes on a grilled flavor. Fava Beans with Yogurt and Garlic (*Bāqillà*; see page 19) would be good to serve alongside it, or the *Shawī* pieces can be dipped into Herb Sauce for Fish (*Ṣalṣ*; see page 38), adding a good tangy flavor to the meat.

1/4 cup olive oil
3 lbs. boneless lamb, chopped into very small pieces
3 tsp. salt
1 cup toasted whole walnuts
1 tsp. ground coriander seeds
1 tsp. caraway seeds
1/2 cup chopped parsley
4 tbsp. chopped fresh mint leaves
1 lime, finely chopped (seeds removed)
1/4 tsp. aṭrāf al-ṭīb

Heat the oil in a saucepan, add meat and salt, and cook over medium heat until brown, about 20 minutes, stirring constantly.

Add the walnuts, coriander, caraway, parsley, mint, and lime. Stir until the spices are absorbed, about 5 minutes.

Stir in the *aṭrāf al-ṭīb* and allow to cook with the meat for 2 minutes more.

Transfer to a serving platter and serve immediately.

Lamb and Sour Apple Tajine

(*Tuffāḥīyah*: Of Apples)

Serves 4–6

> *Cut up fatty meat into small long pieces and throw them into the pot. Add to them a little salt and some coriander. Boil until almost cooked and remove its scum. Then cut up onions in small (pieces) and throw them in it [with] a cinnamon stick, black pepper, mastic, finely pounded ginger, and bunches of mint. Then take sour apples or tart, peel and remove their cores, and pound them in a stone mortar and squeeze out their juice and put it over the meat. Then throw in some almonds adding them to the pot. Rub dried mint into it. If you want to make it with garlic, then do so but add them whole. If you want to make it with chicken, then do so. However, if you make it with chicken do not add garlic.*
>
> *—Kanz al-Fawā'id fī Tanwīʿ al-Mawā'id*

There appear to be two types of *Tuffāḥīyah* recipes in the Arabic medieval source books, one using the juice of sour apples to flavor the meat sauce, the other calling for apple pieces to be cooked with the meat. In both kinds it is essential that the apples be sour on their own or soured with verjuice, vinegar, or lime juice.

According to Ibn Jazlah, *Tuffāḥīyah* balances the humors. We include it here regardless of its medicinal qualities, simply because this tajine tastes good.

This is best served with plain cooked rice.

2 lb. lamb with some fat, sliced into strips 1/2 inch wide and 3–4 inches long
1 tsp. salt
1/2 tsp. ground coriander seeds
2 medium onions finely chopped
1 small cinnamon stick
1/2 tsp. black pepper
1/2 tsp. mastic
1/2 tsp. ground ginger
1/2 cup finely chopped fresh mint leaves
1 1/2 cups unsweetened apple juice to which 1 tbsp. lemon juice has been added

1/2 cup blanched split almonds
1/2 tsp. dried mint
4 cloves garlic, crushed

Place the lamb, salt, and coriander in a saucepan, cover with water, and bring to a boil. Cook 15 minutes, covered, over medium heat, then uncover and cook 15 minutes more, removing the scum as it gathers.

Add the remaining ingredients and return to a boil. Cook over medium heat, uncovered, for 20 minutes or until the lamb is well done and the liquid has thickened, adding a little more water if necessary.

Serve immediately.

Lentil Stew with Lamb and Swiss Chard

(*ʿAdasīyah*: Made of Lentils)

Serves 4–6

> *Its method of preparation is to cut the meat and melt sheep tail fat in the usual way and put the meat in the fat and stew it until it browns. Then, throw on it a little salt, cumin, and ground dried coriander and cover with water. When it is almost cooked, put washed and cut-up chard stalks in it, about the width of four fingers. When the chard is cooked add water as is needed, then boil. When it reaches a full-boil, throw on it cleaned, washed lentils, as much as the water will allow. Then keep the fire going under it until the lentils are cooked. When it is smoothly thickened and it is known that it is cooked, take for it some garlic in the amount the pot will allow, pounding it finely and throw it in. Stir it with the ladle. Then leave it over a quiet fire and remove. When you ladle it, leave on it lemon juice.*
>
> —al-Baghdādi, *Kitāb al-Ṭabīkh*

As its name implies, *ʿAdasīyah* is a type of stew made of lentils. Lentils were commonly identified as an inexpensive pulse, popular among the peasants and associated with those of lesser means, yet so important in the diet of the Arabs that dishes made with them also appear in medieval cookbooks describing what the nobility and even caliphs ate. The irony of the presence of a lowly food on the dining tables of upper Baghdad society is rarely forgotten, however.

Upon being sent *ʿAdasīyah* by the new caliph al-Qādir bi-Allāh (r. 991–1031), the deposed Abbasid caliph al-Ṭāʾiʿ li-Allāh was mortified when he saw the dish of cooked lentils. "Is this what the Prince of Believers eats?" he asked. When it was confirmed that this indeed was the case, al-Ṭāʾiʿ requested that a message be conveyed to the new caliph. If this was the type of food al-Qādir preferred, he was best advised to lie back and not concern himself with the hardship and toil of the caliphate (al-Kutubī II 375–376).

Brown or green lentils can be substituted for the red, but these will have to be cooked longer.

1/4 cup olive oil
1 lb. lamb, cut into 1/2-inch cubes
1 tsp. salt
1 1/2 tsp. cumin
2 tsp. ground coriander seeds
8 cups water
1/2 lb. Swiss chard stalks cut into pieces about 3 inches long and 1/2 inch wide
1 cup split red lentils
6 cloves garlic, crushed
juice of 1 fresh lemon

Heat the oil in a saucepan and brown the lamb over medium heat for about 10 minutes, stirring occasionally. Add the salt, cumin, and coriander and cook for an additional 2 minutes, stirring constantly.

Add 6 cups of water and bring to a boil. Cook over medium heat, stirring occasionally, for 20 minutes, then add the Swiss chard and cook for 20 minutes more, stirring occasionally.

Stir in the lentils and the remaining water and bring to a boil. Cover and cook over medium-low heat for 30 minutes or until the lentils are done, stirring occasionally, making sure that the lentils do not stick to bottom of the saucepan.

Add the garlic and cook over low heat uncovered for 10 minutes, stirring gently.

Ladle into individual bowls and sprinkle with the lemon juice. Serve immediately.

Spiced Lamb and Lentils with Rice

(*Mujaddarah*: "Pockmarked")

Serves 4–6

> *Its preparation is like that of Aruzz Mufalfal except that it is not colored with saffron. Put in it half as much lentils as the rice. Then follow the aforementioned procedure as that of Aruzz Mufalfal.*
>
> —al-Baghdādī, *Kitāb al-Ṭabīkh*

In the Middle East, meatless *Mujaddarah* is one of the oldest and least expensive dishes to prepare. Some say that it is the dish for which Esau sold his birthright to his brother Jacob. Made today with lentils and either rice or burghul, it continues to be one of the most popular dishes in the Arab East. Despite being thought of as a dish of commoners, *Mujaddarah* could be part of the diet of the upper classes with the addition of the luxury item of meat.

Today, when *Mujaddarah* is served, the usual side dishes are sliced raw onion, pickled turnips, and yogurt. For this medieval version we served Pickled Onions (*Baṣal Mukhallal*; see page 26) and Cold Yogurt and Cucumber Soup (*Khulāṭ Baysānī*; see page 40).

5 tbsp. olive oil
1 lb. lamb with a little fat, cut into 1-inch cubes
1 tsp. salt
3/4 tsp. ground coriander seeds
3 cups water
1/4 tsp. cumin
1/4 tsp. cinnamon
1/4 tsp. mastic
1 cup long grain rice, washed
1/2 cup lentils, soaked overnight and drained
1 cinnamon stick

Heat 3 tbsp. oil over medium-high heat in a frying pan, add the lamb, and stir-fry until brown, about 12 minutes.

Sprinkle with 1/2 tsp. salt and 1/2 tsp. coriander and cook, stirring, 1 minute more.

Add the water and cook over medium heat for 40 minutes or until the meat is cooked. Remove the meat from the pan and reserve the broth.

Place the meat on a plate and sprinkle evenly with the remaining 1/4 tsp. coriander, cumin, cinnamon, and 1/8 tsp. mastic.

In a saucepan, place the rice, lentils, cinnamon stick, remaining oil, salt, and mastic. Add 3 cups of the broth, adding more water if necessary, and bring to a boil over medium heat. Reduce heat to medium-low, cover, and cook for 12 minutes.

Remove the cinnamon stick, stir the mixture, and place the cubes of meat evenly over the top. Cover and turn off the heat, allow the mixture to cook in its own steam for 1 hour, then serve.

Browned Lamb with Saffron-Cinnamon Rice

(*Aruzz Mufalfal*: Peppered Rice)

Serves 4–6

> *Its preparation is to take fatty meat and cut into medium-size pieces. Dissolve fresh sheep's tail fat and throw away its cracknels. Throw the meat over it and stir until browned. Sprinkle it with a little salt and finely ground dried coriander. Then cover it with water and boil until cooked, throwing away the scum. Remove from the pot after the water has dried from it, [yet] still moist, not completely dry. Throw in dried coriander, cumin, cinnamon, and finely ground mastic, as much as it can handle, and the same with the salt. When it is completely cooked, remove from the pot, draining off all water and fat, and sprinkle some of those mentioned spices. Then take a* kayl *of rice and 3 1/2* kayls *of water. Dissolve fresh sheep's tail, the weight of 1/3 the amount of the meat. Throw the water into the pot. When it boils, throw the melted fat on it. Add to it mastic and cinnamon sticks and bring it to a full boil. Wash the rice several times, color with saffron, and throw in the water without stirring. Then cover the pot for a while until the rice puffs up and the water boils. Then uncover it and lay that meat in rows on top of the rice and cover. Put a cloth over the cover, wrapping it so that no air goes in. Over a gentle fire, leave the pot for a while on the fire until it settles, then remove. Some people make it plain without coloring it with saffron.*
>
> —al-Baghdādī, *Kitāb al-Ṭabīkh*

The name of this dish is often translated as "Peppered Rice." However, *aruzz mufalfal* can also be construed as "puffed rice" or "rice pilaf," and by using a standard measurement of 2 parts water to 1 part rice the final cooked product is indeed light—puffed—and soft.

5 tbsp. olive oil
1 lb. lamb with a little fat, cut into 1/2-inch cubes
1 tsp. salt
3/4 tsp. ground coriander seeds
1/4 tsp. cumin
1/4 tsp. cinnamon
1/4 tsp. mastic
1 cup long grain rice
1 cinnamon stick
pinch of saffron, dissolved in 2 tbsp. water, optional

Heat 3 tbsp. oil over medium heat in a shallow casserole dish and brown the lamb on all sides, about 10 minutes.

Sprinkle with 1/2 tsp. salt and 1/2 tsp. coriander, barely cover with water, and cook uncovered over medium heat for 10 minutes or until the water has almost evaporated.

Remove the meat with a slotted spoon and place in a mixing bowl. Set the casserole dish with the broth aside.

Mix the remaining salt, remaining coriander, cumin, cinnamon, and 1/8 tsp. mastic with the meat.

Add the rice, 2 cups water, remaining oil and mastic, cinnamon stick, and dissolved saffron to the broth and bring to a boil. Cover, turn heat to medium-low, and cook for 12 minutes.

Stir the rice, then lay the meat evenly over the top. Cover, turn off the heat, and allow to sit for 1 hour before serving.

Lamb and Rice Porridge

(*Harīsah al-Aruzz*: Pottage Made with Rice)

Serves 4–6

> *Take fatty meat and wash and throw into a pot. Pour over it water and salt and boil over the fire until it is cooked [to the point that] its meat shreds and falls off the bones. When it has fallen off the bones, remove it from the fire. If it is still in chunks, then pound it in a mortar. Then take white rice, pick it clean, and wash it three times. Pour strained milk on the meat*

broth. When it comes to a hard boil, throw the rice over it. Once the rice has cooked, throw the pounded meat over it and stir until the rice is crushed. Pour into it butter or clarified butter, or rendered fat with sesame oil in equal portions, or milk. Beat it constantly until it is all crushed, stirring it constantly until it is like nāṭif *and no meat remains in chunks, until it becomes like strings fused together with the rice so that neither (meat and rice) are seen. Serve it with a small bowlful of* murrī, *God willing.*

—al-Warrāq, Abū Muḥammad al-Muẓaffar ibn Naṣr ibn Sayyār, *Kitāb al-Ṭabīkh wa Iṣlāḥ al-Aghdhiyah al-Maʾkūlāt wa Ṭayyibah al-Aṭʿimah al-Maṣnūʿāt*

Harīsah is a smooth porridge-like dish made of pounded boiled wheat or rice and meat or chicken, though a Lenten type in which leeks are substituted for the meat also exists. The name is derived from the Arabic verb *harasa*, meaning "to crush," "mash," or "pound."

When a huge dish of *Harīsah* was set on Caliph Hārūn al-Rashīd's dining table, his guest, Abbān, the Qurʾan reciter, was tempted to reach for its center where the juicy chicken fat sat. Out of respect for the caliph, he at first refrained, but quickly came up with an idea. Taking his finger, he made a little depression so that the fat ran toward him. The caliph noticed and immediately recited a Qurʾanic verse to his guest. "Hast thou scuttled it in order to drown those in it?" Abbān responded, "Indeed, no, O! Commander of the Faithful! 'We are pushing it toward a land parched by drought'" (al-Masʿūdī VIII 244–245).[1]

Enjoyed in the palaces of caliphs and the homes of the general population alike, the dish was also available outside the home at special *Harīsah* shops. In tenth-century Iraq, *Harīsah* sellers would lay out mats and set up tables on the roofs of their shops for their customers. On each table was a bowl of *murrī*, used as a condiment for the *Harīsah*. Waiters were present, and washbasins, pitchers, and potash were provided for customers to use for cleaning their hands before and after they ate: all this costing the diner only 1 *dānaq* (al-Muqaddasī 139).

Today, the dish remains popular throughout the Arab world, differing slightly in ingredients from region to region but always retaining its original base of wheat or rice.

We have tried making *Harīsah* with milk as instructed in the source recipe, and while it was good, it was not thick enough for our tastes. We have opted for yogurt in the recipe below, which makes for a richer, smoother, and very tasty dish. Even though the traditional method is to beat the meat with the rice or wheat until the mixture is smooth and well-blended, we take the easier route and use a food processor.

---

3 lb. lamb with bones and some fat
2 tsp. salt

2 cups plain yogurt, whole or low-fat
1 cup rice, rinsed
2 tbsp. butter
2 tbsp. light sesame oil
2 tbsp. red miso
Arab bread

Place the lamb and salt in a saucepan, cover with about 2 inches of water, and bring to a boil. Cook covered over medium heat for about 2 hours, adding more water if necessary, until the meat is very well done and falling off the bone. Remove the meat, discarding the bones, and reserve 2 cups of the broth in the pan.

Stir the yogurt into the broth and bring to a boil over medium heat, stirring constantly in one direction. Add the rice and cook, covered, over medium-low heat for about 20 minutes, stirring occasionally. Stir in the butter and sesame oil and transfer along with the meat to a food processor. Process 1 minute and transfer to a serving dish.

Serve the miso on the side as a condiment, scooping up the hot *Harīsah* in Arab bread.

Lamb and Cabbage Tajine

(*Luḥūm al-Ḍa'in Yuṭbakh bi-al-Kurunbīyah*: A Baqlīyah of Ziryāb's)

Serves 4–6

> *Take the flesh of a young fat lamb, put in the pot with salt, onion, coriander seed, pepper, caraway, two spoons of oil, and one of* murrī naqī' *[use soy sauce]. Put on a moderate fire.*
>
> *Then take cabbage, its tender parts. Take off the leaves and chop small with the heads, wash. When the meat is almost done, add the cabbage. Then pound red meat from its tender parts and beat in the bowl with eggs and the crumb [that is, everything but the crust] of bread, almonds, pepper, coriander, and caraway. Cover the pot with this little by little and leave on the coals until the sauce dries and the grease comes to the top. Serve.*
>
> *—Anonymous Andalusian Cookbook (Kitāb al-Ṭabikh fī al-Maghrib wa al-Andalus fī ʿAṣr al-Muwaḥḥidīn, li-muʿallif majhūl), page 81, translated by Charles Perry*

This dish is named after Ziryāb and was perhaps introduced to Andalusian cuisine by this famous style-setter. It is similar to contemporary North Africa's tajines in that once it is cooked a little sauce remains to keep the ingredients moist.

3 tbsp. olive oil
1 lb. lamb, cut into 1-inch cubes
2 tsp. salt
1 large onion, finely chopped
2 tsp. ground coriander seeds
1 1/2 tsp. black pepper
1 tsp. caraway seeds
1 tbsp. red miso
4 cups finely chopped cabbage, tough outer leaves removed
1 lb. ground lamb
1 egg, beaten
1/4 cup bread crumbs
1/4 cup blanched split almonds
1 tsp. ground caraway seeds

Heat the oil in a deep saucepan over medium-high heat. Add the lamb cubes, salt, onion, 1 tsp. coriander, 1 tsp. black pepper, caraway seeds, and miso. Reduce heat to medium and simmer for 10 minutes, stirring often.

Stir in the cabbage and reduce heat to low. Cover and cook for 15 minutes, stirring a few times.

Place the remaining ingredients in a bowl and mix well. Crumble this mixture evenly over the top of the lamb and cabbage mixture. Cover and cook over medium-low heat for about 20 minutes or until the meat is done.

Remove the lid, reduce heat to low, and continue cooking until the liquid has almost evaporated.

Transfer to a serving platter and serve immediately.

Lamb with Honeyed Onions

(*Baṣalīyah*: Made of Onion)

Serves 4–6

You will need meat, onions, vinegar, honey, saffron, black pepper, aṭrāf ṭīb, *and mint. Boil the meat, then fry it. Finely chop the onions and boil them by themselves, and then strain them in a sieve. Then add them over the meat and the broth. Mix the honey and vinegar and add to the pot with the saffron and the (other) ingredients. Remove (from the heat).*

—*Kanz al-Fawā'id fī Tanwī' al-Mawā'id*

There are many variations on *Baṣalīyah* in the medieval sources. The recipe in "The Description of Familiar Foods" calls for two parts onions to one part meat, whereas the al-Baghdādi recipe reverses the proportion. We tend in that direction.

The *Baṣalīyah* below is a mild onion-flavored tajine good for light dining.

We enjoy it alongside Tangy Sumac Chicken (*Summaqīyah*; see page 106), as the tastes of sumac and onions go well together.

1/4 cup olive oil
2 lbs. lamb cut into 1-inch cubes
1/2 tsp. black pepper
1 tsp. salt
3/4 tsp. aṭrāf al-ṭīb
1 tsp. dried mint
2 large onions, finely chopped
4 tbsp. honey mixed with 3 tbsp. vinegar
pinch of saffron

Heat the oil in a saucepan over medium heat; add the lamb and sauté for 4 minutes, stirring constantly. Stir in the pepper, salt, *aṭrāf al-ṭīb*, and mint. Sauté for 3 minutes more until the meat has browned on all sides.

Add water to cover by about 2 inches. Raise heat to medium-high and bring to a boil. Stir and cover. Reduce heat to medium-low and cook for about 30 minutes.

Remove the lid and cook over medium heat, stirring occasionally, for 15–20 minutes more or until the liquid has thickened.

While the meat is cooking, bring 4 cups of water to a boil in another saucepan. Add the onions, and cook over medium heat for 5 minutes. Remove and drain in a sieve.

Add the onions to the meat and broth. Stir in the honey/vinegar mixture and saffron and simmer for 10 minutes uncovered, stirring occasionally.

Serve immediately.

Lamb with Greens and Clockwise-Stirred Yogurt

(*Labanīyah Rūmīyah*: Byzantine-Style Yogurt Stew)

Serves 4–6

> *Boil a* raṭl *of meat. Remove the scum. Cook it part way. Add to it chopped green leaves of chard. Cook it until it is well done. Remove the meat, its broth, and the chard. Then put in the pot a pound of yogurt and half an* ūqīyah *of rice. Continue to stir until rice is cooked. Add to it the meat, Swiss chard, and the broth. The broth should be a little. Cook it and remove. Sprinkle mint leaves on it. After ladling it into a bowl, put pounded garlic on top. Turnips can be used instead of chard. The same goes for spinach.*
>
> —Ibn al-ʿAdīm, *Kitāb al-Wuṣlah ilà al-Ḥabīb fī Waṣf al-Ṭayyibāt wa al-Ṭīb*

Milk, both fresh and sour, and particularly in the form of yogurt, is a very ancient ingredient in the cooking of the Arabs. In certain soups, yogurt is added at the end of the cooking and allowed just to become hot without boiling, to avoid any danger of curdling. When yogurt is called for in actual cooking, precautions must be taken so that it does not separate. You will always want to stir the yogurt gently over low heat until it comes to a gentle boil. One of our family members advises, according to tradition, that the yogurt be stirred in a clockwise direction only and with a wooden spoon. We have always followed her instructions just to be on the safe side, as one should not play with popular beliefs!

We serve this as a main dish accompanying Browned Lamb with Saffron-Cinnamon Rice (*Aruzz Mufalfal*; see page 56).

1 lb. lamb, cut into 1/2-inch cubes
1 tsp. salt
4 cups chopped Swiss chard leaves (4 cups chopped spinach or 2 cups finely chopped turnips may be substituted)
2 cups plain yogurt, whole or low-fat
2 tbsp. long grain rice
1 tbsp. finely chopped fresh mint leaves or 1/2 tsp. dried mint
6 cloves garlic, crushed

Place lamb and salt in a saucepan with water to cover, and bring to a boil. Remove scum, cover, and turn heat to medium-low. Cook for 45 minutes, adding more water if necessary to ensure that the meat cooks.

Stir in the Swiss chard, spinach, or turnips and bring to a boil. Cover and cook over medium-low heat for 15 minutes, stirring occasionally. Set aside.

Place the yogurt and rice in another saucepan. With a wooden spoon, stir constantly in one direction over medium heat for 15 minutes or until rice is done.

Stir in the meat and Swiss chard with their broth, then cook over medium heat for 8 minutes, continuing to stir constantly.

Place in a serving bowl, then sprinkle the mint leaves over the top. Spread the garlic evenly over the top and serve.

Fried Bananas with Lamb and Hazelnuts

(*Mawz ma*ᶜ *Laḥm*: Bananas with Meat)

Serves 4–6

> *Peel green bananas. Slice lengthwise like colcosia. Fry them in a lot of sesame oil until the bananas have browned but remain like colcosia. Then, cut the meat and boil it. Fry it in the same way as colcosia [along with] fresh coriander, pounded garlic, and onion. When the meat is brown and cooked through, put the fried bananas on it and a little broth and finely toasted shelled hazelnuts. Let it dry until the broth has evaporated. Then, serve. It is like* Sitt al-Shanᶜ *in color and in taste.*[2]
>
> —Ibn al-ᶜAdīm, *Kitāb al-Wuṣlah ilà al-Ḥabīb fī Waṣf al-Ṭayyibāt wa al-Ṭīb*

It is said that Alexander the Great first tasted the banana in the Indus valley, where it was most likely first cultivated (Watson 51). That was the starting point. From there the banana moved west, and banana production was widespread across the Middle East and in Egypt by the tenth century. Increased cultivation meant easy access to the fruit, and its abundance allowed for its popularity. But it was not only enjoyed as a fruit on its own: it also was used in unique combination with meat in certain medieval Arab dishes. It was a much favored fruit.

Some enjoyed bananas so much that they would serve them to guests. However, according to one story, one guest took offense at their being offered to him. When al-Nūshajānīy placed a bunch of bananas in front of the poet Abū al-ᶜAtāhiyah, the latter accused his host of trying to kill him. Al-ᶜAtāhiyah, it seems, had heard from a worthy source that the great scholar Abū ᶜUbaydah had been carried out of al-Nūshajānīy's house on a stretcher. A bunch of bananas lay near his head and another beside his legs. When asked what had caused him to become ill, the dying Abū ʿUbaydah unhesitatingly blamed his host for offering him too many small bananas that he couldn't resist eating (al-Aghānī IV 12).

We fear no such fate, but assure you that bananas and meat along with hazelnuts yield an intriguing fusion of texture and a subtle flavor.

---

1 cup light sesame oil
4 unripe bananas, peeled and sliced in half, lengthwise
2 lb. lamb with fat removed, cut into 1/2-inch cubes
1 cup chopped fresh coriander leaves
4 cloves garlic, crushed
1 large onion, finely chopped
1 tsp. salt
1/2 cup toasted unsalted hazelnuts

Heat the oil in a frying pan over medium-high heat. Fry the bananas, turning once, to brown on both sides. Remove carefully and drain on paper towels, reserving the oil in the frying pan.

Place the lamb in a saucepan and barely cover with water. Bring to a boil, cover, and cook over medium-high heat until tender, about 20 minutes. Remove the meat with a slotted spoon and retain the broth.

Place the meat in the frying pan with the reserved oil, stirring in the coriander, garlic, onion, and salt and fry over medium-high heat until the meat is browned on all sides and cooked through.

Reduce the heat to low and carefully place the bananas over the meat mixture. Add 1/2 cup of the reserved meat broth. Sprinkle the hazelnuts evenly over the top. Cover and simmer over low heat until the broth has almost evaporated.

Serve immediately.

Spiced Lamb and Fennel Tajine

(*al-Rāziyānaj al-Akhḍar*: Green Fennel)

Serves 4–6

> *Boil the meat and fry with fresh coriander, onions, and hot spices and a little garlic. Then pick out the fennel hearts and cut in half. Put over the*

meat. Put back some of the broth on it along with sheep's tail. Boil until cooked and the broth has been absorbed. Remove [from the heat].

—Ibn al-ʿAdīm, *Kitāb al-Wuṣlah ilà al-Ḥabīb fī Waṣf al-Ṭayyibāt wa al-Ṭīb*

The source recipe for this dish calls for *abzār ḥārrah*, "hot spices." This is a combination of spices such as black pepper, caraway, coriander seed, and cinnamon. We think that the subtle flavor of the cooked fennel along with the spices makes for a distinctive tasting tajine.

2 lb. lamb or beef cut in 1-inch cubes
5 cups water
6 tbsp. olive oil
1/2 cup finely chopped fresh coriander leaves
1 large onion, finely chopped
1 1/8 tsp. black pepper
1 tsp. salt
1/2 tsp. ground caraway seeds
1/2 tsp. ground coriander seeds
1/4 tsp. cinnamon
6 cloves garlic, finely chopped
1 large fennel bulb, washed and cut in half

Place the meat cubes in a saucepan with the water and bring to a boil. Cover and cook over medium heat until the meat is tender, adding more water if necessary. Remove the meat from the saucepan and set the broth aside.

Heat 4 tbsp. oil in a frying pan and add the cooked meat, coriander, onion, black pepper, salt, caraway, ground coriander, cinnamon, and garlic. Sauté together over medium heat for 8 minutes, stirring a number of times.

Place the fennel on top of the meat and add 3 cups reserved broth and the remaining 2 tbsp. oil. Bring to a boil, cover, lower the heat to medium-low, and allow to cook for about 35 minutes or until most of the broth has been absorbed. Serve immediately.

Sweet and Sour Lamb and Vegetable Stew

(*Sikbāj*: Vinegared Stew)

Serves 4–6

> *Cut fatty meat in medium size pieces and put in a pot, covering it with water and a little salt and cinnamon. When it boils, remove the scum. Then put dried coriander on it and take white onions, Syrian leeks, and carrots if they are in season or eggplant and peel all of them. Cut the eggplant lengthwise in quarters and boil it in another pot with water and salt. Add it to the meat, laying it evenly and throw the spices on them. When it is nearly cooked, take some vinegar and fat or honey in the amount needed to make an even combination of sour and sweet. Pour it into the pot and allow it to boil for a while. Then take a little of the broth and dissolve what is needed of saffron and throw it in the pot. Then take peeled almonds split in two, a palm-ful of washed jujubes, dried figs, and raisins and put on top of the pot. Cover it and (allow to cook) for a while. Turn off the fire and wipe the sides with a clean piece of cloth. Sprinkle a little rosewater on it. Allow to sit and then serve.*
>
> *—Kanz al-Fawā'id fī Tanwīʿ al-Mawā'id*

The Persians played a major and influential role in introducing new foods to the Arab world, and prominent among these was *Sikbāj*, a dish that included a broth made from meat juices and vinegar.

One of the most favored dishes among the elite and caliphs alike, *Sikbāj* could be prepared with lamb, veal, beef, or chicken, its sourness sweetened with sugar, syrup, honey, or date molasses—or not sweetened at all (al-Baghdādī 9).

For some, *Sikbāj* epitomized the luxury of the Persian court and its magnificence. The Sassanian Chosroes Anūshirwān once held a contest in which he ordered his cooks to prepare what they each considered to be their best dish. Acting independently of one another, they each presented *Sikbāj*. It was this same king who came to spend 1,000 dirhams a day on *Sikbāj* and prohibited anyone not of his household from eating what he called "The Queen of All Foods" (al-Warrāq 132).

Escabeche, the name for the pickled fish and other meat in modern Spain, originates from the word *al-sikbāj*, as do English caveach, French *escabèche*, Italian *scapece*, and Portuguese *escabe*. In the New World the dish is named *ceviche*. All, like *Sikbāj*, include vinegar.

2 lb. lamb with some fat, cut into 1/2-inch cubes
2 tsp. salt
1/2 tsp. cinnamon
1/8 tsp. pure saffron
1 tsp. ground coriander seeds
2 medium onions, finely chopped
2 cups chopped leeks
2 cups diced carrots
1/4 cup vinegar
4 tbsp. honey
1/2 cup split almonds
1/4 cup jujubes
1 cup chopped dried figs
1/2 cup raisins
2 tsp. rosewater

Place the lamb, salt, and cinnamon in a saucepan, cover with water, and bring to a boil, skimming off any scum. Remove 2 tbsp. broth, dilute with saffron, and set aside.

Add the coriander, onions, leeks, and carrots to the saucepan. Bring to a boil, cover, and cook over medium heat for 40 minutes, stirring a few times. Uncover and cook 20 minutes more.

Stir in the vinegar and the honey, bring to a boil, and continue cooking over medium heat for 10 minutes.

Stir in the diluted saffron and all the remaining ingredients except the rosewater. Cook 20–25 minutes over medium heat, until almost all the liquid is absorbed, stirring occasionally.

Sprinkle with the rosewater and let stand for 5 minutes before serving.

Savory Meatballs and Cubed Lamb with Coriander

(*Tafāyā al-Bayḍāʾ*: White Tafāyā)

Serves 4–6

> *Take meat from a male sheep in its third year, from its breast, its forelegs, and its flanks—whatever choice is available—and cut and clean it and put it in a new pot. Put water and oil on top of it. Take a new piece of cloth and*

put ginger, salt, dried coriander, and a little chopped onion in it. Tie up the piece of cloth and throw it in the pot with the meat and once it is known that the water has been strengthened (by the spices), take it (the cloth spice bag) out of the pot, so that the broth does not change. Leave the meat until it is cooked. Whoever wants to add meatballs to the pot then do so. Once the meat is cooked, leave it for a short time over a low fire until it browns and its fat appears. Then it is finished. Then use it, Almighty God willing. If you want to make this dish with baby kid's meat or with young chickens or with chickens, then do so as I have described with the power of Almighty God.

—al-Tujībī, *Faḍālah al-Khiwān fī Ṭayyibāt al-Ṭaʿām wa al-Alwān*

What identifies a *Tafāyā* is the use of coriander, dried in what are known as white *Tafāyās* and fresh in the green type. Most *Tafāyā* recipes also include meatballs and small *Sanbūsak*. Mint juice was often added to the green variety, while the color of white *Tafāyā* was often imparted through the use of split almonds (*Anonymous Andalusian Cookbook*).

This is a mildly spiced dish with a condensed creamy sauce and is best served with a vegetable appetizer such as Tangy Eggplant Stir-Fry (*al-Bādhinjān*; see page 23) or Honeyed Carrots in Rosewater (*al-Jazar*; see page 27).

For the meatballs:

1/2 lb. ground lamb
1/2 tsp. miso
2 tsp. vinegar
1 tbsp. olive oil
2 cloves garlic, crushed
1/2 tsp. black pepper
pinch of saffron
1/2 tsp. cumin
1/2 tsp. ground coriander seeds
1/2 tsp. rosewater
1/4 tsp. cinnamon
pinch of ground cloves
2 tbsp. butter at room temperature
1 egg, beaten
olive oil for frying

For the *Tafāyā*:

2 lbs. lamb or skinless, boneless chicken, cut into 1-inch cubes
1/4 cup olive oil
2 tbsp. grated fresh ginger
1 1/2 tsp. salt
1 1/2 tsp. ground coriander seeds
1 medium onion, finely chopped

Mix the ingredients for the meatballs. Form into 1/2-inch balls. Fry in olive oil over medium heat until browned. Set aside.

Place the lamb or chicken and oil in a saucepan, cover with water, and bring to a boil. Remove any scum.

Place the ginger, salt, coriander, and onion in a spice bag and secure tightly. Add the spice bag to the saucepan with the lamb or chicken and cover. Cook over medium-low heat for 45 minutes.

Remove the spice bag and stir in the meatballs. Cook uncovered over medium-high heat for another 45 minutes or until the liquid has almost evaporated, stirring often to ensure the meat does not stick to the bottom of the saucepan.

Serve hot.

Spice-Infused Cucumbers with Lamb and Walnuts

(*ʿAjūrīyah*: of Cucumber)

Serves 4–6

> *Cut meat into small pieces. Boil and fry until browned. Section the cucumber into a cross. Take dried coriander, black pepper, salt, and Chinese cinnamon and stuff the cucumber. Arrange them one over another until their water comes out. In the pot, put with it sliced onions, fresh coriander, and pounded garlic. Throw it over the meat. Return to it a little broth and sheep tail fat. Allow to gently dry until the broth dries out and is cooked. If desired, add to it finely pounded walnuts.*
>
> —Ibn al-ʿAdīm, *Kitāb al-Wuṣlah ilà al-Ḥabīb fī Waṣf al-Ṭayyibāt wa al-Ṭīb*

When, in a story of *The Thousand and One Arabian Nights,* Judar pulled from the magical saddlebags one of the foods known as *ʿAjjūrīyah,* his mother was shocked since this cucumber-based dish was considered very fine and elegant. In general, we admit, cucumbers are bland cooked on their own. However, in this recipe, the cucumber is transformed into something luxurious, prepared with spices and garnished with walnuts. Just as eggplant came to be accepted and enjoyed on the tables of nobility, so did the cucumber chart a course of upward culinary mobility.

Although this preparation may take a little while, the end result is well worth the time and effort.

---

4 cucumbers, 6 inches long
1 lb. ground lamb
3 1/2 cups water
7 tbsp. olive oil
1 tsp. ground coriander seeds
3/4 tsp. black pepper
1 1/2 tsp. salt
1/2 tsp. cinnamon
2 medium onions, thinly sliced
3/4 cup finely chopped fresh coriander leaves
4 cloves garlic, crushed
2 tbsp. finely ground walnuts

Starting about 1/8 inch from the bottom end of each cucumber, make a lengthwise slit to 1/8 inch from the top. Slit again crosswise, making a cross shape. Set aside.

Place the lamb and 1 1/2 cups water in a saucepan and bring to a boil, turn heat to medium-low, and cook for 8 minutes. Drain the meat and set aside, reserving the broth.

Heat 5 tbsp. of the oil in a frying pan and sauté the meat over medium heat for about 3–4 minutes or until light brown. Set aside.

Combine the ground coriander, black pepper, salt, and cinnamon and rub into the slits of the cucumbers. Place cucumbers carefully on a rack over a tray and allow to drain for 1 hour.

Carefully place the cucumbers in a saucepan and cover them with the onions, fresh coriander, garlic, meat, remaining oil, reserved broth, and the 2 remaining cups of water. Bring to a boil, cover, and cook over medium-low heat for 40 minutes.

Carefully transfer onto a serving platter. Sprinkle the walnuts over the top and serve immediately.

Asparagus Wrapped in Lamb

(*Luḥūm al-Ḍaʾin Yuṭbakh bi-al-Isfarāj*: Preparing Asparagus with Meat Coating)

Serves 4–6

> *Take asparagus, the largest you have, clean and boil it. Take tender meat and pound fine. Throw in pepper, caraway, coriander seed, cilantro juice, some oil, and egg white. Take the boiled asparagus, one after another, and dress with this ground meat, and do so carefully. Put an earthenware pot on the fire, and put in it water, salt, a spoon of* murrī *and another of oil, cilantro juice, pepper, caraway, and coriander seed. Little by little, while the pot boils, throw in it the asparagus wrapped in meat. Boil it in the pot and throw in it meatballs of this ground meat. And when it is all evenly cooked, cover with egg, bread crumbs, and some of the stuffed meat already mentioned and decorate with egg, God willing.*
>
> *—Anonymous Andalusian Cookbook (Kitāb al-Ṭabikh fī al-Maghrib wa al-Andalus fī ʿAṣr al-Muwaḥḥidīn, li-muʿallif majhūl), page 104, translated by Charles Perry*

The Abbasid poet Kushājim described asparagus as one of nature's most beautiful vegetables and wrote that God, excelling in its creation, dressed it in a cloak of green silk brocade. For him, when placed on a table, asparagus appeared lance-like, the tops layered like "a coat of mail" or woven in the manner of gold. Decorated with yellow and dressed in oil, its color shone, and the sight alone was enough to satisfy. In fact, the devout person, upon seeing asparagus, would prostrate himself before it (al-Masʿūdī VIII 399–400).

We confess that our own reactions are somewhat more reserved, but for those who enjoy a tasty and spicy dish, the time involved in preparing this recipe will be well spent.

---

1 1/2 tsp. salt
1/2 lb. large asparagus, washed and ends snipped
1 1/2 lb. finely ground lamb
1 tsp. black pepper
1 tsp. ground caraway seeds
1 tsp. ground coriander seeds
4 tbsp. finely chopped fresh coriander leaves
2 tbsp. olive oil
whites of 2 eggs

1 tsp. red miso
2 eggs, beaten
2 tbsp. bread crumbs
2 boiled eggs, chopped

Bring at least 4 1/2 cups water to boil in a large saucepan with 1/2 tsp. salt. Add asparagus, and bring to a boil again. Cook for 5 minutes. Remove and drain asparagus, reserving 4 cups water.

Mix the lamb, 1/2 tsp. black pepper, 1/2 tsp. caraway, 1/2 tsp. ground coriander, 2 tbsp. fresh coriander, 1 tbsp. oil, and egg whites. Knead well, divide into two parts, and set aside.

Using half the meat, wrap each asparagus stalk carefully, allowing the ends to show.

Divide the remaining meat, forming half of it into small meatballs about 1/2 inch in diameter. Set aside.

Put reserved water into wide, deep casserole and stir in miso and remaining salt, black pepper, caraway, ground and fresh coriander, and oil. Bring to a boil, lower heat to medium-low, and carefully add the meat-wrapped asparagus and meatballs. Cover and cook for approximately 30 minutes.

Pour beaten eggs evenly over the contents of the casserole and sprinkle with bread crumbs. Top with the remaining pieces of meat, flattened as thin as possible.

Cover and cook for 15 minutes more over medium-low heat. Remove from heat, sprinkle evenly with the chopped boiled eggs, and serve immediately.

Ground Meat with Fried Halloumi Cheese and Spices

(*Badīʿīyah*: Marvelous or Unprecedented: A Dish from the Western Arab Lands)

Serves 4–6

> *Fry the meat, that has been pounded and mixed with spices, until it browns. Take* khaysī *cheese; it is the type that can be fried. Bring water to a strong boil for it. Cut (the cheese) and throw it in it and leave for a while. Drain it in a sieve. Fry it in sesame oil. Arrange the meat and cheese in a frying pan. Beat whole eggs with hot spices and chopped parsley and a little saffron. Leave an amount of egg yolks on the side. Fold the beaten eggs with spices and the ingredients into the meat and cheese until all is well-coated. Drizzle onto it a little broth and a lot of sheep tail fat. Leave it until it is*

cooked (after having added to it the egg yolks) and put over them some of the pounded (meat) and some of the fried cheese and the other ingredients. Remove.

—Ibn al-ʿAdīm, *Kitāb al-Wuṣlah ilà al-Ḥabīb fī Waṣf al-Ṭayyibāt wa al-Ṭīb*

The *khaysī* called for in this recipe is a solid type of cheese that can be fried. We substitute a more available type of cheese called halloumi (*ḥālūm*), which was known in the Middle Ages and is widely available in Middle Eastern grocery stores, and popular in Arab cooking.

As its name implies, the dish is excellent. We recommend serving it with Pickled Onions (*Baṣal Mukhallal*; see page 26), which will add a good tartness to the taste, and with a vegetable dish such as Honeyed Carrots in Rosewater (*al-Jazar*; see page 27).

---

2 lb. ground lamb or beef
1/2 tsp. salt
1/4 tsp. black pepper
1/4 tsp. cinnamon
1/4 tsp. caraway seeds
1/4 tsp. ground coriander seeds
1/4 tsp. ground ginger
1/2 cup + 2 tbsp. light sesame oil
1 lb. halloumi cheese, cut in 1/2-inch cubes
4 eggs beaten with 2 egg whites and mixed with 1/8 tsp. cayenne, 1/8 tsp. cumin, 1/8 tsp. black pepper, and pinch of saffron
4 tbsp. finely chopped fresh parsley
4 tbsp. butter, melted
2 egg yolks

Combine the meat, salt, black pepper, cinnamon, caraway, coriander, and ginger.

In a large frying pan, heat 4 tbsp. oil over medium heat. Add meat mixture and cook, stirring constantly, for 12 minutes. Set aside but keep warm in the pan.

Bring 2 cups water to boil in a small saucepan. Add the cheese. Bring to a boil again, cook for 1 minute, remove from heat, drain, and set aside.

Heat the remaining oil in a small frying pan over medium heat and sauté the cheese for 5–6 minutes, until browned on both sides, turning over once.

Add half the cheese to the meat. Fold in the beaten egg mixture, parsley, and butter, then stir-fry over medium-low heat for 1 minute.

Place the egg yolks over the meat mixture, breaking up the yolks to allow them to spread. Cover and continue to cook until the eggs are done, about 2 minutes.

Spread the remaining cheese over the top and serve immediately from the pan.

The Caliph's Wife's Eggplant and Lamb Stir-Fry

(*Būrānīyah*: of Būrān)

Serves 4–6

> *Cut meat into small pieces and boil. It will be fried with onions, fresh coriander, and hot spices after having pounded the meat with the fresh coriander, onions, and hot spices. Fry the meat with them. Then fry for it dried onions and eggplants that have been pierced with a knife and that have been thrown into water and salt in order that the black water comes out of them and it is then pressed out, and fried in sheep tail fat or sesame oil enough to cover them. When it is brown and has reached the right consistency, place the eggplant over the meat. Sprinkle on it dried coriander and sheep tail fat. Add to it the measure of 6 or 7 spoonfuls of meat broth. Simmer over the fire. Turn it every once in a while until the broth is absorbed. Spoon it out. Sprinkle on it dried coriander, Chinese cinnamon, and black pepper.*
>
> —Ibn al-ʿAdīm, *Kitāb al-Wuṣlah ilà al-Ḥabīb fī Waṣf al-Ṭayyibāt wa al-Ṭīb*

This delicious eggplant and lamb dish is attributed to the wife of Caliph al-Maʾmūn, Būrān, who is said to have made it first, on the occasion of her marriage in 825 to the caliph in Baghdad (al-Rāghib al-Aṣbahāni II 617).

6 small eggplants, about 5 inches long
2 1/2 tsp. salt
1 lb. lamb, cut into 1/2-inch cubes
3/4 cup light sesame oil
2 medium onions, finely chopped
1/2 cup finely chopped fresh coriander leaves
1 1/2 tsp. black pepper

1 tsp. ground ginger
3/4 tsp. ground coriander seeds
1/4 tsp. cinnamon

Pierce the eggplants in several places with a fork or knife and soak in water with 2 tsp. salt for one hour. Remove from the water and press out the water by placing the eggplants under a weight for at least one hour.

Place the lamb in a saucepan, cover with water, and bring to a boil, skimming off any scum. Cover and cook over medium heat for 30 minutes. Drain the meat, reserving the broth.

Heat 4 tbsp. oil in a large frying pan over medium heat. Add the meat, remaining salt, onions, fresh coriander, 1 1/4 tsp. black pepper, and ginger and stir-fry for 10 minutes. Set aside but keep warm.

Fry the eggplants in remaining oil over medium heat for 10 minutes, turning them over to brown all over.

Place the eggplants over the meat in the frying pan. Sprinkle with 1/2 tsp. ground coriander. Add a cup of the reserved broth; simmer over medium-low heat for 10 minutes covered and another 10 to 15 minutes uncovered, or until the broth has been absorbed, turning eggplants over several times.

Transfer to a serving platter, sprinkle with remaining 1/4 tsp. black pepper, remaining 1/4 tsp. ground coriander, and cinnamon, and serve.

Stuffed Eggplant

(*Madfūnah*: Buried)

Serves 4–6

Its procedure is to cut up fatty meat in small pieces. Dissolve sheep tail fat and fry the meat until moist. Then cover with water. Add to it a dirham of salt, a dirham of finely ground dried coriander, and a cinnamon stick. Once it boils, take its scum and throw it away. Take red meat and pound finely. Boil in water and salt and add to it a handful of skinned and coarsely ground chickpeas that have been soaked in water for a while. Then take large eggplants and cut off their stems and remove all that is in their core of their seeds preserving (its exterior) so that it does not get pierced. Then stuff them with that meat adding to it the well-known spices. Then lay them in the pot after having chopped for it a little onion that was first put in the pot before it (the meat). Then color the pot's broth with a little saffron. Sprinkle over it a dirham of powdered dried coriander and powdered cinnamon. Wipe its sides with a clean piece of cloth and allow it to sit over a gentle fire for a while and then remove.

—al-Baghdādi, *Kitāb al-Ṭabīkh*

For medieval Arabs, the eggplant was one of the popular vegetables for stuffing. Still today, a stuffed eggplant makes a tempting entrée, especially since whatever is buried within it is quickly discovered with the first bite.

For Arab mothers teaching their children the key points of cooking, the first lesson is usually how to make Arabic coffee, and the second how to core an eggplant or squash properly. When coring any type of vegetable to prep it for stuffing, the goal is to hollow it out as thin as possible, without piercing the outer skin.

The stuffing in al-Baghdādī's *Madfūnah* is made of a spicy meat-chickpea blend. The trick is to place a thick stuffing gently and carefully into a thin sleeve of vegetable without tearing.

1 lb. lamb with some fat, cut into 1/2-inch cubes
1/4 cup cooking oil
1 medium onion, finely chopped
2 tsp. salt
1 tsp. ground coriander seeds
1 cinnamon stick
2 eggplants, 1 lb. each
1 lb. ground lamb
1/2 cup dried chickpeas, soaked overnight, drained, skins removed, then coarsely ground
1 tsp. cumin
1 tsp. black pepper
1/2 tsp. aṭrāf al-ṭīb
pinch of saffron dissolved in 2 tbsp. hot water
1/4 tsp. cinnamon

Place the cubed lamb and oil in a saucepan large enough to hold the eggplants; stir-fry over medium heat for 5 minutes. Add water just to cover the meat. Bring to a boil and remove any scum.

Add the onion, 1 tsp. salt, 1/2 tsp. coriander, and cinnamon stick. Cover and cook over medium-low heat for 40 minutes. Remove cinnamon stick, remove saucepan from heat, and set aside.

Core eggplants, making sure not to pierce the exterior. Reserve the caps.

Place the ground lamb and remaining salt in a small saucepan. Barely cover with water and bring to a boil. Cover and cook over medium-low heat for 30 minutes, stirring a few times, adding a little more water if needed.

Remove from heat. Stir in the chickpeas, then add the cumin, black pepper, and *aṭrāf al-ṭīb*. Set aside and allow to cool.

Stuff the eggplants with the ground meat-chickpea mixture, then carefully seal with their caps. Place lengthwise in the saucepan with the cubed meat and its liquid. Add the dissolved saffron, remaining coriander, cinnamon and enough water to barely cover the top of the eggplants. Bring to a boil, cover, and cook over low heat for 40 minutes, occasionally stirring the sauce and gently moving the eggplants to prevent their sticking to the bottom.

Place the eggplants on a serving platter and spoon the sauce over them. Slice into one-inch rounds and serve immediately.

Lamb and Vegetables with Spiced Onion Sauce

(*Dīkabrīkāt* or *Dhājibrijah* of Ibrāhīm ibn al-Mahdī, who made it for al-Muʿtaṣim)

Serves 4–6

Take three raṭls *of scalded lamb. Put it in a pot. Pour over it three* ūqīyahs *of oil that has been washed of all impurities and moistures, a piece of galangal root, a* raṭl *of whole onions and two dirhams of* andarānī *[snow-white] salt and a measure of fresh coriander that the palm and fingers can hold. Cover everything with water amounting to four fingers wide. Boil until the onions are almost cooked. Then remove the whole onions and put aside. Pour into the pot a* raṭl *of wine-vinegar and stir until the meat cooks or is almost done. Add a bunch of leeks or carrots and Syrian leeks or eggplants or gourds.*[3] *Then cover. Mash the onions that were put aside with a measure of five dirhams of dried coriander, a half dirham of black pepper and five dirhams of caraway. Put all of this in a large bowl and pour over it two* ūqīyahs *of Nabatean* murrī *and some of the pot's sauce. Then mix it well together and return it to the pot leaving it to boil. Remove it from the fire while it is still boiling and sprinkle over it some chopped fresh coriander and cover it until it settles. Then ladle it and present it, God willing!*

—al-Warrāq, Abū Muḥammad al-Muẓaffar ibn Naṣr ibn Sayyār, *Kitāb al-Ṭabīkh wa Iṣlāḥ al-Aghdhiyah al-Maʾkūlāt wa Ṭayyibah al-Aṭʿimah al-Maṣnūʿāt*

The origin of the name of this dish is obscure, although the etymology seems to be Persian. Whatever its source, we can be sure that Ibrāhīm ibn al-Mahdī enjoyed it, describing it as an orchard flower or the glow of gardens (al-Warrāq 151). The dish is actually tart and tangy and makes for a full meal when rice is served alongside.

For those cooks who wish to follow tradition we recommend using a mortar and pestle to mash the onions with the spices; for those who favor contemporary technology, a food processor serves the same purpose.

3 lb. lamb, cut into 1-inch cubes
3 tbsp. olive oil
3/4 tsp. ground ginger
1 lb. onions, peeled and left whole
1 1/2 tsp. salt
3/4 cup finely chopped fresh coriander leaves
1 cup wine vinegar
3 cups chopped leeks, green parts only
2 cups peeled eggplant, cut into 1-inch cubes
2 tsp. ground coriander seeds
1 tsp. black pepper
2 tsp. ground caraway seeds
1 tbsp. red miso

Place the lamb, oil, ginger, onions, salt, and 4 tbsp. fresh coriander in a saucepan, and water to cover to 2 inches. Bring to a boil, cover, and cook over medium heat for 40 minutes.

Remove the onions with a slotted spoon, place in a strainer, and set aside. Skim off any excess froth or scum.

Add the vinegar to the saucepan contents and cook over medium-low heat for 5 minutes, stirring a number of times. Stir in the leeks and the eggplant, then cover and cook for a few minutes.

Place the onions in a bowl and mash them, adding the ground coriander, black pepper, caraway, miso, and 2 cups of the broth from the saucepan. Combine well.

Pour onion mix into the saucepan and bring to a boil. Cook for 5 minutes or until the meat and vegetables are done. Sprinkle with the remaining fresh coriander leaves and serve hot.

Garlicky Spinach with Buttered Lamb and Chickpeas

(*Isfānākh*: Spinach)

Serves 4–6

> *Cut meat in large pieces and boil with chickpeas. When it is cooked, remove the meat and fry it in fat and good oil. Stir its broth into it. Wash rice and put it in until it is cooked. Throw in it a lot of whole garlic cloves. On the side, boil whole spinach in water until it is cooked. When it is done, put it over the rice and allow it to sit until it dries and is firm. There should be a lot of fat in it.*
>
> —Ibn al-ʿAdīm, *Kitāb al-Wuṣlah ilà al-Ḥabīb fī Wasf al-Ṭayyibāt wa al-Ṭīb*

Al-Isfānākh is a meal in itself. The chickpeas and rice with the spinach are flavored with a hefty amount of garlic. Another version of this dish, called *Isfānākhīyah*, is prepared in the same way but with more spices (al-Baghdādī 26) or with the addition of hazelnut-size meatballs ("Description" 331).

1/2 cup dried chickpeas, soaked overnight and drained
1 lb. lamb, cut into serving pieces
1/4 cup olive oil
1 cup long grain rice, rinsed
1 1/4 tsp. salt
cloves of one head of garlic, peeled
2 bunches spinach, or 2 10 oz. bags spinach leaves, thoroughly washed and stemmed
4 tbsp. butter, melted

Place the chickpeas in a large saucepan and cover with 4 inches of water. Bring to a boil and remove the scum. Cover and cook over medium heat for 40 minutes.

Add the lamb, bring to a boil over medium-high heat, and cook for 1 hour over medium heat, adding more water if necessary. Set saucepan aside.

Remove the meat with a slotted spoon. Heat the oil in a frying pan over medium-high heat, and brown the meat on all sides, for a total of about 5 minutes. Return the meat to the chickpeas and broth, and stir in the rice, salt, and garlic, adding extra water to cover if needed. Bring to a boil, cover, and cook over medium-low heat for 12 minutes. Stir, turn off the heat, and allow to cook in its own steam in the covered saucepan for 30 minutes.

In the meantime, bring water to a boil in another saucepan, add the spinach, and cook for 5 minutes. Remove, place in ice-cold water for 1 minute, and drain well.

Spoon the meat/chickpea/rice mixture onto a serving dish and drizzle with the butter. Place the spinach evenly over the top and serve immediately.

Spiced Lamb with Honeyed Apricots

(*Mishmish Yābis*: Dried Apricots)

Serves 4–6

Chop meat in small pieces and boil. Put the broth aside. Cook the onions, fresh coriander, and spices until limp and until the meat browns and changes color and the onions have shrunk. Then take dried sweet-kernelled apricots and wash them in hot water for a while just until the pits can be easily removed without damaging the apricots. Arrange them on the fried meat and add enough broth to cover them. Turn over every once in a while in order that the apricots are cooked very well. When they are cooked add honey and lemon juice. If sour grape juice is available it is better than lemon juice because its aftertaste is distinct and sweet. Cook it until its broth has dried up. Add to it mint and fresh coriander. If lemon juice is not used then replace it with the sour grape juice to make it more potent. Add finely pounded spices, mint, fresh coriander and onions. Cook, simmer, and spoon into a serving bowl and sprinkle on it both dried and chopped fresh coriander. If dry apricot paste is available, the kind made in Byzantium or in Medina, this is better than [sweet-kernelled] apricots.

—Ibn al-ʿAdīm, *Kitāb al-Wuṣlah ilà al-Ḥabīb fī Waṣf al-Ṭayyibāt wa al-Ṭīb*

The versatility of ingredients was a hallmark of cooking during the Abbasid period. Seasonings, condiments, and aromatic spices were used in ever-changing combinations in these dishes. Drying fruits was a popular method to preserve them for later use, and their abundance, especially in Syria and Iraq, encouraged cooks to find innovative ways of including them in main dishes. A repertoire of sweet and sour or spicy and sweet meat dishes was developed, and some of the most delectable used dried apricots.

Called by the Persians the "golden seeds of the sun," apricots are one of the earliest fruits known to man. Some even believe that they were the "apples" in the Garden of Eden.

This dish below combines dried apricots with lamb to excellent advantage. A version continues to grace the Arab tables in North Africa; in Iraq today, another variant is a stew of lamb meatballs, apricots, sugar, and tomato paste.

---

2 lb. lamb, cut into 1-inch cubes
1/4 cup olive oil
2 medium onions, finely chopped
1 1/4 cups finely chopped fresh coriander leaves
1 tsp. cumin
1 tsp. black pepper
1 1/4 tsp. ground coriander seeds
1 lb. dried apricots, soaked in hot water for 1 hour
2 tbsp. honey
2 tbsp. lemon juice
1 tsp. dried mint
1 tsp. salt

Place the lamb in a saucepan, cover with water, and bring to a boil, skimming off any scum. Cover and cook over medium heat for 40 minutes. Drain but reserve the broth. Return the meat to the saucepan.

Add the oil, all but 2 tbsp. onions, 1/2 cup fresh coriander, 1/2 tsp. cumin, 1/2 tsp. black pepper, and 1/2 tsp. ground coriander, and fry, stirring occasionally for 8 minutes.

Add the apricots and barely cover with the reserved broth. Cover and cook over medium-low heat for 15 minutes or until the apricots are cooked but not overcooked, stirring a number of times.

Stir in the honey and lemon juice and cook for 15 minutes more or until only a little broth remains.

Stir in the mint, salt, the remaining 2 tbsp. onions, 1/2 cup of the remaining fresh coriander and the remaining cumin, black pepper, and 1/2 tsp. of the remaining ground coriander. Cook, stirring, for 2 minutes, then transfer to a serving bowl. Sprinkle with the remaining ground and fresh coriander and serve.

Sweet and Meaty Lamb and Date Kebabs

(*Ruṭabīyah*: Made of Dates)

Serves 6–8

> *Its method of preparation is to cut red meat into small, long, thin slices. Then melt fresh sheep tail fat, discarding its residue. Throw the meat into the fat. Add to it half a dirham of salt, and the same for finely ground dried coriander. Stir until browned. Then cover with tepid water. When it boils, remove its scum. Put in a handful of almonds and pistachios that have been peeled and coarsely ground. Color with a little saffron. Throw into it finely ground cumin, coriander, cinnamon, and mastic, about two and half dirhams in all. Take finely pounded red meat as required, and make into long kebabs placing inside each a peeled sweet almond and put into the pot. Take* ṭabarzadh *or another (sweet) type, a cluster of dates. Remove the stone from the bottom of the date with a large needle, and put in its place a peeled sweet almond. When it (the meat) is cooked and its liquid has evaporated so that only its fat remains, arrange these dates over it. Sprinkle over it about ten dirhams of sugar that have been scented with a* dānaq *of camphor. Spray a little rosewater over it. Wipe the sides of the saucepan with a clean rag, and leave to settle over the fire for a while, then serve.*
>
> —al-Baghdādī, *Kitāb al-Ṭabīkh*

So important were dates for the Bedouin that a little milk with water and five small dried dates would make them "kings of the earth" (*Rasā'il al-Jāḥiẓ* II 394–395). Dates are exceedingly rich and nourishing, ideal for the daily diet. If need be, one can subsist for many months on a menu of only dates and milk—a diet eaten for centuries in the Arabian Peninsula. It is little wonder, then, that the Bedouin came to call dates the "bread of the desert," considering them a miracle food.

Ruṭabīyah is one of those richly flavored tajines with the unique taste of a sweet meat dish. In the words of one of our guests as he clamored for seconds, "I've never eaten an entrée and dessert together in one dish!"

We recommend Mejdoul dates to guarantee the full flavor of this dish.

1/4 cup olive oil
1 lb. lamb, sliced in about 4-inch thin strips
2 tsp. salt
2 tsp. ground coriander seeds
1/3 cup blanched almonds, coarsely ground
1/3 cup pistachios, coarsely ground
pinch of saffron
1 1/2 tsp. cumin
1 1/2 tsp. cinnamon
pinch of mastic
1 lb. finely ground lamb
48 whole blanched almonds
32 Mejdoul dates, pitted
2 tbsp. sugar
1/2 tsp. dried mint
2 tbsp. rosewater

Heat the oil in a saucepan over medium heat. Add the lamb strips and sprinkle with 1 tsp. salt and 1/2 tsp. coriander. Stir-fry until the meat is lightly browned, cover with 2 inches of water, and bring to a boil, removing the scum as it gathers.

Stir in the ground almonds, pistachios, saffron, 3/4 tsp. cumin, 3/4 tsp. cinnamon, mastic, and 1/2 tsp. coriander. Remove from heat.

In a mixing bowl, combine the ground lamb and the remaining salt, coriander, cumin, and cinnamon, and mix well. Form into 16 long kebabs, inserting 1 blanched almond into each.

Carefully add the kebabs to the saucepan. Cook uncovered over medium-low heat for 30 minutes. Turn the kebabs over and cook 30 minutes more or until most of the liquid has evaporated and the meat is done.

While the meat is cooking, prepare the dates by placing one almond inside each. Once the meat is cooked, place the dates evenly over the top of the meat, then sprinkle evenly with the sugar, mint, and rosewater.

Turn off the heat, cover, and allow to sit for 10 minutes before serving.

Spicy Lamb Sausage

(*Ṣiffah Ḥashū Maṣīr al-Duwwārah*: Manner of Preparing the Stuffing for the Small Intestine: Making Sausages)

About 44 patties 2 inches in diameter

> *Take red meat and chop up very fine along with the same amount of sheep tail fat. Then take fresh herbs, onions, and rue and chop very finely. Then pound them very finely with a knife until they become the texture of ointment. Add to it cassia, black pepper, caraway,* kāmakh *sauce, a little vinegar, and olive oil and knead until it is mixed. Then stuff large intestines (of sheep) with their fat and stuff small intestines. Cook them with whatever dishes you like, God willing.*
>
> —al-Warrāq, Abū Muḥammad al-Muẓaffar ibn Naṣr ibn Sayyār, *Kitāb al-Ṭabīkh wa Iṣlāḥ al-Aghdhiyah al-Ma'kūlāt wa Ṭayyibah al-Aṭ'imah al-Maṣnū'āt*

Sausages in the medieval Arab world were of a spicy type. The casings were made from the large or small intestine. The smaller sausages were and are still known as *Laqāniq*, *Maqāniq*, and *Naqāniq*. In al-Andalus and the Maghrib these were known as *mirqās*, although al-Tujībī has a recipe labeled *Laqāniq* in which he states that they are made like *mirqās* (146). Today, in North Africa, one finds "*mergaz*" (or *merguez*), featuring such ingredients as sumac, paprika, and harissa, a hot chili paste. Not surprisingly, they have caught on in the large cities of France, thanks to the steady influx of immigrants from North Africa to the country.

If one prefers to shy away from "intestines," the meat can be formed into patties or long kebabs and fried or baked in the oven. Their uses are many: think of serving them as appetizers or alongside Fried Eggs with Vinegar and Spices (*Bayḍ Maṣūṣ*; see page 17) for breakfast.

2 lb. ground lamb
1/4 lb. lamb or beef fat, ground (not suet)
1/2 cup finely chopped fresh coriander leaves
1 medium onion, very finely chopped
2 tbsp. finely chopped rue or dandelion leaves
1 tsp. cinnamon
1 tsp. black pepper
1/2 tsp. ground caraway seeds

3 tsp. soy sauce
2 tbsp. vinegar
2 tbsp. olive oil
sheep intestine casings
oil for frying

Place all the ingredients, except the intestine casings and the oil for frying, in a food processor and process for one minute, then remove.

Stuff the intestine casings thoroughly, leaving a little space at the top. Twist the top end of the casing to secure the filling. Or, if casings are not used, form into patties or long kebabs.

Fry the sausages in oil over medium heat until browned, turning them over once.

Arrange on a serving platter and serve immediately.

Fried Lamb Turnovers (Two Ways)

(*Sanbūsaj* and *Sanbūsak*: Triangular Turnovers with Meat Filling)

Makes 22–25

Sanbūsaj

Take meat from the back between the two shoulders, the inner thighs, the rump and some sheep's tail fat. Remove the veins. Pound (the meat) very well on a board, with a knife. Then pound with them, the whites (of onions), leek leaves, fresh coriander, rue, and some mint. Pound them extremely well. Pour over them Nabatean murrī, *as much as is needed. Throw into it dried coriander, black pepper, cassia, cloves, what you prefer of aromatic spices, and ginger, kneading them well with spices and oil. Cook them well until done. This (preparation) is* Isfīdhāj. *If you would like it to be sour, then throw into it some pounded (dried) yogurt whey,*[4] *as much as you like, or some dried buttermilk*[5] *or some sumac juice or any other souring agent, as you like, God willing. When you have finished doing that then fill thin sheets of bread with it, folding them into triangles, squares, or rectangles. If you would like to add some dried fruits, then throw into it that which you would like of walnuts, almonds, coconut, pistachios, hazelnuts, pine nuts, and anything else. If you would like to decorate it with eggs as is done during feasts and banquets, then do so. If you prefer to make them in the Bābakī manner, then take yeast dough and roll it out thin. Cut out rounds with a round wooden mold similar to a small hollowed bowl. Stuff it with meat and seal the edges together with fingernail impressions. Deep-fry in washed olive oil or sesame oil. Once they are browned, then remove them and eat them with what you like made of vinegar and mustard. This is the method of preparing* Sanbūsaj *and its various types except for how to make them sweet.*

—al-Warrāq, Abū Muḥammad al-Muẓaffar ibn Naṣr ibn Sayyār, *Kitāb al-Ṭabīkh wa Iṣlāḥ al-Aghdhiyah al-Ma'kūlāt wa Ṭayyibah al-Aṭ'imah al-Maṣnū'āt*

Sanbūsak

Take meat from the legs (from the thigh area) and lean rounds of meat, pound on a block of wood with a cleaver. Boil it until it is done, then drain the water from it. Pound it in a mortar until it is finely pounded. Then put it in a large pot. Mix sheep's tail fat, dried coriander, cassia, mastic and black pepper with it and fry. When browned add two parts finely chopped parsley, one part mint and half part rue. Let it come to a boil. Then add lemon juice and vinegar. Simmer until the vinegar and lemon juice are reduced. After that, stuff the Sanbūsak *(dough) as usual. Indeed it is the best.*

Another type: Add sumac, almonds, and pistachios to this filling.

—Ibn al-'Adīm, *Kitāb al-Wuṣlah ilà al-Ḥabīb fī Waṣf al-Ṭayyibāt wa al-Ṭīb*

The popularity of *Sanbūsaj* is evident by the number of recipes included in all the medieval Arabic cookbooks. Still today, in the eastern Arab world, they are enjoyed as appetizers or as part of the main meal, stuffed with meat and spices, or served for dessert filled with nuts or cheese such as Fried Nut Turnovers (*Sanbūsak Ismuhu Fāḍil*; see page 171).

The Arabic term derives from the Middle Persian word *sanbūsah*, meaning a small triangular pie. Given the Persian origin, it is feasible that al-Warrāq's reference to the "Bābakī" method refers to the third-century king Ardashīr I son of Bābak, the founder of the Sassanid Empire. According to Nasrallah, it is possible that this "King of Kings" who defeated the Parthian Empire is remembered by the shape of his crown in this turnover.

Al-Warrāq also offers a Lenten *Sanbūsaj* stuffed with prawns, colocasia, sumac, onions, *murrī*, and spices as one of the dishes prepared by the Arab Christians during their times of abstention due to religious obligations (123).

There is a poem composed by Isḥāq ibn Ibrāhīm al-Mawṣilī extolling the virtues of *Sanbūsaj*, which is also a recipe for the turnover (al-Masʿūdī VIII 398–399; al-Warrāq 90). We have enjoyed the challenge of translating it into English:

Oh you who ask about the tastiest of foods
You've asked the most qualified of men to conclude
You resolve upon meat that is red and not tough
Pound it with its fat, not a lot but enough
An onion that's cut in rounds in it is thrown
And very green cabbage that's been freshly grown
After, throw in the rue, an amount that is plentiful
And cinnamon and coriander an amount of a handful
Then somewhat of cloves after this do you add
And ginger and black pepper of good quality not bad
And cumin a handful and murrī *but a slight*
And a measure of two handfuls of salt from Palmyra
Then pound them, my lord, pound them a lot
Then kindle a fire for them, a fire that's hot
Place it all in a pot and over it pour water
Then place over it a lid to form as a cover
When it appears that the water is gone and is few
And the fire beneath it has dried it all up too
Then roll it, if you wish, in dough that is thin
Then seal up the edges in what you've put the meat in.
Or, take an even portion of dough, if you fancy
Rub with the hands softly and gently.
Roll it out with the rolling pin until it is round
Then with fingernails scallop the edges around
Into the frying pan pour in oil that is good
Then fry them, fry well, this understood
Put them in a bowl that is delicate and dainty
In its middle is mustard, its pungency tasty
Eat them, a food delicious with mustard aflurry
Indeed this is the best for those in a hurry.

We redacted two different recipes, to decide which would taste better. In the end, it was a draw, and we present both below. Both are spicy, slightly tart, and filling. Al-Warraq's addition of coconut to the stuffing shows the creativity of Baghdad's tenth-century kitchen.

Dough:

See dough for Fried Nut Turnovers (*Sanbūsak Ismuhu Fāḍil*; page 171)

Stuffing as per al-Warrāq:

5 tbsp. olive oil
1 lb. ground lamb
1 onion, finely chopped
1/2 cup finely chopped greens of leeks
1/2 cup finely chopped fresh coriander leaves
1 tsp. finely chopped rue or dandelion
1 tbsp. finely chopped fresh mint leaves
1 tbsp. red miso
1 tsp. salt
1/2 tsp. ground coriander seeds
1/2 tsp. cinnamon
1/4 tsp. ground cloves
pinch of saffron dissolved in 1/2 tsp. rosewater
1/4 tsp. ground nutmeg
1/2 tsp. ground ginger
2 tbsp. sumac
1/4 cup pine nuts and/or chopped walnuts, slivered almonds, chopped pistachios, chopped hazelnuts
1/4 cup unsweetened shredded coconut
2 hard boiled eggs (optional)

Cook the lamb in oil over medium heat for 5 minutes, stirring occasionally. Add the onion and leeks and cook 3 minutes more.

Stir in the chopped coriander, rue, and mint, cooking for 1 minute. Stir in the remaining ingredients except the eggs and set aside to cool.

For stuffing and cooking procedure follow instructions for Fried Nut Turnovers. Once the *Sanbūsaj* is ready to serve, if using the boiled eggs, crumble them evenly over the turnovers.

Stuffing as per Ibn al-ʿAdīm:

5 tbsp. olive oil
1 lb. ground lamb with fat

1 tsp. salt
1/2 tsp. ground coriander seeds
1/2 tsp. cinnamon
1/2 tsp. mastic
1/2 tsp. black pepper
1/2 cup finely chopped parsley
4 tbsp. finely chopped fresh mint leaves
1 tsp. finely chopped rue or dandelion
1 tbsp. lemon juice
1 tbsp. vinegar
2 tbsp. sumac
4 tbsp. ground almonds
2 tbsp. ground pistachios

Cook the lamb in oil over medium heat, for 5 minutes, stirring occasionally. Stir in the salt, ground coriander, cinnamon, mastic, and black pepper, and cook for 3 minutes, stirring a few times.

Add the parsley, mint, and rue, cook for 1 minute, and stir in remaining ingredients. Allow to cool, then use for stuffing.

For stuffing and cooking procedure follow instructions for Fried Nut Turnovers.

Serve hot.

Hearty Stuffed Tripe with Lamb, Chickpeas, and Rice

(*Sukhtūr*: Also Called Kībā)

To prepare it: cut fatty meat into small pieces. Take the small stomachs of sheep and wash once with hot water and soap, a second time with hot water and citron leaves, and a third time with water and salt, until they are clean. Then coat their inside and outside with saffron and rosewater. Then pound red meat with spices and make them into small meatballs and throw them into hot water until they are firm. Remove and then throw them on that cut up meat. Then take twice the amount of rice as the meat, and chickpeas, one-quarter of the amount, and wash them a number of times. Then mix with the aforementioned meat. Put on it, as much as needed, salt and thin shavings of cinnamon sticks. Color all of these with saffron and sprinkle dried coriander, cumin, mastic, black pepper, cinnamon, and finely pounded ginger. Some people add to that plucked (and cleaned of its hair) chicken that has been cut at its joints. Then take those stomachs and cut into medium-sized pieces and stuff with that meat. Join them and sew them with linen thread or skewer them with a dried stick. Arrange them in the pot and cover them with water, salt and the above mentioned spices. Colour the water also with a little saffron and put in it pieces of fatty meat cut into long and thin strips. Increase the water, as much as needed, after it boils. Then put it in the tannūr *(cylindrical clay oven commonly known as tandoor) and cover (the top of) it (and cook it) overnight until the morning. Then remove and use. Whoever wants (to make) it without the stomachs, (then) put that (previously) described meat, rice and chickpeas in a small mouthed pot and leave it in the* tannūr*—the amount of water is four-finger width more than it. When it boils, stir it and over the top of the pot and leave it in the* tannūr *until the morning. Then remove it.*

—al-Baghdādi, *Kitāb al-Ṭabīkh*

According to al-Jāhiẓ, the caliph Muʿāwiyah was fond of tripe (Arabic *qibbah*) stuffed with rice and meat. One day Ṣaʿṣaʿah ibn Ṣawḥān/Ṣūḥān was having lunch with him and took the food that lay in front of the caliph. Muʿāwiyah's response? "Indeed you seek far for food." To which Ṣaʿṣaʿah retorted: "One who experiences drought goes out seeking food" (*al-Bukhalāʾ* 150).

Even in the stories of the *Arabian Nights*, stuffed lamb, ribs, and poultry were considered luxurious rich dishes eaten in the households of the high and noble. Over time, these elaborate dishes would trickle down to the everyday household, which still held them in their original esteem, serving them on special occasions, holidays, and festivities, as is done today.

We have included, as a recipe of interest, al-Tujībī's elaborate description of preparing stuffed stomach, which involves a number of steps. A stuffed chicken is placed into the stomach, the type of stuffing being the cook's choice chosen from among the options provided in his book (see Regal Recipes for Stuffed Meats, p. 188). Al-Baghdādi, on the other hand, gives a recipe for the preparation of stuffed stomach which, in comparison, seems to border on the simple.

For our redaction, we have chosen al-Baghdādī's, as it appears to be the forerunner of the modern-day stuffed stomach of the Arab world.

Stuffed tripe is juicy, meaty, and spicy. Serve with a side salad such as one made with tomatoes and cucumbers to cut the taste of any fat from the lamb.

1 sheep stomach, scraped, then scrubbed with soap and very thoroughly washed a number of times until totally clean (available at most Mediterranean meat markets)
5 tsp. salt
peel of one lemon
1/4 cup vinegar
1/4 tsp. saffron dissolved in 3 tbsp. rosewater
1/4 lb. finely ground lamb
3/4 tsp. cumin
3/4 tsp. black pepper
3/4 tsp. ground coriander seeds
3/4 tsp. cinnamon
3/4 tsp. ground ginger
1/4 lb. lamb, cut into 1/4-inch cubes
1 cup cooked chickpeas
2 cups long grain rice, rinsed
1/4 tsp. saffron, diluted in 2 tbsp. water
1/4 tsp. mastic
1/2 lb. lamb with some fat, cut into 2-inch strips

Cut the stomach into four pieces, then rub with 4 tsp. salt. Place in a bowl, rub with lemon peel, add vinegar, and cover with water. Allow to stand refrigerated overnight, then drain and wash thoroughly. Dry with paper towels.

Coat the inside and outside of the stomach pieces with the saffron and rosewater mixture and set aside.

For the stuffing, thoroughly combine the ground lamb, 1/4 tsp. salt, and 1/4 tsp. each cumin, black pepper, coriander, cinnamon and ginger. Form into meatballs the size of small marbles. Place in a saucepan and cover with water. Bring to a boil, then cook over medium heat for 5 minutes. Drain and place in a mixing bowl; add the cubed lamb, chickpeas, and rice. Add 1/8 tsp diluted saffron, mastic, 1/2 tsp. salt, 1/4 tsp. cumin, 1/4 tsp. black pepper, 1/4 tsp. coriander, 1/4 tsp. cinnamon, and 1/4 tsp. of the ginger, thoroughly mix, and set aside.

Using a needle and a strong thread (preferably nylon), sew the stomach pieces into the form of bags.

Fill the stomach bags with the stuffing until nearly full, and sew the openings closed. Place in a large saucepan and cover with 3 inches of water. Add the remaining saffron, salt, cumin, black pepper, coriander, cinnamon, ginger, and the strips of lamb, and bring to a boil. Cover and cook for 1 hour over medium heat or until well cooked, adding more water if necessary to keep the stomach covered.

Carefully remove the stomach-bags from the saucepan with a slotted spoon and place on a serving dish. Remove the thread and slice the stomachs vertically into serving portions. Ladle a little of the stomach broth from the saucepan on top.

Serve hot along with the "stomach water" as a soup.

Aromatic Couscous with Veal and Vegetables

(*Kuskusū*: Couscous)

Serves 10–12

The way to cook it is to take the choicest of fatty calf meat along with large bones and put these into a large pot. Add to them salt, oil, black pepper, dried coriander, a little chopped onion, and water enough to cover plus a little more. Put the pot on the fire and when the meat begins to cook, add to it the vegetables that are easily found at the time such as cauliflower, turnips, carrots, lettuce, fennel, green fava beans, gourd, and eggplants. When the meat and the vegetables are cooked, take the special pot for the couscous that is perforated at its bottom, and fill it carefully with couscous. Then put it on top of the large pot that contains the meat and vegetables. Stick the edges of the two pots together with dough until no steam from the pot escapes. Pull tightly around the mouth of the couscous pot a thick cloth to keep back its steam and to strengthen its cooking. The sign that it is cooked is the strength of the steam that rises at the mouth of the pot and if the couscous is tapped by hand, there will be a sound. When it is cooked, empty it into a mixing bowl so to rub it with both hands with clarified butter, cinnamon, mastic, and spikenard until each is separated from each other. Put it in a serving bowl and do not fill the bowl without having taken into consideration that liquid will be added to it. Then check the meat broth to see whether there is enough or not. If there is not enough, add water to the pot and leave it until it boils. When it boils, remove it from the fire and leave it until it settles. Then, first put the broth into the middle of it then evenly along the sides of the bowl. Cover it and leave it for a while until it absorbs the broth and a dent will form if pressed with the finger once it has reached its right consistency of moisture unless more than the required amount had been added. Then take the bones and stand them up in the middle of the bowl and arrange the meat and vegetables on top. Sprinkle over it cinnamon, black pepper and ginger and it is eaten happily, Almighty God willing. Whoever wishes to make it with lamb or with chicken then do so in same manner mentioned above, with the power and strength of God.

—al-Tujībī, *Faḍālah al-Khiwān fī Ṭayyibāt al-Ṭaʿām wa al-Alwān*

A staple food for the whole of North Africa, couscous is a type of semolina usually made from a hard wheat (durum) and believed to have been invented by the Berbers and embellished by the Arabs.

The name *Kuskusū* may be derived from the Arabic *kaskasa* (to pound small) or the Berber *seksu*, but whatever its etymology, it was and remains popular throughout North Africa and beyond. The Moroccans gently blend numerous spices into theirs; the Algerians often include sausage among the ingredients; Tunisian couscous is spicy; Sicilian couscous is made like a soup; the West African type made with sorghum. In Syria, Lebanon, and the Palestinian territories small round balls known as *maghribiyah* or *maftūl* are made of moistened semolina. The same is popular in Israel, where it was introduced by the North African Jews. In Brazil, where it was introduced by West African slaves, it is made with cornmeal, fish, or other meat, and called *cuzcuz*. In most other parts of the world, the preparation of couscous follows the Moroccan style.

In this source recipe the cook is instructed to take the bones from the cooked meat and to position them standing in the middle of the serving dish, surrounded by the couscous ingredients, a presentation designed for those who enjoy extracting the scrumptious marrow from the bones.

The source recipe calls for spikenard, which is difficult to find even in Middle Eastern speciality shops. In place of this bitter and strong aromatic, we have substituted the gentler and more familiar cloves.

You will need a couscousier, available from any outlet that specializes in North African products, for this preparation.

If you enjoy modern-day couscous, you will find its origin in this dish which, seemingly, has not changed over the centuries.

---

1 lb. veal shoulder with bones and some fat, with the meat cut into large pieces but the bones whole
2 tsp. salt
2 tbsp. olive oil

1 1/2 tsp. black pepper
1 1/2 tsp. ground coriander seeds
1 medium onion, finely chopped
5 cups water
1 cup chopped cauliflower
1 cup carrots cut into 1/2-inch cubes
1 cup squash cut into 1-inch cubes
1 1/2 cups fresh or frozen green lima beans
1 cup peeled, 1/2-inch turnip cubes
1/2 cup finely chopped fennel
2 cups couscous
4 tbsp. butter, melted
1 tsp. cinnamon
1/2 tsp. mastic
1/4 tsp. ground cloves
1/4 tsp. ground ginger

Place the veal, salt, oil, 1 1/4 tsp. black pepper, coriander, onion, and water in the bottom part of a *couscousière*. Bring to a boil, cover, and cook for 40 minutes over medium heat. Add the vegetables.

Place the couscous in the upper part of the *couscousière*. Fit the upper part to the bottom part and seal the two parts together with a flour-impregnated piece of cloth (this is necessary only if steam is escaping between the two parts). Cook over medium heat for 30 minutes, stirring the couscous every few minutes to make sure the kernels do not stick together.

Transfer the couscous to a mixing bowl and add the butter, 1/2 tsp. cinnamon, mastic, and cloves, and thoroughly combine. Stir in 1 cup of the broth from the stew and allow to stand for 10 minutes.

Transfer the couscous to a serving platter. Then take the bones from the meat and stand them up in the middle of the couscous. Arrange the meat and the vegetables on top of the couscous, and sprinkle the remaining black pepper, the remaining cinnamon, and the ginger over it.

Serve immediately.

Stuffed Dumplings in Yogurt

(*Shushbarak,* commonly now known as *Shīsh Barak)*

Serves 4–6

> *You take minced meat and stuff it in dough rolled out like cut noodles. Cook it in water until done. Then take it off the fire and put yogurt, garlic, and mint with it.*
>
> —Ibn al-Mabrad (or Ibn al-Mubarrad), *The Book of Cookery (Kitāb al-Ṭibākhah), page 473, translated by Charles Perry*

The modern version of this dish is common in the eastern Arab world, where it has evolved into something richer and tastier than its medieval ancestor, due to the addition of spices and, more specifically, to the final step, cooking the dumplings in yogurt. Our redaction embellishes the original by including the spices used in the contemporary dish that graces the tables of the Middle East.

These dumplings are best served alongside a dish of plain rice.

1 lb. fresh or frozen bread dough, thawed
1 lb. ground beef or lamb
2 tbsp. butter
2 tsp. salt
3/4 tsp. black pepper
3/4 tsp. ground coriander seeds
1/2 tsp. cinnamon
3 cups plain yogurt, whole or low-fat
5 cloves garlic, crushed
3 tsp. dried mint

Form the dough into 3/4-inch balls, cover with a towel, and allow to rest for 1 hour.

In the meantime, make a filling by frying the meat in the butter until light brown, then adding 1 tsp. salt, black pepper, coriander, and cinnamon, stirring constantly for 5 minutes.

Roll out the dough into circles 1/8 inch thick. Place 1 level tsp. of filling on each circle, fold dough over filling, and pinch the edges to seal. Fold in half again and pinch to close, then let sit for 10 minutes.

Place the dumplings in a saucepan, cover with water, and bring to a boil. Cover and cook over medium-low heat for 15 minutes, then uncover and cook for 15 minutes more. Remove from the heat and gently remove the dumplings to a strainer, reserving 1 cup of the water in the saucepan.

Add the remaining salt, yogurt, garlic, and mint to the water in the saucepan. Cook over low heat for 2 minutes, stirring constantly. Remove from the heat, then very gently stir in the dumplings.

Serve immediately.

CHICKEN

Herbed Chicken Pita Rolls

(*Bazmāward bi Ḥummāḍ Yuʿrifu bi-al-Maʾmūnī*: A Bazmāward Made with Citron Pulp Known as al-Maʾmūnī)

Serves 4–6

> *Cut up chicken and arrange it on thin, flat bread, after having spread beneath the chicken skinned walnuts, citron pulp, mint, tarragon, basil, and salt and roll it up.*[6]
>
> —al-Warrāq, Abū Muḥammad al-Muẓaffar ibn Naṣr ibn Sayyār, *Kitāb al-Ṭabīkh wa Iṣlāḥ al-Aghdhiyah al-Maʾkūlāt wa Ṭayyibah al-Aṭʿimah al-Maṣnūʿāt*

Bazmāward is grilled meat rolled in thin bread. In the eleventh century it was referred to as the "narcissus of the table" (al-Rāghib al-Aṣbahānī II 612). These rolled sandwiches reached the level of the aristocracy, and were called "tidbits of the judge" and "tidbits of the caliph" (*Tāj*). The Arabic term is derived from the Persian *razmāwardāy*, Arabized as *zumāward*, a food consisting of eggs and meat and known colloquially as *Bazmāward* (612; *Tāj*). However, Perry's origin for the Arabic term differs: it is taken from the Persian *bazm* (banquet) and *āward* (bringing) ("Description" 381).

Related to *Bazmāward* are *Awsāṭ*. While the former are made with thin sheets of bread (*ruqāq*), then rolled and sliced, *Awsāṭ* (*Wasṭ*, sing.) are made with a thicker bread (*raghīf*), where the loaf is split, the pith removed, the stuffing then added and the top crust of the loaf returned to cover the stuffed loaf. There is also an open-faced version of the *Wast* that al-Warrāq describes, with a spread made of egg yolks and pounded cheese, which is then grilled. Prince Ibrāhīm ibn al-Mahdī dedicated a poem to these (58). *Shaṭā'ir*, another type, was one of the types of sandwiches eaten by the monks and Christians during fast times ("Description" 448).

Today, in Iraq, sandwiches are occasionally referred to as *al-Shāṭir wa al-Mashṭūr wa Baynahumā al-Kāmikh*, literally "the halved and the divided and between the two the relish-spread." With such a long descriptive name for a simple sandwich, no wonder that modern Arabic has redeveloped the phrase into the more familiar *Sandwīj*.

Although this may appear to be "only a chicken sandwich," the surprise is its distinct taste and texture. Nothing goes better with cooked chicken on pita than fresh basil, mint, and tarragon.

---

1 lb. cooked chicken, deboned and cut into very small pieces
*2 thin fresh loaves of pita, 12 to 15 inches in diameter, or 2 soft Arab thin bread (*marqūq*), similar to soft lavash bread, 12 to 15 inches in diameter*
1 cup ground walnuts
1/4 cup fresh lemon juice
4 tbsp. finely chopped fresh mint leaves
4 tbsp. finely chopped fresh tarragon
4 tbsp. finely chopped fresh basil
1/2 tsp. salt

Split the two loaves of bread open. Sprinkle all the ingredients except the chicken evenly over the four bread rounds. Divide the chicken into 4 portions and spread evenly on each bread round. Tightly roll each piece into a cylinder, slice into small sandwiches, and serve.

Chicken Stew with Pomegranate Juice and Pumpkin

(*Ṭabīkh Ḥabb Rummān*: A Cooked Dish of Pomegranate Seeds)

Serves 4–6

> *Finely pound pomegranate seeds and strain. Thicken with shelled almonds. Add sugar, mint, cinnamon, and mastic, allowing it to congeal over the fire.*

Mix it with chicken which has been boiled and baked. Boil it. If you want to put pumpkin with it, do so.

—Ibn al-ʿAdīm, *Kitāb al-Wuṣlah ilà al-Ḥabīb fī Waṣf al-Ṭayyibāt wa al-Ṭīb*

Pomegranate seeds can be eaten raw, served as a garnish, or used as an ingredient in other dishes. A sweet, tangy crimson liquid is obtained from the seeds' transparent outer gel, and the Arab cook will sometimes scent the seeds with rose or orange blossom water to make a tasty and refreshing drink. The juice can be easily removed from the ovules by placing a cupful in a piece of muslin cloth and squeezing out the fluid.

Today, in Europe and North America, pomegranate syrup, also known as grenadine syrup, is made from the liquid of the fruit, usually mixed with artificial flavors and used as a base for drinks. In the Middle East, where the fruit is popular, a similar concentrate called *dibs rummān* is prepared by boiling the juice until it becomes thick and turns brownish, a great additive when cooking meat.

As in the kitchens of the medieval Arab world, today's Middle Eastern cooks use this condensed juice to make drinks or to give soups and sauces a pleasing and somewhat tart taste. In certain recipes, it can be substituted for lemon juice.

---

1 cup pure pomegranate juice
1/2 cup blanched split almonds
1 tbsp. sugar
1 tsp. dried mint
1/2 tsp. cinnamon
1/2 tsp. ground mastic or 1 tbsp. cornstarch
2 cups finely chopped baked chicken
1 cup 1/2-inch pumpkin cubes (optional)

Place the pomegranate juice and almonds in a saucepan and bring to a boil. Lower heat to medium-low and stir in the sugar, mint, cinnamon, and mastic or cornstarch. Continue to simmer, stirring a number of times until mixture begins to thicken.

Add the chicken, simmering and stirring for five minutes. If using pumpkin, add with the chicken and continue to simmer and stir and until the pumpkin is cooked.

Spoon into a serving dish and serve immediately over rice or mashed potatoes.

Savory and Sour Chicken, Lamb, and Egg Casserole

(*Bustānīyah*: [Produce] of an Orchard, from the book of Abū Samīn)

Serves 4–6

> *Take small sour plums and wash them. If they are dried, then wrap them in a damp thin scarf. If they are fresh, mash them in water, then strain them through a sieve. Then take chicken breasts and cut them in the length of fingers. Then put with them as much meat as you wish. Then throw in the plums and boil them together. Season the pot with black pepper and liquid of* kāmakh, *olive oil, some spices, some sugar, wine vinegar, and five [shelled] walnuts that have been finely pounded. Then add them to it. Break eggs over it and allow them to set, God willing.*
>
> —al-Warrāq, Abū Muḥammad al-Muẓaffar ibn Naṣr ibn Sayyār, *Kitāb al-Ṭabīkh wa Iṣlāḥ al-Aghdhiyah al-Ma'kūlāt wa Ṭayyibah al-Aṭʿimah al-Maṣnūʿāt*

The main souring agent in this recipe is the juice from what al-Warraq calls *al-ijjāṣ al-sighar al-ḥamid* , a variety of sour plum, also called *khawkh al-dubb*. However, as Nasrallah correctly points out, thirteenth-century Ibn al-ʿAdim equates the *khawkh al-dubb* with *qarāṣiyah*, which are either cherries (Nasrallah 630) or types of plums or service-tree berries (Perry, "Studies," n. 4). In any event, the fruit needed to make the recipe should be sour.

To simplify this recipe, we have replaced *kāmakh* with the souring agent sumac.

---

2 lb. chicken breasts, boned and skinned, cut into 1/4 x 3-inch strips
1/2 lb. lamb, cut into 1/4 x 3-inch strips
2 lb. black plums, still sour, pits removed, boiled for 10 minutes, then drained and mashed through a sieve
1 tsp. salt
1/2 tsp. black pepper
2 tbsp. sumac
1 tsp. salt
1/2 tsp. cumin
1/2 tsp. ground caraway seeds
1/2 tsp. ground coriander seeds
1/2 tsp. ground ginger
1 tbsp. sugar

1 tbsp. wine vinegar
2 tbsp. olive oil
1/2 cup ground walnuts
4 eggs

Place chicken and lamb in a saucepan. Add the strained plum juice, topping it with enough water to cover the meat. Bring to a boil, skimming any scum.

Add all the remaining ingredients except the eggs, and bring to a boil. Cover and cook over medium-low heat for 50 minutes or until chicken and lamb are done, stirring occasionally.

Preheat oven to 350° F.

Transfer the saucepan contents to a casserole. Break the eggs over the top and bake uncovered for 10 minutes or until the eggs are firm.

Serve immediately.

Grilled Chicken in Yogurt

(*Dajāj ʿAmrūs*: an Eastern Way of Preparing Chicken called "Chicken ʿAmrūs")

Serves 4–6

> *Take a chicken as described above [fat and young] and kill it. Prepare it the way that it was prepared previously (i.e., wash and clean it from its organs). Grill it whole. Then take it and mount it on a skewer of any kind. Grill it on a low fire. When it is almost fully cooked, remove it from the skewer, and cut off its meat as thinly as possible. Then put the chicken pieces in a new pot and add salt, oil, dried coriander, and a little onion. When the chicken is cooked and the pot boils take yogurt and strain it. Put it in a serving dish. Break an egg over it and add to the egg and yogurt, some yeast and mix them all together well until all parts are well mixed. Then add this to the pot over the chicken and stir the pot slowly. Shut off the fire under it keeping it there until it is cooked. And eat it happily God the Most High willing!*
>
> —al-Tujībī, *Faḍālah al-Khiwān fī Ṭayyibāt al-Ṭaʿām wa al-Alwān*

Umayyad caliph Sulaymān ibn ʿAbd Al-Malik enjoyed eating, and supposedly ate 100 Iraqi *raṭls* of food daily. One claim is that the caliph's cooks would bring him piping hot grilled chickens still on spits and the ruler would pounce on them. Despite his elegant dress, he would use the end of his sleeves to grab the hot chickens to break them into pieces. A little over seventy years later, al-Aṣmaʿī would claim to have seen Sulaymān's cloaks with traces of chicken grease still on the sleeves (al-Masʿūdī V 400–401).

Yeast may sound out of place as an ingredient in this dish; it serves as a thickening agent for the yogurt sauce. Remember too, when cooking yogurt, that it should be stirred in one direction to avoid curdling.

3–4 lb. chicken, cleaned and washed, rubbed with 1 tsp. salt and 3 tbsp. olive oil
1 1/4 tsp. salt
1/2 cup olive oil
3 tsp. ground coriander seeds
1 medium onion, finely chopped
1 cup plain yogurt, whole or low-fat
1 egg, beaten
1/2 tsp. yeast

Place the chicken on a skewer and grill rotisserie-style in the oven or on a barbecue until cooked. Remove the skin, debone, and slice as thin as possible.

Heat the oil in a saucepan over medium heat, and add the chicken, salt, ground coriander, and onion. Sauté for about 10 minutes, stirring a number of times.

In a separate bowl, combine the yogurt, egg, and yeast.

Turn the heat to low under the chicken, and slowly stir in the yogurt mixture with a wooden spoon, continuing to stir in one direction for 2 minutes. Turn off the heat and allow to stand for 5 minutes before serving.

Fried Meatballs with Pistachios and Honey

(*Dajāj Mudaqqaqah*: Pounded Chicken)

Serves 4–6

> *Make meatballs in the size of hazelnuts from chicken breasts and baby lamb meat adding the proper spices. Then sizzle and fry in sheep tail fat. Throw over them bee's honey, sugar, a lot of boiled and softened pistachios,* aṭrāf

al-ṭīb, *saffron, and lemon juice in the amount needed, making enough broth. Cook and add a sprig of mint to it. Sprinkle rosewater on them and allow to settle then serve.*

—Ibn al-ʿAdīm, *Kitāb al-Wuṣlah ilà al-Ḥabīb fī Waṣf al-Ṭayyibāt wa al-Ṭīb*

The eastern Arabic medieval cookbooks include many recipes using *kubāb* (also *kubub*) in the preparation of meat. These are small balls of ground or pounded (*mudaqqaqah*) meat. Their size is clearly given when the cook is instructed to form them into the shape of a hazelnut (*al-bunduq*).

The Arabs brought their recipes for meatballs from Baghdad to Andalusia, and the Spaniards passed them on to Latin America. *Albóndigas*, Spanish for meatballs, is derived from the Arabic *al-bunduq* (hazelnut), referring to the small size of the meatball. Today, Spanish *Albóndigas* can be served as an appetizer or a main course, often in a tomato sauce, while Mexican *Albóndigas* are commonly served in a soup with a light broth and vegetables. In al-Andalus, lamb and chicken were the most popular meats used for Arab cooking. Beef, according to medieval Arabic medical texts, was heavier on the digestive system.

Ibn al-ʿAdīm's chicken and lamb version makes for a tender meatball, along with what are normally reserved as dessert ingredients, rosewater, honey, sugar, and pistachios.

1/2 lb. ground chicken breast
1/2 lb. ground lamb
1 1/2 tsp. salt
1/2 tsp. black pepper
1/2 tsp. cumin
1/2 tsp. ground coriander seeds
1/2 tsp. caraway seeds
1/4 cup olive oil
3 tbsp. honey
1 tbsp. sugar
1 cup unsalted pistachios, boiled for 15 minutes over medium heat and drained
1/2 tsp. aṭrāf al-ṭīb
pinch saffron dissolved in 2 tbsp. hot water
1 tbsp. lemon juice
10 fresh mint leaves
1 tsp. rosewater

Place the chicken, lamb, salt, pepper, cumin, ground coriander, and caraway in a bowl and mix thoroughly. Form into hazelnut-size balls.

Fry balls in oil in a saucepan over medium heat, turning them over a few times until evenly light brown. Cover with water and bring to a boil. Cover and cook over medium heat for 35 minutes, then stir in the honey, sugar, pistachios, *aṭrāf al-ṭīb*, dissolved saffron, and lemon juice. Cover and cook for an additional 20 minutes, then stir in the mint and sprinkle with rosewater. Allow to stand for 10 minutes before serving

Pistachio-Stuffed Roasted Chicken

(*Fustuqīyah*: Made of Pistachios)

Serves 4–6

> *Take shelled pistachios and finely pound some with sugar in the mortar. Add to it musk and camphor and knead with a little rosewater. Stuff the cavity of the chicken with it. For each chicken let there be one* ūqīyah *of sugar and the same applies to almonds and pistachios after having fried the chicken until it has cooked and browned in two* ūqīyahs *of sesame oil. Move the syrup onto the fire. Take the remaining pistachios and finely pound them then put the syrup over them. Then take chard leaves, pound them, and drain them from their water. Add them to the syrup in order to make it green. When it turns green in the pot and its color changes, then take the chicken and arrange it in the bowl covering it with the said syrup. Allow it to settle and serve. Be careful that not too much camphor is used otherwise it will be bitter. Instead, it should be made with an amount of one seed.*
>
> *—Kanz al-Fawā'id fī Tanwī' al-Mawā'id*

Pistachios were considered a luxury, often used in the lavish sweets and desserts made for the caliphs and nobility, but also when salted served as *naql* or part of the dry fruits offered with wine. For one poet, pistachios are likened to emeralds wrapped in green silk (al-Rāghib al-Aṣbahānī II 625).

Chicken stuffed with pistachios appears in the fictional *1001 Arabian Nights* as a lavish dish. In the story of the "Barber's Tale," Shakashik dines in the home of a rich Barmakid notable and feasts upon it; likewise, in the story of the "Nazarene Broker," a rich woman of Cairo presents it to a young Baghdadi merchant. Ibn al-ʿAdīm includes a number of chicken recipes that use not only pistachios, but also hazelnuts or almonds, ground or whole.

We have replaced the musk and camphor called for in the recipe with almond extract and cinnamon for the sake of simplicity and availability. The source recipe calls for frying the chicken, but we have opted to roast it in sesame oil instead for a less greasy result. We recommend that when roasting the chicken, it be rubbed well with oil, salt, and black pepper.

Fustuqīyah is slightly sweet and with a smooth crunch of ground nuts; an unusual taste and texture combination indeed.

---

5 tbsp. sugar
2 cups finely ground pistachios
2 cups packed Swiss chard leaves, processed in a blender with 3/4 cup water, then drained
1/2 tsp. almond extract
1/2 tsp. cinnamon
1 tbsp. rosewater
3 lb. whole roasted chicken
1 tbsp. ground almonds

Prepare the syrup by dissolving 4 tbsp. sugar in 1/4 cup water, bringing to a boil, and simmering on low heat for 10 minutes. Stir in 1 tbsp. pistachios and Swiss chard. Set aside.

Mix together remaining pistachios, remaining 1 tbsp. sugar, almond extract, cinnamon, and rosewater, and then stuff the chicken with the mixture and place on a serving platter.

Spread the syrup over the chicken and serve.

Chicken and Vegetables in a Tart and Creamy Sauce

(*Kishk*)

Serves 4–6

> *You will need meat or young pigeons or chicken or stomach,* kishk, *lemon or verjuice or citron, black pepper, garlic, chickpeas, onions, eggplant, chard,*

white turnips, and mint. Boil the meat and chickpeas until cooked. Pour out the broth. Throw the eggplant on it or the other (ingredients) until cooked. Dissolve the kishk that has been soaking in a little meat broth. Add it to it and cook and throw the black pepper, garlic, mint, and lemon on it. If unripe sour grapes are used, boil them and strain them in a sieve and then add it to it (the dish).

—Kanz al-Fawāʾid fī Tanwīʿ al-Mawāʾid

Kishk is a fermented wheat and milk mixture. The grains of wheat are softened by parboiling and air-dried, with the bran removed by winnowing. These are then moistened with yogurt and allowed to dry in natural sunlight over a period, in some cases, of six days (al-Warrāq 102–103). In the medieval period, *kishk* was stored as a dough, formed into disk-shaped patties, or even dried, strung together by thread in necklace form, and used as needed.

It is much simpler, of course, to buy *kishk* already made. It is available in most Middle Eastern grocery stores. If kept refrigerated it can last for months.

Although identified as a simple peasant food, *kishk* was elevated in the medieval Arab culinary texts with the addition of various ingredients. There is a *Kishkīyah* of the son of the caliph Hārūn al-Rashīd, a future caliph himself, that includes meat, chickpeas, onions, seasonal greens, and fresh herbs (al-Warrāq 165). Another type is a soupy variety served over noodles ("Description" 323–324). And yet another is a *kishk* dish recommended for hangovers (al-Warrāq 165).

Kishk has a distinct taste best described as that of a strong and tart cheese. Yet in this dish the sourness is toned down by the other hearty ingredients. For a vegetarian version, the dish can be prepared without chicken.

---

2 cups peeled eggplant cut into 1/2-inch cubes
1 lb. boneless and skinless chicken breast, cut into 1/2-inch cubes
1 cup dried chickpeas, soaked overnight, drained, and split
1 tsp. salt
4 tbsp. kishk
1 medium onion, finely chopped
2 cups chopped tender Swiss chard leaves and ribs
1 cup peeled 1/2-inch turnip cubes
1/2 tsp. black pepper
6 cloves garlic, crushed
1 tbsp. finely chopped fresh mint leaves
2 tbsp. lemon juice

Sprinkle the eggplant with 1/2 tsp. salt and allow to sit for one hour. Drain on paper towels.

Meanwhile, place the chicken and chickpeas in a saucepan and cover with 4 inches of water. Bring to a boil, removing any scum. Add the remaining salt, cover, and cook over medium-low heat for 1 hour or until almost done.

Drain the broth, reserving 4 cups of the liquid. Dissolve the *kishk* in the reserved broth.

Add the broth with the *kishk*, onion, Swiss chard, and turnips to the chicken and chickpeas and bring to a boil. Cover and cook over medium heat for 15 minutes, stirring occasionally.

Add the eggplant and cook uncovered for an additional 15 minutes, stirring often. Stir in the remaining ingredients and cook for 2 minutes more, then serve immediately.

Tangy Sumac Chicken

(*Summāqīyah*: Made of Sumac)

Serves 4–6

> *Take a chicken as described above, slaughter it and prepare it as previously presented. Put it in a new pot and put over it water, salt, good oil, black pepper, dried coriander, and a little onion. Take the pot to the fire to cook it. When it is nearly cooked, take good sumac free of sediment, clean it and thresh it. Put in a clean piece of cloth and tie it. Keep it in the pot until the chicken cooks. Then taste the [contents of the] pot. If you find the sumac is strong enough, take out the piece of cloth from the pot and keep the pot on a gentle fire until it is evenly cooked then empty into a large bowl. Eat happily, All Mighty God willing.*
>
> —al-Tujībī, *Faḍālah al-Khiwān fī Ṭayyibāt al-Ṭaʿām wa al-Alwān*

Sumac, derived from the Arabic *summāq*, may be the last of the great condiments still to be widely taken up in the West. Middle Eastern cooks have employed it for thousands of years in numerous dishes as a replacement for lemon juice or vinegar. This sour seasoning, obtained from the *Rhus coriaria*, a species of sumac, is as indispensable to modern Middle Eastern cuisine as it was to the kitchens of the Sumerians, ancient Egyptians, and medieval Arabs. Its berries are gathered a little before maturity, dried in the sun, and crushed to remove the seed. The dried fruit pulp is then pulverized to make the brick-red sumac seasoning.

As a seasoning, sumac lends a tart taste to barbecues, chicken, curries, fish, salads, sauces, stews, stuffing, and vegetables. In the eastern Arab countries and adjoining lands, it is also extensively combined with onions and salt as a savory spice for roasts. The national Palestinian dish *Musakhkhan* retains the basic ingredients of the medieval *Summāqīyah* except that it is served on thin loaves of Arab bread. Arab gourmet cooks are convinced that there is no substitute for this tangy condiment.

---

3 lb. chicken, cleaned, skinned, and jointed, or 3 lb. skinless, boneless chicken breasts, cut into medium-sized pieces
1 1/2 tsp. salt
2 tbsp. olive oil
1 1/2 tsp. black pepper
1 1/2 tsp. ground coriander seeds
1 medium onion, finely chopped
4 tbsp. sumac

Place the chicken, salt, olive oil, black pepper, ground coriander, and onion in a saucepan and cover with water. Bring to a boil and remove any scum. Cover and cook over medium heat for 30 minutes.

In the meantime, place the sumac in a clean piece of cloth, tie it, and place it in the saucepan. Cook over medium-low heat for a further 30 minutes or until the chicken is well cooked, stirring occasionally and adding a little more water if necessary. Remove the sumac bag from the saucepan, transfer the saucepan contents to a serving bowl, and serve over plain rice.

Saffron Chicken Tajine

(*Jaʿfarīyah*: "That of Jaʿfar" or "The Golden One")

Serves 4–6

> *Take a chicken as described previously [i.e., plump and young], kill it and prepare it as it was prepared previously. Put them (the chicken pieces) in a new deep bowl and cover them with water, salt, a lot of oil, black pepper, dried coriander, and a little cumin, likewise with onion, peeled almonds, soaked chickpeas, some cloves of garlic,* murrī *which has been soaked in a bowl, citron leaves, and fennel stalk. Put the bowl on the fire to cook. When*

it is cooked and well done, add to it a ladle of good vinegar after having colored it with saffron. Leave it to boil. Then remove it from the fire and remove them gently and put them into a glazed earthenware pot. Add to them some of the broth which has been strained and the almonds and first-rate chickpeas. Put the pot in the oven. When it has finished cooking and the chicken is browned all over and the water from its broth has dried up and the oil and fat remain, remove it from the oven. Put it in a large bowl and put over it chopped eggs and the choicest of mint. And eat it happily God, the Most High willing!

—al-Tujībī, *Faḍālah al-Khiwān fī Ṭayyibāt al-Ṭaʿām wa al-Alwān*

Although there is a similar recipe in the *Anonymous Andalusian Cookbook*, it is not clear whether the tajine-like dish was named after an individual with the name Jaʿfar, or from the Arabic word *jaʿfar* meaning golden. With the addition of saffron, the dish presents itself as golden in color.

Today, in Morocco, tajine dishes are prepared in a similar manner using fish, chicken, lamb, or other meats and a wide variety of vegetables. Tajine stews are fragrant, tart, spicy and at times sweet if stewed with fruits. Ideally they are cooked in a tajine, a special shallow earthenware utensil with a cone-shaped lid that captures the steam and juices from all the ingredients. These are simmered together for long hours over very low heat.

To cook these types of stews, a tajine is recommended. However, any covered casserole dish or Dutch oven will do.

3–4 lb. chicken, washed with salted water, patted dry, and cut into serving pieces
2 tsp. salt
1/4 cup olive oil
1 1/2 tsp. black pepper
1 1/2 tsp. ground coriander seeds
1 1/4 tsp. cumin
1 medium onion, finely chopped
1/2 cup blanched almonds
1/2 cup dried chickpeas, soaked overnight in water with 1/2 tsp. baking soda, then drained
6 whole cloves garlic
1 1/2 tbsp. red miso
4 tsp. lemon or lime peel, grated

1/2 cup finely chopped fennel stalk
1/4 tsp. crushed saffron, dissolved in 1/2 cup vinegar
2 tbsp. vinegar
2 hard boiled eggs, chopped
2 tbsp. finely chopped fresh mint leaves

Place the chicken in a saucepan and cover with water. Bring to a boil and remove any scum.

Add the remaining ingredients, except the saffron solution and vinegar, eggs, and mint, and bring to a boil. Cover and cook over medium heat for 30 minutes.

Stir in the saffron solution and vinegar, bring to a boil, then remove from the heat. With a slotted spoon, remove the chicken pieces and place in a tajine or casserole.

Preheat oven to 350° F.

Strain broth and set aside. Spread strained almonds and chickpeas over the chicken pieces. Pour 2 cups of the clear broth over the top of the casserole contents and bake uncovered for one hour or until most of the sauce has evaporated.

Remove from the oven and place the casserole contents on a serving platter. Spread the eggs over the top, sprinkle with mint, and serve.

Zesty Almond and Chicken Pie

(*Maghmūm*: The Veiled or Covered One)

Serves 4–6

> *Take a cleaned chicken and put it, as is, whole, with its breast split, in a pot with salt, oil, black pepper and dried coriander and a small onion. Cook half way. Then, take it out and put it in another pot and put on it its broth, macerated* (naqīʿ) murrī,[7] *saffron, rue, thyme, and citron leaves. Put in its cavity a lime. Scatter over it peeled almonds and cover the top of the pot with dough. Place it in the oven until it is cooked, then use.*
>
> —al-Tujībī, *Faḍālah al-Khiwān fī Ṭayyibāt al-Ṭaʿām wa al-Alwān*

Sometime in the late seventh century, an Iraqi merchant arrived in Medina with a large batch of veils. He sold all of them except the black ones. The veil-seller needed help and sought out

Miskīn al-Dārimī (d. 708), the Umayyad poet who had given up his art to live a life of piety and prayer.

The one-time poet agreed to help.

So it was that he doffed his clothing of piety and one more time took on his role as poet. He approached a friend who was a singer and recited the following lines:

Tell the beautiful woman in the black veil
What did you do to a worshipping hermit?
He had tucked up his garment to begin his prayers
When you came to his mind at the door of the mosque
Give back to him his prayer and his fasting
Do not kill him in the name of the religion of Muḥammad.

The song spread throughout Medina, as did the rumor that the famous al-Dārimī had returned as a result of falling in love with a lady in a black veil. Soon, no woman remained in Medina who did not purchase a black veil. The Iraqi merchant sold his entire stock. As for al-Dārimī, he donned once more the clothing of a pious hermit and returned to his life of asceticism and worship (Ibn ʿAbd Rabbih VI 15–16). Even today these famous lines continue to be sung throughout the Arab world.

The veil in the recipe below may not be so romantic, but beneath the layer of dough lies a mystery of ingredients that remains unknown until the cover is lifted.

There are different versions of the "veiled dish" *Maghmūm* in the medieval Arabic cookbooks. Ibn Jazlah has meat and eggplant as the main ingredients; this is the most typical variant in eastern Arabic recipes. The *Anonymous Andalusian Cookbook* and al-Tujībī give poultry as the meat base, however, and al-Baghdādī recommends using fatty meat.

Ibn Jazlah is vague on the particular spices to be used in the preparation. Al-Baghdādī's version advises that these spices include the fine-ground seasonings of dry coriander, cumin, caraway, black pepper, cinnamon, ginger, and salt; in the "Description" caraway is omitted, but mastic is added. We have decided on an edited list, drawing from both recipes.

3–4 lb. whole chicken
1 medium onion
1 tsp. salt
1 tsp. black pepper
1 tsp. ground coriander seeds
3 tbsp. light sesame oil
1 tsp. red miso
pinch saffron or 1/2 tsp. turmeric

1/2 tsp. chopped rue
1 tbsp. finely chopped fresh thyme
1/2 tsp. zest of lime
1/2 lime
1/2 cup blanched split almonds
3/4 lb. frozen bread dough, thawed

Wash the chicken, split the breast, and lay it in a saucepan, skin-side up. Add the onion and enough water to cover, and bring to a boil. Remove any scum.

Combine the salt, black pepper, ground coriander, and sesame oil and pour over the chicken. Cover and cook over medium heat for 40 minutes. Carefully remove the chicken and transfer to a casserole, reserving 2 cups of the chicken broth in the saucepan.

Add the miso, saffron or turmeric, rue, thyme, and zest of lime to the reserved broth. Place the lime underneath the chicken and pour the broth over it. Spread the almonds over the chicken.

Preheat the oven to 350°F.

Roll out the dough and place over the top of the casserole. Pinch the edges all around, ensuring that the dough is secured to the casserole edge.

Bake for 50 minutes to 1 hour or until the dough is evenly browned.

Serve immediately, using the topping for scooping up the chicken and the sauce.

Aromatic Chicken with Fried and Boiled Eggs over Toasted Pita

(*Tharīdah bi-al-Dajāj*: Soaked Bread with Chicken)

Serves 4–6

> *Take chicken and prepare it, as described previously, in the method of cleaning and separating it into pieces [slaughter it and boil it and open its stomach and remove its inners and separate it bone by bone]. Then put it into a large pot with salt and a lot of oil, black pepper, coriander, cumin and a little bit of chopped or pounded onion, soaked white chickpeas, boiled almonds, citron leaves, fennel stalk, and a head of garlic unpeeled. Carry the pot to the fire. Then take flour or semolina and knead it with water and salt and yeast and leave it until it rises in the kneading bowl. Upon rising punch*

it down again and pinch into medium size, between thick and thin, loaves and pierce and wipe on top [of them] water. Cook in the oven. Then wipe them and break up as small as possible. When the chicken is nearly cooked dissolve enough of an amount of saffron in cold water and be careful, too much of it will ruin it. Put it in a pot and stir until the saffron changes the color of everything in it. Leave it for a short while. Then put in it that which makes it delicious of good vinegar and boil it well. Then take some eggs, enough to cover the pot. Break in a dish and add on them salt, black pepper, ginger, and cinnamon and beat it with a spoon until well mixed together. Add diluted saffron to color it and add all of this to the pot and stir. Then, leave on a low fire and boil eggs and cut them with a string in four. Put them in a large enough bowl. Then grind the gizzards and liver until they become like marrow and add to them salt and enough mixed spices with egg whites. Then prepare patties from it and fry them in a frying pan in clear oil until they brown. Then, cut them lengthwise and add them to the sliced eggs. Then, fry the amount of four egg yolks in clear oil until they brown and add them to the sliced eggs. Then, remove as much fat as possible from the pot. Moisten the broken bread pieces with the remaining broth until they are well soaked. Place the meat on top and garnish with the sliced eggs mixed with the aforementioned egg yolks and the pieces that were prepared of gizzards and pour the fat on top of all of it. Sprinkle on top of it cinnamon and ginger and eat it happily, God the most High willing!

—al-Tujībī, *Faḍālah al-Khiwān fī Ṭayyibāt al-Ṭaʿām wa al-Alwān*

Tharīdah (also known as *Tharīd* and *Thardah*) can generally be described as a stew of broken bread pieces soaked with a rich meat or vegetable broth, considered ideal for the toothless adult and the child whose teeth have not yet developed (*al-Bukhalāʾ* 74).

The Prophet Muhammad's great-grandfather Hāshim ʿAmr ibn ʿAbd Manāf is credited with being the first to introduce *Tharīdah* to Mecca after having shredded (*hashama*) bread for his tribe (*al-Bukhalāʾ* 74). However, it was the noble Banū Ghassān who received the highest praise for their *Tharīdah*. Known for specializing in delicious dishes, this tribe's *Tharīdah* became proverbial among all Arabs. Neither the common man's *Tharīdah* nor that of the elite could compare to *Tharīdah Ghassān*. Some say that it was made with bone marrow, making it the tastiest (*Thimār* 122).

The taste for *Tharīdah* was a common bond between the elite and the Bedouin. As one Bedouin proclaimed, "I would lunge into it the way an evil guardian would lunge at the property of an orphan" (*al-Bukhalāʾ* 179; Ibn Quṭaybah III 198).

It is more than likely that bread was baked fresh daily for the tables of the caliphs and used in dishes that required it. Although our source recipe includes this baking stage, stale bread or bread that has been dried in the oven is more typically used in *Tharīdah* dishes.

3–4 lb. chicken, cleaned and washed and cut into serving pieces, with gizzards ground and set aside
3 tsp. salt
1/4 cup olive oil
1 1/2 tsp. black pepper
1 tsp. ground coriander seeds
1 tsp. cumin
1 small onion, finely chopped
1/2 cup dried chickpeas, soaked overnight and drained
1/2 cup blanched whole almonds
2 1/2 tbsp. ground lemon rind
1 cup finely chopped fresh fennel
1 head peeled garlic
2 pinches saffron, dissolved in 2 tbsp. water
1/4 cup vinegar
10 eggs (4 hard boiled, 4 with whites and yolks separated, and 2 whole)
3/4 tsp. ground ginger
1/2 tsp. cinnamon
1/2 tsp. ras al-hanout
cooking oil
2 10-inch toasted pita loaves, broken into small pieces
2 tbsp. melted clarified butter

Place the chicken, 2 1/2 tsp. salt, olive oil, 1 tsp. black pepper, ground coriander, cumin, onion, chickpeas, almonds, lemon rind, fennel, and garlic in a large saucepan, cover with water, and bring to a boil. Cover and cook over medium-low heat for 40 minutes.

Stir in half the dissolved saffron and cook for 5 minutes more, then stir in the vinegar and cook an additional 5 minutes.

Beat the 2 whole eggs in a small bowl, then beat and stir in 1/4 tsp. salt, remaining 1/2 tsp. black pepper, 1/2 tsp. ginger, 1/4 tsp. cinnamon, and remaining saffron.

Stir the mixture into the saucepan with the chicken. Cook over low heat for 15 minutes or until the chicken and the chickpeas are done. Keep warm, removing any fat that gathers on top of the broth.

Quarter the 4 boiled eggs and place in a bowl.

In another bowl place the ground gizzards, remaining 1/4 tsp. salt, ras al-hanout, and the 4 egg whites, and mix. Heat the cooking oil in a frying pan over medium heat and spoon the mixture into the oil, forming patties. Fry until golden brown. Cut into strips and add to the boiled eggs in the bowl.

Fry the 4 egg yolks and add to the quartered eggs and patty strips.

Spread the broken pita on a large serving platter and moisten with the broth until the bread is well soaked, then place the chicken pieces on top.

Garnish with the egg mixture and sprinkle butter evenly on top. Sprinkle with remaining ginger and cinnamon and serve.

Creamy Stew with Meat and Vegetables

(*Maḍīrah*: Meat Cooked with Yogurt)

Serves 4–6

> *Its method of preparation is: cut fat meat into medium-sized pieces with tail-fat and if chickens are used then cut at the joints. Then throw them in the pot with a little salt and cover with water. Then boil it and remove its scum. When it is almost cooked, take large onions and large Nabatean leeks also, and peel and cut off their ends, then wash with water and salt and dry and put into the pot. Throw on it dried coriander, cumin, mastic, and finely ground cinnamon. Once it is cooked and the water has dried from it and only the fat remains, ladle into a dish. Then take Persian milk (yogurt), as much as is needed and throw it into the pot. Add to it salted lemon and fresh mint. Leave it until it boils. Then lower the heat and stir. Once its boiling has subsided, return that meat and the ingredients back into it. Cover the pot and wipe its sides and then let it simmer over the fire. Then remove.*
>
> —al-Baghdādī, *Kitāb al-Ṭabīkh*

The cuisine in pre-Islamic Arabia was simple. Although dairy products were used, it was not until the Umayyad period that cooks became well versed in preparing meat with milk products (*albān*) and greens (Maḥjūb/Khaṭīb 177, 193). The Abbasids continued the tradition and with versatility as an ingredient, dishes such as *al-Maḍīrah* became foods fit for nobility.

Maḍīrah is a warm, rich, thick stew made with soured milk or yogurt and meat, so delicious that one poet claimed that had the companion of the Prophet, Abū Hurayrah (603–681), been given the chance to eat it, he would have lost his will to fast (al-Masʿūdī VIII 404). It was this same Abū Hurayrah who was given the nickname "Sheikh of *Maḍīrah*" because of his great love for the dish. During the conflict between Muʿāwiyah and ʿAlī, Abū Hurayrah supported both in his own way. He enjoyed eating Muʿāwiyah's rich and tasty *Maḍīrah*, but for the hour of prayer ʿAlī was preferable (al-Thaʿālabī *Thimār* 112).

This creamy and slightly tart stew goes well served with rice.

1/4 cup. olive oil
one 3–4 lb. chicken, cleaned and jointed, or 2 lbs. lamb shoulder cut into 1-inch cubes
2 1/2 tsp. salt
2 large onions, quartered
2 leeks, green parts only, washed and cut in half, ends trimmed
1 1/2 tsp. ground coriander seeds
1 1/2 tsp. cumin
1/4 tsp. mastic
1/2 tsp. cinnamon
2 cups plain yogurt, whole or low-fat
3 tbsp. lemon juice
3 tbsp. finely chopped fresh mint leaves

Place the oil, chicken pieces or lamb, and 1 1/2 tsp. salt in a deep saucepan and cover with water. Bring to a boil, removing the scum as it gathers. Lower the heat to medium-low, cover, and simmer for 50 minutes, stirring occasionally.

Add the onions, leeks, 1/2 tsp. salt, ground coriander, cumin, mastic, and cinnamon, and cook over medium heat uncovered, stirring gently and occasionally, for 30 minutes or until very little liquid remains. Remove the chicken or lamb and the vegetables with a slotted spoon and set aside.

Add the yogurt, lemon juice, mint, and remaining salt to the broth and stir constantly with a wooden spoon in one direction over medium heat, bringing the mixture to a gentle boil. Remove from the heat for 5 minutes, then return the chicken or lamb and the vegetables to the saucepan. Cook over low heat for 10 minutes.

Serve immediately.

Ginger-Fried Shrimp for Lent

(*Ṭabāhajah min al-Rūbiyān*: Fried Dish Made from Shrimp)

Serves 4–6

> *Take shrimp, shell them, boil them and remove them from the water. Gently drain them or be patient until they dry from their water then place them in a pot. Chop onions for them. Fry in olive oil and throw in dried spices. Sprinkle with vinegar and scatter rue over the top of it . Then serve.*
>
> —al-Warrāq, Abū Muḥammad al-Muẓaffar ibn Naṣr ibn Sayyār, *Kitāb al-Ṭabīkh wa Iṣlāḥ al-Aghdhiyah al-Ma'kūlāt wa Ṭayyibah al-Aṭ'imah al-Maṣnū'āt*

This dish was one of those prepared during Lent, when Christians abstained from meat and dairy products.

Lenten meals in the medieval Arab world might incorporate shrimp, truffles, beans, lentils, chickpeas, leeks, carrots, Swiss chard, eggplant, and coconut milk. *Maḍīrah*, for example, would be made with flour and vinegar and either ground sesame, almonds, or hazelnuts instead of milk or yogurt, while the meat would be replaced with sprouted fava beans (al-Warrāq 124; "Description" 446).

We set aside our forks for this tasty meal and opt for Arab bread as our scooping utensil in order not to miss out on a drop of the sauce.

2 lb. large shrimp, shelled and deveined
1/2 cup olive oil
2 medium onions, finely chopped
1 tbsp. grated fresh ginger
1/2 tsp. salt
1/2 tsp. ground coriander seeds
1/2 tsp. caraway seeds

2 tbsp. vinegar
2 tsp. finely chopped rue

Place the shrimp in a saucepan, cover with water, and bring to a boil. Cook over medium heat for 2 minutes, then drain and set aside.

Heat the oil over medium in a frying pan. Add the onions and stir-fry for 3 minutes. Stir in shrimp and ginger and stir-fry for 3 minutes.

Add the salt, coriander, and caraway, and stir-fry for a minute longer.

Transfer to a serving platter, sprinkle with the vinegar and rue, and serve.

Fried Fish with Garlic and Coriander Sauce

(*al-Samak al-Kizbarīyah*: Coriandered Fish)

Serves 4–6

> *You will need a tender fish and black pepper, garlic, fresh coriander, sesame oil, and onions. Wash the fish and dredge in flour. Fry in the sesame oil, piece by piece, and allow to cool. Take the onions and chop finely. Pound the fresh coriander and garlic and add, stirring together until cooked. Add broth, as much as you need, to it then pour over the fish.*
>
> *—Kanz al-Fawā'id fī Tanwīʿ al-Mawā'id*

The Tigris and Euphrates Rivers were home to a multitude of varieties of fish, and it is not surprising that a great number of fish-based recipes were created for the tastes of the upper classes.

We find nothing tastier than the combination below, of garlic and fresh coriander with fried fish.

3–4 lb. whole fish (red mullet or any similar fish will do), cleaned and washed with water and salt
3/4 tsp. salt
flour for dredging
1/2 cup light sesame oil
1 1/4 tsp. black pepper

2 medium onions, finely chopped
1/2 cup finely chopped fresh coriander leaves
10 cloves garlic, crushed
1 cup fish broth

Sprinkle the salt over the fish and allow to sit for 1/2 hour. Dredge the fish in flour and set aside.

Heat the oil in a frying pan and fry the fish over medium-high heat until brown, turning to ensure both sides are browned. Set aside on a serving platter, reserving about 4 tbsp. oil in the frying pan.

Place the onions, pepper, coriander, and garlic in the frying pan and sauté over medium-low heat for 10 minutes or until the onions begin to brown, stirring occasionally.

Stir in the broth, bring to a boil, and simmer for 2 minutes. Pour over the fish and serve.

Poached and Baked Fish with Fennel

(*Basbāsīyah*: Made of Fennel)

Serves 4–6

> *Take a large variety of [fish], remove the skin and wash it. Cut it into pieces and boil it lightly in water and salt. Remove it then put in a tajine. Pound some fresh fennel and squeeze its juice enough to cover it. Add a lot of oil, black pepper, dried coriander, ginger, salt, onion water, and a little mastic gum. Put it in the oven until it browns on top and its sauce reduces. Remove it and use it.*
>
> —al-Tujībī, *Faḍālah al-Khiwān fī Ṭayyibāt al-Ṭaʿām wa al-Alwān*

In recipes calling for large fish, al-Tujībī recommends sturgeon, grouper, or shad, all types with good, tasty, and fatty meat.

As the name implies, fennel is the strongest flavor in this particular dish, but it is mellowed by the coriander and ginger. If your preference is for fresh herbs, replace the 1 teaspoon of ground coriander with a half cup of finely chopped fresh coriander leaves.

1 whole grouper or similar fish, about 3 lbs., cleaned, skinned, washed, and cut into serving pieces
1 1/2 tsp. salt
3 cups chopped fresh fennel
1 cup water
5 tbsp. olive oil
3/4 tsp. black pepper
1 tsp. ground coriander seeds
1 tbsp. grated fresh ginger
1 medium onion, puréed
1/2 tsp. ground mastic

Sprinkle the fish pieces with 1 tsp. salt and allow to sit for 1 hour.

Preheat the oven to 350° F.

Bring enough water to a boil in a saucepan and to cover the fish. Add the fish pieces and boil gently over medium heat for 2 minutes, gently stirring once. With a slotted spoon, carefully remove the fish pieces and place in a casserole. Retain 1 cup of the broth.

Combine the fennel and the reserved broth in a food processor, process for 1 minute, then spoon evenly over the fish pieces.

Combine the remaining ingredients, including remaining 1/2 tsp. salt, and spoon evenly over the fish pieces. Bake for 30 minutes, uncovered, or until the sauce is reduced.

Serve hot from casserole.

Fried Fish with Tahini and Onions

(*al-Samakah al-Ṭaḥīnīyah*: Fish with Tahini)

Serves 4–6

> *Vinegar,* aṭrāf ṭīb, *black pepper, saffron, and onions: wash the fish then dredge in a little flour and fry in sesame oil. Pound the black pepper and* aṭrāf ṭīb *and put over the onions and mix (together). Dilute the tahini with the vinegar and the saffron and put over the said ingredients and boil. Once cooked, place the fish on it.*
>
> *—Kanz al-Fawāʾid fī Tanwīʿ al-Mawāʾid*

The contemporary eastern Arab kitchen includes a dish somewhat similar to this one, called *Samak Ṭājin*. It is a fish baked with tahini and onions, and a possible descendant of our thirteenth-century recipe. It is quite customary for the Syrians, Lebanese, Jordanians, and Palestinians to eat fish, whether baked or fried, with some sort of tahini-based sauce, either served on top or as a side dip known as *ṭaraṭūr*, tahini mixed with lemon juice and garlic.

3–4 lb. whole fish such as red snapper or grouper, cleaned, scaled, and washed in salted water
1 tsp. salt
flour for dredging
1 1/2 cups light sesame oil
1 medium onion, finely chopped
1 tsp. black pepper
1/2 tsp. aṭrāf al-ṭīb
4 tbsp. tahini, diluted in 1 cup water
3 tbsp. vinegar
pinch of saffron

Sprinkle fish on both sides with salt. Allow to sit for 1 hour. Dredge lightly in flour and set aside.

Fry fish in oil over medium heat in a large frying pan until light brown, turning once. The fish is done when easily flaked with a fork. Remove and drain on paper towels.

Place the onion in a saucepan, stir in black pepper and *aṭrāf al-ṭīb*, and mix thoroughly.

Stir together the tahini-water mixture, vinegar, and saffron and pour into onion mixture. Stirring constantly over medium heat, bring the contents of the saucepan to a soft boil, and immediately remove from the heat.

Spoon the sauce evenly on a serving platter, place the fish on top, and serve immediately.

Walnut-Stuffed Roasted Fish

(*Samak Mashwī*: Roasted Fish)

Serves 4–6

> *Take black pepper, cinnamon, caraway, ginger, sumac, dried coriander, thyme, and a little cumin. Pound all of them with a little mint and sift. Then*

take garlic and peel then finely pound with rock salt and fresh oil in the mortar and add to it from the ingredients in an amount enough to knead it. While you are kneading it, take walnuts and pound and add them. Take lemon, oil, and tahini in an amount that you need and mix all together and knead with these kneaded spices. Then take the fish and stuff its sides and belly well. Beneath the baking dish set thin pieces of wood or a thin wooden plank so that it does not stick. Then take it to the oven. When it is cooked on one side, take it out and allow it to cool on that plank for a while. Then return it to the oven until it is cooked as desired.

—*Kanz al-Fawāʾid fī Tanwīʿ al-Mawāʾid*

Although Caliph al-Muʿtaṣim was careful with what he ate, depending heavily on the advice of his physician Ibn Māsawayh, a time came when he decided to eat only what he wanted. During this period Aḥmad ibn Abī Duʾād came to visit the caliph and found the ruler with the doctor.

When the caliph left the room, Aḥmad remarked to the physician that the ruler seemed pale and not alert. Ibn Māsawayh responded that the caliph was like a piece of iron from an iron bar, but that it was the caliph who was holding the axe that was chipping away at the piece of iron. Confused, Aḥmad asked the doctor what he meant.

Ibn Māsawayh explained that what was happening to the caliph, he was doing to himself. "At one time, when the caliph wanted to eat fish, he would eat it prepared with a sauce of vinegar, caraway, cumin, rue, celery leaves, mustard, and walnuts. He would eat it this way to avoid any harmful effects of the fish, to prevent anything that would damage the nervous system. If dishes of sheep or beef heads were served to him, the seasoned sauces served with them would make this type of food lighter and harmless. He used to take care of himself and consult with me regularly about his meals. However, today, when I advised him not eat one of the dishes, he disobeyed and told me, 'I will eat it, in spite of the nose of Ibn Māsawayh!' I, thus, do not know what to do, as I cannot violate the word of the ruler. Do you have any suggestions?"

Despite knowing the doctor's fear of angering the caliph, Aḥmad's advice to the physician was to stand up to him like a man and "Put your finger in his eye!" so that he would listen.

Neither man knew that the caliph was behind a curtain and had heard the entire conversation. The caliph then appeared and asked Aḥmad what the two had been discussing. Aḥmad was straightforward and told the caliph he had noticed his pale complexion and his lack of appetite, which in turn had troubled him. Furthermore, he told him that Ibn Māsawayh was also worried because at one time the caliph had followed the physician's dietary advice. Now, it seemed, the caliph was disobeying what was only being advised for his own good.

When al-Muʿtaṣim asked Aḥmad how he had responded to the physician, Aḥmad attempted to change the subject. The caliph, however, interjected almost immediately and with a laugh asked "Was this before or after he was supposed to thrust his finger in my eye?" (al-Masʿūdī VII 104–107).

Surely Ibn Māsawayh would have nodded his head in approval had *al-Samak Mashwī* been presented to Caliph al-Muʿtaṣim, but the virtues of the dish extend far beyond its perceived health benefits. It has a subtle nutty yet creamy taste due to the tahini and the walnuts—and we find it delicious.

3–4 lb. whole grouper, or any type of whitefish, scaled, cleaned, washed, and patted dry
1/2 cup olive oil
1 1/2 tsp. salt
1 tsp. black pepper
1/2 tsp. cinnamon
1/2 tsp. ground caraway seeds
1/2 tsp. ground ginger
3 tbsp. sumac
1/2 tsp. ground coriander seeds
1 tbsp. ground dried thyme
1/4 tsp. cumin
1/2 tsp. dried mint
4 garlic cloves, crushed
1/2 cup ground walnuts
2 tbsp. lemon juice
3 tbsp. tahini

Rub the fish all over with 1 tbsp. olive oil and 1/2 tsp. salt, and place in a baking pan that has been greased with 2 tbsp. of the oil. Set aside for 1/2 hour.

Preheat oven to 400° F.

Thoroughly combine the remaining ingredients, including the remaining oil and salt, to form a paste, adding a few more drops of oil if necessary. Stuff the fish with the mixture. Seal the belly of the fish with toothpicks and bake uncovered for 15 minutes. Carefully turn the fish over and bake 30 minutes more or until the fish is done.

Serve hot or cold.

Summertime Fried Fish

(*Samak al-Sikbāj*: Fish Made like Sikbāj)

Serves 4–6

> *You will need a fresh fish, vinegar, honey,* aṭrāf ṭīb, *black pepper, onion, saffron, sesame oil, and flour. Wash the fish. Cut up and fry in the sesame oil after having dredged it in flour. When it has cooked, remove it. Mince the onions and fry in the sesame oil until they brown. Pound the black pepper and add the* aṭrāf ṭīb. *Dissolve the saffron in the vinegar and honey and add (to the onions). When they are cooked put the fish into it.*
>
> *—Kanz al-Fawā'id fī Tanwīʿ al-Mawā'id*

In ninth-century Baghdad, we read, the Christian community purchased its fish on Fridays, Sundays, Mondays, and Wednesdays. On those days, the price for fish soared in the souks. Because the demand on those days was so high, the non-Christian communities preferred to shop for fish on the remaining days of the week, when both the demand and the price were lower (*Ḥayawān* IV 431–432).

Ibn Quṭaybah recommends that fish be eaten hot in the winter and with mustard, but in the summer, with vinegar and spices (III 297). Ibn Sīnā concluded that fresh fish is a healthy meal when cooked in a sauce with a little vinegar. If they are to be trusted, the fish dish below—a vinegar-based *sikbāj* type of fish stew—makes for a perfect and salubrious summer meal.

3 lb. fresh grouper or similar fish, scaled, cleaned, washed, and cut into serving pieces
1 1/2 tsp. salt
flour for dredging
2 cups light sesame oil
2 medium onions, finely chopped
1 1/2 tsp. black pepper
1/2 tsp. aṭrāf al-ṭīb
pinch of saffron dissolved in 1/4 cup vinegar and 4 tbsp. honey

Sprinkle the salt over the fish pieces and set aside for 1/2 hour.

Dredge the fish pieces in flour and fry in oil over medium heat until brown, turning once. Transfer to a serving platter.

Fry the onions in the same pan, over medium-low heat for 8 minutes or until they turn light brown, adding more oil if necessary.

Stir in remaining ingredients and cook for 1 minute. Spoon the sauce over the fish and serve immediately.

Fried Salmon with Raisins and Almonds

(*Zabībīyah*: Made of Raisins)

Serves 4–6

> *You need a fresh fish, raisins, wine vinegar,* aṭrāf ṭīb, *saffron, black pepper, almonds, and sesame oil. Wash the fish and fry it after having dredged it in a little flour. Cool. Boil the vinegar, and add the raisins, the ground black pepper and the* aṭrāf al-ṭīb *to it. Prepare the almonds and color them on the outside with a little saffron. Throw them on the fish.*
>
> *—Kanz al-Fawā'id fī Tanwīʿ al-Mawā'id*

The combination of raisins and vinegar here makes an unusual type of sauce for fish.

3–4 lb. whole salmon or similar type fish, cleaned, scaled, and washed
1 tsp. salt
light sesame oil for deep frying
flour for dredging
1/2 cup wine vinegar
2 tbsp. water
1/2 cup raisins
1 tsp. black pepper
1/2 tsp. aṭrāf al-ṭīb
1/2 cup whole blanched almonds soaked in 3/4 cup water diluted with 1/8 tsp. saffron, 2 hours before preparation

Sprinkle the fish on both sides with the salt and set aside for 1/2 hour.

Heat the oil in a saucepan over medium heat. Dredge the fish in flour and deep-fry until golden brown, turning over once to crisp both sides. Place on a serving platter and set aside to cool.

Place the vinegar and water in a small saucepan and bring to a boil. Add the raisins, black pepper, and *aṭrāf al-ṭīb*, turn the heat to low, and cover, stirring occasionally. Cook for 8 minutes, then spread evenly over the fish.

Drain the almonds, spread evenly over the fish, and serve.

VEGETARIAN

Sweet Tooth Rice and Yogurt

(*Aruzz bi-al-Laban al-Ḥalīb*: Rice with Yogurt)

Serves 4–6

> *Wash white rice in hot water a number of times until its water is free of dirt and clean then put it in an earthenware bowl. Let it dry up until all its water is dried off. Then pour sheep's yogurt in a tightly-woven cloth. Yogurt made of sheep's milk is the best for cooking it; cow's yogurt is the next best; and if neither are available, use goat's yogurt. The amount of yogurt needed is six* raṭls *to one* raṭl *of rice. Put the rice in a large pot with a little bit of hot water then pour onto it all the yogurt, if the pot is large enough. Leave the pot on the fire until the yogurt is heated through. Shut off the fire under it and leave it on the cinders or on enough of a temperature. Cover with a piece of clean cloth. If the fire dies down, add to it more cinders and if the yogurt dries up in the pot, add more of the yogurt. Continue doing so until the rice is cooked. Then sprinkle a suitable (amount of) salt in it, stirring the rice gently with the handle of the ladle until the salt flavors it. Then empty it into a bowl and place a vessel filled with honey in the middle. Sprinkle sugar over it for those who wish that and eat it with clean wooden spoons, in good health with the power of God.*
>
> —al-Tujībī, *Faḍālah al-Khiwān fī Ṭayyibāt al-Ṭaʿām wa al-Alwān*

In the Muslim world, sheep and goat milk were much more popular than cow's milk for drinking and cooking because of their rich flavor. The meat of lamb, goat, and sheep was also considered healthier than beef, which was, according to medieval Arab physicians, much more difficult to digest.

Ibn Jazlah offers a simple rice with yogurt dish made of only two ingredients. We have opted for a version from al-Tujībī, which is somewhat more complicated to prepare, but appealing to our sweet tooth. It calls for honey, with the optional addition of sugar. We choose to add both.

Today the Arabs continue the tradition of their medieval ancestors in that almost always when rice is served, whether on its own or as part of a stuffing, there stands beside it a plate or bowl of homemade yogurt.

1/2 cup honey
1/2 cup long grain rice, rinsed and drained well
1 cup hot water
3 cups plain yogurt, whole or low-fat (sheep or goat if possible)
1/2 tsp. salt
1 tbsp. sugar (optional)

Place the honey in a small bowl on a serving platter.

Place the rice and water in a saucepan, stir in the yogurt, and cook over medium heat, stirring continuously in one direction until the yogurt begins to bubble.

Turn the heat to very low and cover, stirring occasionally, until the rice is cooked, about 15 minutes. If the yogurt begins to dry up, add a little water.

Add the salt and transfer to a serving platter, spooning the rice-yogurt mixture around the bowl of honey. Each diner will add honey to taste to his or her portion of the rice-yogurt.

If sugar is desired, sprinkle over the rice.

Sautéed Aphrodisiac Greens

(*Muzawwarah Mulūkhīyah*: "Vegetarian" Mulūkhīyah)

Serves 4–6

> *You will need Jew's mallow, sesame oil, mastic, cinnamon, an onion, and dried coriander. Fry the onion in the sesame oil until it is done with the aforementioned ingredients.*
>
> *—Kanz al-Fawā'id fī Tanwīʿ al-Mawā'id*

Melokhia, also called *meloukhia*, *melokhiya*, or *milookhiyya*, is a potherb also called Jew's mallow, Jute mallow, and Nalta jute. It is found in most Middle Eastern groceries either dried or fresh. It can also be purchased frozen and canned.

From Fatimid Egypt a decree was issued on the 7th of Muḥarram in the year 1005 by caliph al-Ḥākim bi ʾAmr Allāh (996–1020) prohibiting eating *mulūkhīyah*, said to be a favorite dish of Umayyad caliph Muʿāwiyah ibn Abī Sufyān (al-Maqrīzī 53). His successor later permitted the herb to be eaten again. Why the prohibition? Popular Arab lore attributes the caliph's ban to the notion that this green serves as an aphrodisiac. Not many foods can lay claim to such fame. Today, in spite of the decree of al-Ḥākim, per capita consumption of *mulūkhīyah* in Egypt is perhaps the highest in the world.

As the name of this dish implies, this recipe simulates a more popular medieval dish, the main ingredients of which were meat and *mulūkhīyah*. *Muzawwar*—"imitation" or "deceptive"—signals that this is a meatless preparation used for medicinal purposes or during times of fasting, when meat and dairy products were not permitted.

A warning: the texture of cooked melokhia is unusual, and people tend either to love or to detest it. If, on first trial, its slimy quality is not to your liking, we suggest replacing it with fresh or frozen spinach.

1/4 cup + 2 tbsp. light sesame oil
2 medium onions, finely chopped
2 tsp. ground coriander seeds
1 1/2 tsp. salt
1/2 tsp. mastic
1/2 tsp. cinnamon
1 1/2 lb. fresh mulūkhīyah *leaves or 2 packages (13 ounces) each frozen* mulūkhīyah*, thawed at room temperature and not drained*
1 cup water (if using fresh mulūkhīyah*)*

Fry the onions in oil over medium heat in a saucepan for 8 minutes, or until they begin to brown.

Add remaining ingredients, cover, and simmer over medium-low heat for 20 minutes, stirring occasionally.

This goes well served hot with cooked rice.

Garlicky Yogurt and Chard

(*Silq bi-Laban*: Swiss Chard in Yogurt)

Serves 4–6

> *Take chard with large stalks. Cut off the ends of its leaves and cut into pieces the span of a hand and wash. Then boil in water and salt until they are cooked. Dry them from the water and put them in Persian milk*[8] *and garlic. Sprinkle black caraway (*nigella sativa*) on it and serve.*
>
> —al-Baghdādī, *Kitāb al-Ṭabīkh*

Yogurt remains the most important milk product in the Arab world. Mixed with honey, it serves as a refreshing breakfast dish; diluted with water and a sprinkle of salt, it becomes a refreshing beverage; eaten on its own, it is enjoyed as a snack. For centuries, it has been referred to as "the miracle milk product," the "mystery food," or sometimes even "the elixir of life." Medieval physicians lauded its curative powers, either on its own or when mixed with meat and garlic and eaten for three straight days.

This is a light garlic-flavored yogurt dish. The Swiss chard adds a little bounce to the texture. It can stand alone as a meal in itself or is a good side dish with any meat-based entrée, spooned on top of kebabs or used as a marinade for various cuts of meat.

1 large bunch Swiss chard, washed and tips snipped, and chopped into large pieces
2 1/2 tsp. salt
2 cups plain yogurt, whole or low-fat (preferably sheep or goat)
4 cloves garlic, crushed
1 tsp. black caraway seeds (also called black cumin)

Put enough water to cover the Swiss chard in a large saucepan; add salt and bring to a boil. Add the chard, lower heat to medium-low, and simmer for 5 minutes.

Place the yogurt in a serving bowl, stir in garlic, and set aside.

Drain the Swiss chard and allow it to cool, then stir into the yogurt. Sprinkle with black caraway and refrigerate covered until ready to serve.

Spiced Chickpea Patties

(*ʿUjjah min Ghayr Bayḍ*: An Omelet Without Eggs)

Makes 12 patties

> *Take chickpeas and boil them until they become like the texture of marrow. Boil some onion and pound it with them. Pour over them a little olive oil,* murrī, *coriander seed, black pepper, and gum Arabic dissolved in water. Put it in a frying pan and fry in olive oil until cooked, God willing!*
>
> —al-Warrāq, Abū Muḥammad al-Muẓaffar ibn Naṣr ibn Sayyār, *Kitāb al-Ṭabīkh wa Iṣlāḥ al-Aghdhiyah al-Maʾkūlāt wa Ṭayyibah al-Aṭʿimah al-Maṣnūʿāt*

To eastern Christians in the Middle East, the Great Fast beginning seven weeks before Easter is the most important part of the year. When this time approaches, preparations for Lent begin in the kitchen. All types of meats, cheese, eggs, and milk are excluded from the family diet. Rich traditional dishes are replaced by a variety of less extravagant, but often quite delicious vegetarian foods.

Many Lenten dishes are the same as those recommended for those who are sick and need proper nourishment. Known popularly as "*muzawwarāt*" or "*kadhdhābah*" (imitation, mock, simulated) dishes, we find them listed as such in al-Warrāq (Chapters 46 and 105), in the *Kanz* (100–101), and in the "Description" (443–450), which includes many of the recipes found in the ninth-century Christian monk ʿAbdūn al-Naṣrānī's cookbook *Mā Yaʾkuluhu al-Mardà wa al-Ruhbān wa al-Naṣārà* (What the Sick, the Monks, and the Christians Eat) (*Zayyāt* 17).

Lenten dishes are always cooked with oil, usually olive oil. This acts as a natural preservative that makes it possible to keep food fresh and tasty for long periods of time—an important consideration, since Lenten foods are often eaten cold.

In this recipe al-Warrāq calls for *māʾ al-ṣamgh*, gum Arabic dissolved in water. Because gum Arabic is difficult to find and its function here is as a binding ingredient, we have replaced it with flour.

Simply put, *ʿUjjah min Ghayr Bayḍ* is a tasty chickpea patty, crunchy and spicy.

1 cup dried chickpeas, soaked overnight and drained
1 large onion, peeled and left whole
1 cup olive oil
3/4 tbsp. red miso

1/2 tsp. salt
1/2 tsp. ground coriander seeds
1/2 tsp. black pepper
1 1/2 tbsp. flour

Place the chickpeas in a saucepan and cover with 4 inches of water. Cook over medium heat for 1 1/2 hours or until soft. Remove from heat and drain.

While the chickpeas are cooking, boil the onion with 2 tbsp. oil over medium heat for 1/2 hour or until soft, then remove from the heat and drain.

Place the chickpeas and onion in a food processor and process well. Transfer to a bowl, add remaining ingredients except the oil, and mix well.

Form the mixture into patties, using a little flour on the palms of hands, and set aside.

Over medium heat, heat enough of the remaining oil to fry a first batch of the patties until brown, gently turning over once. Add more oil and fry the remainder of the patties. If the patties begin to fall apart before cooking, add a little flour to the palms of hands and re-form them.

Serve immediately.

Gardener's Vegetable Tart

(*Jannānīyah*: Gardener's Dish)

Serves 4–6

It was the custom among us to make this in the flower and vegetable gardens. If you make it in summer or fall, take saltwort, Swiss chard, gourd, small eggplants, fennel, fox-grapes, the best parts of tender gourd, and flesh of ribbed cucumber and smooth cucumber; chop all this very small, as vegetables are chopped, and cook with water and salt; then drain off the water. Take a clean pot and in it pour a little water and a lot of oil, pounded onion, garlic, pepper, coriander seed, and caraway; put on a moderate fire and when it has boiled, put in the boiled vegetables. When it has finished cooking, add grated or pounded bread and dissolved [sour] dough, and break over it as many eggs as you are able, and squeeze in the juice of tender coriander and of mint, and leave on the hearthstone until the eggs set. If you make it in spring, then [use] lettuce, fennel, peeled fresh fava beans, spinach, Swiss chard, carrots, fresh coriander, and so on; cook it all and add the spices already indicated, plenty of oil, cheese, dissolved [sour] dough, and eggs.

—Anonymous Andalusian Cookbook (Kitāb al-Ṭabikh fī al-Maghrib wa al-Andalus fī ʿAṣr al-Muwaḥḥidīn, li-muʾallif majhūl), page 59, translated by Charles Perry

This is an interesting recipe, variable according to the season in which it is prepared. One common denominator for all three versions—spring, summer, and fall—is *silq*, presumably Swiss chard.

In the contemporary Arab kitchen, *silq* can be not only Swiss chard, but also the leaves of spinach, beet, kohlrabi, radish, dandelion, or any other greens. *Silīqah*, a preparation of greens sautéed in olive oil with onions and garlic, is a basic side dish in Lebanon.

Two types of small cucumber appear in the source recipe for summer and fall, the ribbed type used most commonly today in the Arab East for pickling and for salads and snacking, and the smoother-skinned variety known as *khiyār*. We have opted to replace the two varieties with only one. If saltwort is unavailable, we suggest spinach as a perfectly acceptable replacement.

In summer or fall:

2 cups finely chopped tender saltwort leaves or fresh spinach
2 cups finely chopped Swiss chard leaves
2 cups peeled pumpkin or zucchini, cut into 1/2-inch cubes
1 small peeled eggplant, about 1/2 lb., cut into 1/2-inch cubes
1 cup finely chopped fennel
2 cups sour grapes
2 cups 1/2-inch cubed cucumbers
2 1/2 tsp. salt
1/4 cup olive oil
1 large onion, very finely chopped
6 cloves garlic, crushed
1 tsp. black pepper
1 tsp. ground coriander seeds
1 tsp. ground caraway seeds
1/2 cup fine bread crumbs
2 tbsp. sourdough starter dissolved in 1/2 cup water
4 eggs

4 tbsp. very finely chopped fresh coriander leaves
2 tbsp. very finely chopped fresh mint leaves

In spring:

2 cups finely chopped lettuce, packed tightly
2 cups finely chopped fennel
1 cup shelled green fresh fava beans or baby lima beans
2 cups finely chopped spinach, packed tightly
2 cups finely chopped Swiss chard leaves, packed tightly
1 cup carrots, diced into small cubes
1/2 cup plus 4 tbsp. finely chopped fresh coriander leaves
1/2 cup finely chopped leeks
2 cups chopped asparagus, bottom ends removed
2 1/2 tsp. salt
1/4 cup olive oil
1 large onion, very finely chopped
6 cloves garlic, crushed
1 tsp. black pepper
1 tsp. ground coriander seeds
1 tsp. ground caraway seeds
1/2 cup fine bread crumbs
2 tbsp. sourdough starter
2 tbsp. finely chopped halloumi cheese
4 eggs
2 tbsp. very finely chopped mint leaves

Fill a large saucepan with water and bring to a rolling boil. Add the first seven summer/fall ingredients or first nine spring ingredients (reserving 4 tbsp. chopped coriander leaves) and bring to a boil again. Turn heat to medium and cook for 5–8 minutes, or until the vegetables soften. Drain and set aside in a strainer.

Heat the oil in a frying pan over medium heat and add the onion, garlic, black pepper, ground coriander, and caraway. Sauté for 3 minutes, stirring often.

Add the cooked vegetables and stir-fry for 3 minutes.

Stir in the bread crumbs and sourdough starter, adding the cheese if using spring vegetables.

Break the eggs evenly over the top and sprinkle the remaining coriander leaves and mint over the eggs. Cook for a few minutes over low heat until the eggs are set. Serve warm.

Desserts

BASIC DESSERT ELEMENTS

Sugar Syrup

(*Qaṭr*)

2 cups sugar
1 cup water
2 tsp. lemon juice
1 tbsp. orange blossom water or rosewater

Stir the sugar and water in a saucepan and bring to a boil over medium heat. Simmer for 10 minutes. Stir in the lemon juice and simmer 1 minute more.

Stir in the orange blossom or rosewater. Set aside until ready to use.

Honey Syrup

(*'Asal*)

2 cups honey
1/4 cup butter

Combine the honey and butter in a saucepan. Bring to a boil over medium heat, stirring constantly. Reduce the heat and keep warm.

Rosewater and Orange Blossom Custard Cream

(*Qashṭah*: Thick Custard-Like Cream)

1 1/2 cups cornstarch
6 cups homogenized milk
1 1/2 cups heavy whipping cream
4 tbsp. sugar
1/4 cup rosewater
1/4 cup orange blossom water

Mix the cornstarch and 1 1/2 cups milk. Stir until smooth, making sure there are no lumps. Set aside.

Combine the remaining milk and cream in a large saucepan. Add the sugar and mix well. Stir in the rosewater and orange blossom water.

Place over medium-low heat and continue to stir until the liquid is heated through, almost hot to the touch. Add the cornstarch mixture and continue stirring until the mixture is thick and begins to bubble.

Remove from the heat, pour into a bowl, and allow to cool. Cover and refrigerate for at least two hours before using. The mixture will thicken as it cools, and can remain refrigerated for up to a week, covered with plastic wrap.

Sugared Lettuce

(*Khassīyah*: Made of Lettuce)

Serves 4–6

> *Take a bunch of lettuce, peel and cut it up and boil in syrup. Take starch and dissolve it into some of the syrup in which the lettuce has been boiled. Then pound poppy seeds and throw them all into the syrup and stir them around in sesame oil. When it is done, fry the boiled lettuce in it. Stir it and perfume it then remove it.*
>
> —Ibn al-ʿAdīm, *Kitāb al-Wuṣlah ilà al-Ḥabīb fī Waṣf al-Ṭayyibāt wa al-Ṭīb*

A word of advice from the tenth-century *ʿUyūn*: eating lettuce on an empty stomach eases the stress of puberty. A drink of lettuce seeds mixed with cold water will take away the craving for sexual intercourse (III 290). We're not sure if this lessens or increases the appeal of lettuce. What is certain is that this is an unusually sweetened, syrupy vegetable dessert. Our own lettuce-related advice? Forgo the extra sugar in your coffee or tea when savoring this very sweet dessert.

1 large head romaine lettuce, washed, drained, dried, and ends trimmed
*Sugar Syrup (*Qaṭr*) recipe (see page 133)*
1 tbsp. cornstarch
1 tbsp. ground poppy seeds
2 tbsp. light sesame oil
1/4 tsp. anise seed
1/4 tsp. cinnamon
1/4 tsp. ground ginger

Separate the lettuce leaves and slice into 1 1/2-inch wide strips. Set aside.

In a saucepan, bring the syrup to a boil over medium heat. Add the lettuce and cook over medium-low for 5 minutes, stirring constantly. Drain the lettuce, reserving the syrup.

Return 1/4 cup of syrup to the saucepan and stir in the cornstarch. Mix well until smooth, then stir in the poppy seeds and sesame oil.

Add the boiled lettuce and the remaining ingredients and sauté over medium heat for 2 minutes, stirring constantly. Transfer to a serving dish and serve warm.

Honey and Almond Candy

(*Fālūdhaj*: "Strained" or "Refined")

Makes approximately 30 1-inch pieces

> *Take good white honey as much as you wish and pour it into a large copper pot with a rounded bottom and light a gentle fire beneath it. Take off its froth, strain it and discard. Take washed olive oil or the oil of hulled sesame seeds. If the amount of honey is one* raṭl, *then take half a* raṭl *of sesame oil or olive oil. Take starch in the amount of a quarter of the honey allowing it to absorb lest it become sour. Take the amount of saffron that you want and add it to the cornstarch. Pour it into the pot over the honey and sesame oil and stir gently over a gentle fire until it pulls from the sides. Add almonds, as much as you prefer, letting it thicken until the sesame oil is absorbed and hardens and is ready. Remove from the heat. Spread on a platter, God willing.*
>
> —al-Warrāq, Abū Muḥammad al-Muẓaffar ibn Naṣr ibn Sayyār, *Kitāb al-Ṭabīkh wa Iṣlāḥ al-Aghdhiyah al-Ma'kūlāt wa Ṭayyibah al-Aṭʿimah al-Maṣnūʿāt*

In the seventh century, while visiting Persia and dining at the court of the Persian king, ʿAbd Allāh ibn Judʿān, leader of Mecca's prominent Banū Quraysh tribe and chief inspector of Souk ʿUkāẓ, tasted a fabulous dessert. Impressed with this sweet of wheat flour mixed with honey, he received permission from the king to return to Mecca with one of the court cooks who specialized in its preparation. There he ordered the cook to prepare a very large quantity of the dish for the people of Mecca. The party was a great success, and so it was that *Fālūdhaj* took its place on the dessert tables of the Arabs from then on (al-Isfahānī, *al-Aghānī* VIII 331–332). This pudding was so well received that it continued yet developed into another variety, a type of candy.

There are many recipes for *Fālūdhaj* in the source cookbooks, including variations made with watermelon or with rice, and eleven recipes in al-Warrāq alone. We have chosen one that pays special attention to details of quantities and methods. It can be thickened, according to al-Warrāq, with cornstarch, rice flour, ground almonds, or ground dried melon. In its dense and chewy texture, we may compare it with today's Turkish Delight.

We suggest that you offset its sweetness with a good cup of hot mint tea.

2 cups honey
1 cup olive, light sesame or vegetable oil
1/2 cup cornstarch dissolved in 6 tbsp hot water
pinch of saffron
1 cup whole or slivered blanched almonds

Bring the honey to a boil in a saucepan over medium heat.

Stir in the oil, dissolved cornstarch, and saffron and continue cooking over medium heat, stirring constantly, until the mixture thickens, about 12 minutes.

Remove from heat and stir in almonds.

Spread the mixture on a platter to a thickness of 1/4 inch. Allow to cool, then cut into serving pieces.

Chewy Fruity Nut Candy

(Ḥalwà)

Makes approximately 30–35 1-inch pieces

> *Its varieties are many. Among them are the sweets made of* nāṭif.[1] *You put* dibs *[date molasses], honey, sugar or* rubb *[boiled-down fruit juice] in the pot then you put it on a gentle fire and stir until it takes consistency. Then you beat egg whites and put them with it and stir until it thickens and becomes* nāṭif. *After that, if you want almond candy, you put in toasted almonds and* ʿallaftahu *[literally, "you feed it"]; that is, you bind them. Walnuts, pistachios, hazelnuts, toasted chickpeas, toasted sesame seeds, flour. You beat the* nāṭif *until it thickens. For* duhniyah, *you put in flour toasted with fat [*duhn*]. As for* ḥalāwah ʿajamīyah, *toast flour with sesame oil until it becomes slack, and boil* dibs *or another sweet ingredient and put it with it.*

As for khabīṣ *[pudding], take* dibs *and put it on the fire until its scum rises, and skim it. Dissolve starch in water and put it with it.*

—Ibn al-Mabrad (or Ibn al-Mubarrad), *The Book of Cookery (Kitāb al-Ṭibākhah), pages 471–472, translated by Charles Perry*

Ḥalwà is a dense confection, the root of the word from the Arabic *ḥ l w* meaning to be sweet. Its variations are many. Made with sugar, honey, or *dibs* (see below), it can also include nuts or poppy seeds and be flavored with rosewater or musk. The fourteenth-century traveler Ibn Baṭṭūṭah spoke of Baalbek's popular *Ḥalwāʾ bi-al-Malban* or *Jild al-Faras* (skin of the horse), made with grape pulp *dibs* to which pistachios and almonds were added (83). In Nablus, carob *dibs* was used to make *Ḥalwāʾ al-Kharrūb*, which was exported to Damascus and other places (61).

Caliph al-Muqtadir bi-Allāh (r. 908–932) arrived one day unannounced at his *Zubaydīyah* orchard. Hungry, he ordered the servants to bring him food, which they did. However, *Ḥalwà* was not part of the meal. Disappointed, the caliph exclaimed that he could not believe anyone could eat without having *Ḥalwà* served for dessert (al-Tanūkhī III 189–191).

Ibn al-Mabrad's version is a tasty, light, chewy candy, simple to make but a little tricky because one needs to work quickly to produce the proper results.

2 cups dibs *(date, carob, grape, or corn syrup)*
3 egg whites, beaten until stiff peaks form
2 cups chopped walnuts (or toasted almonds, pistachios, hazelnuts, roasted chickpeas, or sesame seeds)

In a deep saucepan, bring the *dibs* to a boil over medium heat, stirring constantly. Lower heat to medium-low and continue to stir until the syrup begins to thicken. The *dibs* will be ready when a little dropped into cold water forms a hard ball. Remove from heat.

Quickly fold the *dibs* into the egg whites and stir quickly until smooth.

Quickly stir in the nuts, chickpeas, or sesame seeds, then spread the mixture evenly on a greased 8- or 9-inch round serving platter. While still warm, cut into serving pieces with an oiled knife.

Keep refrigerated until ready to serve.

Muḥammad's Wedding Cookies

(*Hays*)

Makes 35 balls

> *Take dry good bread or biscuits and pound fine. For each* raṭl *of it take half a* raṭl *of dates. Remove their pits. Rub (the dates with) the pounded biscuits. Then take one* ūqīyah *each of finely ground walnuts, almonds, pistachios, and toasted sesame seeds and throw them on (the mixture). Take sesame oil and boil over a calm fire. Then pour it over (the mixture) continuing to rub and rub with the hands until well blended. Make it into kebabs. Sprinkle with finely ground sugar and take up.*
>
> *—Kanz al-Fawā'id fī Tanwī' al-Mawā'id*

According to tradition, *Hays* was served in the seventh century at the wedding of the Prophet Muḥammad and Ṣafīyah. A basic Bedouin sweet made of bread crumbs or dried curd, clarified butter, and dates, it traveled with time to the tables of the affluent, with the addition of expensive ingredients such as pistachios, almonds, and spices—and continued to travel from there, often packed as a provision by pilgrims on their way to Mecca and beyond. Portuguese *bolas de figo e almêndoa* (fig and almond balls) may be distant descendants.

We suggest that a food processor be used to ensure that the date-nut mixture is blended thoroughly. If you are adventurous, however, the mixture can be worked rigorously by hand.

3/4 lb. soft pitted dates, chopped
2 cups finely ground bread crumbs
1/4 cup ground walnuts
1/4 cup ground almonds
1/4 cup ground pistachios
1/4 cup ground toasted sesame seeds
1/2 cup + 2 tbsp. light sesame oil
confectioner's sugar or superfine sugar

Place the dates, bread crumbs, walnuts, almonds, pistachios, and sesame seeds in a food processor and process for 2 minutes.

Pour the sesame oil evenly over the mixture and process for 5 minutes more.

Test the mixture by pressing a small amount in the palm of the hand to make sure it sticks together. If not, process the mixture further until it begins to bind.

Form the mixture into balls about the size of a walnut, roll in confectioner's or superfine sugar, and place on a serving plate. *Hays* will keep well for about two weeks if stored in an airtight container.

Fried Rosewater Melts

(*Kāhīn*)

Makes 15–20 pieces

> *Take for each egg white, two dirhams of starch. Pound starch finely and mix with the egg whites in a cup. Throw on it a little rosewater—not too much because it will become thin. Take a new whisk made of husk used to make mats. Beat the egg whites and starch until all parts are mixed and it has foam. Then take a frying pan and put it on a gentle fire. When the sesame oil is heated, drop in it with a small spoon the egg whites and starch. Fry until they brown. Do not let them stick to each other. Remove them from the frying pan. Put them in boiling syrup. Eat them while they are hot. Frying them in butter is tastier than in sesame oil. If eaten cold, they will not be tasty.*
>
> —Ibn al-ʿAdīm, *Kitāb al-Wuṣlah ilà al-Ḥabīb fī Waṣf al-Ṭayyibāt wa al-Ṭīb*

Kāhīn are meringue-like cookies. The origin of the name is obscure, perhaps derived from that of the sweet's creator or from a place where it was first developed. But be forewarned: it is also possible that the term derives from the Arabic colloquial form of *k h n*—repulsive and ugly, due to the sweet's non-uniform shape and color.

Although these little delights are quick and easy to prepare, it is important that you butter the serving platter well, because they are very sticky. It is important that they be eaten immediately while they are warm.

Ibn al-ʿAdīm notes, they taste better if fried in butter instead of oil, and we concur. If fried in oil, they tend to be a bit heavy; in butter, they are moderately and pleasantly sweet.

*half Sugar Syrup (*Qaṭr*) recipe (see page 133)*
3 egg whites
1 1/2 tsp. cornstarch

1/4 tsp. rosewater
1 cup light sesame oil or 1–1 1/2 cups butter, melted

Keep the syrup on low heat while preparing the egg white mixture.

Mix the egg whites, cornstarch, and rosewater in a bowl, stirring until there are no lumps. Beat the mixture with an electric beater until stiff peaks form.

Heat the oil or butter in a saucepan over medium-low heat. Drop a teaspoonful of the egg white mixture into the oil or butter and fry until it begins to turn slightly golden, turning over once. Gently remove with a slotted spoon, immediately dip into the warm syrup, and place on a well-greased serving platter.

Continue until all the *Kāhīn* are made, then serve immediately.

Honeyed Sesame Patties

(*Juljulānīyah al-Bayḍā'*: White Sesame)

Makes approximately 20 patties

> *Strain the honey as was mentioned previously and stir in the pot over a gentle fire. Judge by finger (that it is ready) when it sticks to it, then remove it from the fire. (When over the fire) it should be stirred often. Then beat egg whites, five eggs per* raṭl, *and four if the honey is white, until white froth forms on top and then pour over the honey that is lukewarm. Put the pot over the fire and stir often with the spoon until it turns white and thickens. Then put in the honey enough of peeled sesame and stir until thickened. Remove from the fire and spread over a marble slab in patties.*
>
> —al-Tujībī, *Faḍālah al-Khiwān fī Ṭayyibāt al-Ṭa'ām wa al-Alwān*

One of the surviving traces of the two and a half centuries of Arab rule in Sicily is the sweet known as *Cubaita di Giuggiulena*. Popular all over the island, its Arab origin may be discerned not only in its ingredients and method of preparation, but also in its name: the *Cubaita* of the Sicilian dialect is derived from the Arabic term *qubbayṭ*, meaning "cubes"; *Giuggiulena* is derived from *juljulān jiljilān*, or sesame.

Farther west, in Spain, a similar candy, *guirlache*, a blend of walnuts, honey or sugar, and sesame, is believed to be one of the culinary contributions brought by the ninth-century

Ziryāb, when he immigrated to al-Andalus from Baghdad (Lebling 33). In Morocco, *Ḥilū di al-Juljulān*, a mixture of sugar or honey melted and then mixed with sesame seeds and almonds, is also, no doubt, a relation.

These come out chewy and pleasantly sweet. For a slightly different taste, try using toasted sesame seeds.

---

1 cup honey
2 egg whites
1 cup sesame seeds

Bring the honey to a boil in a saucepan over medium heat, stirring constantly. Lower heat to medium-low and continue stirring for 10 minutes. Remove from heat and cool to lukewarm.

Beat the egg whites to stiff peaks, and fold into the honey.

Return the saucepan to the stove over medium heat and stir the mixture for 4 minutes. Stir in the sesame seeds, mixing well, for 4 minutes more. Remove from heat.

Drop the mixture by tablespoonfuls onto a greased tray, flattening slightly to form patties. Allow to cool, then transfer to a serving platter, or store refrigerated in an airtight container.

Adult Butter Cookies

(*ʿAdhārī*: The Virgins)

Makes 24 pieces

> *Take one part flour, one part clarified butter, and one part sugar. Rub them together. Knead well, then form like breasts [of the virgins], without water. Bake on a tray in the oven.*
>
> —*Kanz al-Fawāʾid fī Tanwīʿ al-Mawāʾid*

The name of this cookie describes its shape, to a certain extent. *Al-ʿAdhārī*, the virgins, or more precisely, *Nuhūd al-ʿAdhrāʾ*,[2] breasts of the virgin, are so named because of the small, round, firm shape of the cookie.

These cookies are similar to shortbread in texture and taste but are guaranteed to be a conversation piece because of their shape.

2 1/4 cups flour
3/4 cup clarified butter
1 cup confectioner's sugar

Preheat oven to 300° F.

Mix the ingredients to form a dough and divide into 24 balls.

Shape each ball into the form of a breast and bake on an ungreased tray for 30 minutes or until the "breasts" begin to brown underneath.

Remove the tray from the oven and allow to cool. Carefully place on a serving platter.

Caliph's Favorite Shortbread

(*Khushkanānaj Gharīb*: Strange or Foreign Dry Bread)

Makes approximately 25 1-inch cookies

> *Take three* raṭls *of good quality sugar, and pound it and sift it using a fine mesh sieve. Take one and half* raṭls *of white flour and mix it well with the sugar. Knead it with one quarter* raṭl *of fresh sesame oil just as you would with flour. Then take a mortar and put it in it and pound it until all ingredients come together. Then take a small mold, the smallest possible, or in place of it, something like a small wooden or a copper container with a wide rim and a round bottom. Stuff it with this flour and sugar [mixture], then turn the mold upside-down on a wide, low table in order that it comes out on it. Continue to do this until all of the flour/sugar mixture is used up. Then, take a wide frying pan with low sides and in it, one at a time, arrange that which came out of the molds, not letting them stick together. Then, put it in a low burning tannur. When they are lightly browned remove them from the pan with a long, thin flat spatula inserting it beneath them, one at a time and put them on a clean platter and arrange them, God willing.*
>
> —al-Warrāq, Abū Muḥammad al-Muẓaffar ibn Naṣr ibn Sayyār, *Kitāb al-Ṭabīkh wa Iṣlāḥ al-Aghdhiyah al-Ma'kūlāt wa Ṭayyibah al-Aṭ'imah al-Maṣnū'āt*

In the court of the caliph al-Wāthiq was a young lad, learned, intelligent, with a magnificent memory, and able to recite poetry and sayings that few others could recall so well. When he spoke, all eyes and ears were on him. Yet, he was not permitted to sit beside the caliph or among the assembly of the court. He was too young.

It was on an occasion when the caliph asked his guests their favorite sweet tidbits that the young man's status would change. Responses varied from pomegranates to apples to crystallized vegetables flavored with rosewater and even wine, but the young lad, when pressed for his opinion, responded that he preferred *Khushkanānaj.*

With this, the caliph invited the boy to sit alongside him, for as it turned out, this was the ruler's favorite sweet (al-Masʿūdī VII 170-171).

Although we cannot guarantee that *Khushkanānaj* will grant you access to the highest echelons of society, we can recommend it on culinary grounds.

We use a very small mold for forming the cookies since they are very sweet. They are especially good eaten as soon as they are removed from the oven, but they are still delicious when they have cooled down.

The sesame oil is the only liquid used in the source recipe. However, we find that adding butter or shortening to the oil makes the dough easier to handle. Also, the taste of sesame oil on its own may be too strong for some.

This recipe is for the *Khushkanānaj* prepared for the caliph al-Wāthiq by his court cook Abū Samīn.

---

1 cup superfine sugar
3/4 cup flour
2 tbsp. light sesame oil
4 tbsp. shortening or butter

Preheat oven to 300°F.

Combine sugar and flour in a mixing bowl. Add the oil and shortening (or butter) and mix by hand until dough has a crumbly texture. Transfer to a food processor and process until the dough binds (pinch the dough with your fingers to see if it sticks together and add a little oil or shortening if it doesn't).

Press the dough into a cookie mold and turn out onto an ungreased baking sheet.

Bake for 20 minutes or until bottoms are slightly browned. Allow to cool for about 10 minutes, then carefully remove cookies from the baking sheet.

Sesame-Nut Shortbread

(*Khubz al-Abāzīr*: Bread of Spices or Seeds)

Makes 20

> *Take first-rate flour, and on every* raṭl *put four* ūqīyahs *of sesame oil, an* ūqīyah *of sesame seeds, and a handful of pistachios and almonds. When it rises, make patties from it and bake them until brown. This is* Khubz al-Abāzīr.
>
> —Ibn al-ʿAdīm, *Kitāb al-Wuṣlah ilà al-Ḥabīb fī Waṣf al-Ṭayyibāt wa al-Ṭīb*

Although the name of this cookie may be translated "spice bread," spices are notably absent from the list of ingredients. Perhaps "seed bread" would be a better rendering, as the medieval Arabic recipes for the cookie include sesame seeds in addition to almonds and pistachios.

Where the source recipe states that the dough must "*yakhtamar*" or be allowed to rise, one might at first assume that yeast is needed. Not so. Long-time Arab cooks realize almost immediately that this term denotes that some non-yeast doughs just need to rest to absorb any liquid or binder mixed with them.

The original recipe calls for sesame oil as the binding ingredient. This works, but the cookies turn out especially dry and crumbly. When we tried to adjust the measurements, the results were dry and brittle. Finally, we created another version by replacing the sesame oil with unsalted butter. Although less authentic, it was much more palatable, yielding something more like shortbread and not too heavy. We have given two redacted versions of the original recipe: the first with sesame oil and just a little butter, the second with butter alone.

With sesame oil:

2 cups flour
2 tsp. sesame seeds
2 tbsp. chopped pistachios
2 tbsp. chopped almonds
4 tbsp. butter, melted
1/4 cup light sesame oil
6 tbsp. water

Mix flour, sesame seeds, pistachios, and almonds in a bowl. Form a well and add the butter, sesame oil, and water. Knead to form a dough, adding more flour or water if necessary. Cover and let rest for 2 hours.

Preheat oven to 350° F.

Form the dough into 20 balls and shape into rounded buns, and place on greased baking sheet. Bake for 40 minutes or until the cookies begin to brown.

Allow to cool for a few minutes, then remove and place carefully on a serving platter.

With unsalted butter:

1/2 lb. unsalted butter
2 1/2 cups flour
1 tbsp. sesame seeds
2 tbsp. chopped pistachios
2 tbsp. chopped almonds

Preheat oven to 350°F.

In a bowl, mix all the ingredients by hand, adding more butter or flour if necessary to form a dough. Cover and let rest for 2 hours.

Shape into 20 round patties and place on an ungreased baking sheet. Bake for 40–45 minutes, or until the cookies begin to brown. Allow to cool for a few minutes, then remove and carefully place on a serving platter.

Hazelnut Filo Dough Cake

(*Akhmīmīyah*: A Type of Cake)

Serves 8–10

> *A* raṭl *of* kunāfah *broken into pieces: put into a pot with four* ūqīyahs *of sesame oil and fry for a short time. Then add on it a* raṭl *of ground sugar and stir together until the sesame oil that had been absorbed reappears, this being the sign that it no longer needs to be fried. Then add to it four* ūqīyahs *of bees' honey and stir. Then add four* ūqīyahs *of ground roasted hazelnuts. Remove from the fire. It is perfumed with musk and rosewater.*

Take it up. This method has never changed for years. Every time it is presented, it is enjoyed.

—Ibn al-ʿAdīm, *Kitāb al-Wuṣlah ilà al-Ḥabīb fī Waṣf al-Ṭayyibāt wa al-Ṭīb*

The name of this crispy and tasty cake-type dessert may be derived from Akhmīm, a region of Egypt. Although Ibn al-ʿAdīm calls for hazelnuts, other medieval sources note that other types of shelled nuts can be used.

We have replaced the musk of the original recipe with cinnamon, the former being almost impossible to find in any grocery store.

---

5 tbsp. light sesame oil
1 pound filo dough unrolled and cut into small pieces
2 cups sugar
5 tbsp. honey
5 tbsp. ground roasted hazelnuts
1/2 tsp. cinnamon
2 tsp. rosewater

In a large saucepan, heat the oil over medium heat. Add the filo pieces and fry until golden brown, about 8 to 10 minutes, stirring gently and constantly.

Add the sugar and gently stir until some of the oil that has been absorbed begins to reappear, about 3 to 4 minutes. Immediately remove from heat.

Gently stir in the honey and hazelnuts to coat the filo pieces.

Stir in the cinnamon and rosewater. Transfer quickly to a serving platter and mold into an 8-inch round cake.

Slice and serve immediately; otherwise the *Akhmīmīyah* will become too hard.

Fried Filo Dough with Pistachios and Rosewater

(Kul wa Ushkur! Eat and Give Thanks!)

Serves 8–10

They are also called the horns of Yārūq. Mix flour with butter and knead with water. Stretch with a rolling pin similar to ṭuṭmāj. *Melt butter and brush the leaves of the* ṭuṭmāj *dough with it. Fold the dough in layers making sure that the width of each layer is four fingers. Cut into triangles. Fry in sesame oil until they become rose-colored. Put them in a plate. Sprinkle sugar, boiling syrup, and peeled pistachios on them.*

—Ibn al-ʿAdīm, *Kitāb al-Wuṣlah ilà al-Ḥabīb fī Waṣf al-Ṭayyibāt wa al-Ṭīb*

Ṭuṭmāj, the dough called for in this recipe, is also used in a meat broth today served in modern Central Asian cuisine. The name survives in Armenian and Serbo-Croatian to describe a thick, spicy soup of broth or hot yogurt mixed with noodles made from this dough.

We read the original recipe for this sweet as calling for the dough to be rolled out thinly so that it may be folded many times. To simplify the process, we suggest using ready-made filo dough.

The original recipe instructs that hot syrup be poured over the fried dough, while the *Kanz* directs that the pastries be dipped in either a rose-flavored syrup or honey mixed with rosewater and musk, and then sprinkled with sugar.

We find that to maintain the crispness of the fried pieces it is best to pour cold syrup over the pastry.

---

*half Sugar Syrup (*Qaṭr*) recipe (see page 133) using rosewater, cooled*
1 pound package filo dough
1 cup clarified butter, melted
oil for deep frying
1/4 cup fruit (caster) sugar
1 cup coarsely ground pistachios

Place a sheet of filo dough on a flat surface and brush lightly with butter. Place another sheet over the buttered sheet and butter lightly. Continue the process until you have used all the sheets.

Lift the right side of the buttered filo and fold a 3-inch width toward the center of the pastry sheet. Lift the folded portion and fold again toward the center, and again and again until you have a 3-inch wide panel. Cut the panel twice, forming 3 even squares. Cut each square diagonally into four equal triangles.

Heat the oil in a saucepan over medium-low heat. Place the triangles, two or three at a time, in the oil and fry until the filo begins to turn golden. Each triangle will separate in the oil as it is frying, creating many more triangles (lightly tap the top of any triangles that do not separate, to allow them to fan out; you may also want to score folded edges of the triangles before frying to help them brown evenly).

Remove with a slotted spoon and drain on paper towels. Transfer to a serving platter. Pour the cooled syrup evenly over the triangles. Sprinkle the fruit sugar and pistachios evenly over the triangles and serve.

Honey-Cream Crunch

(Kunāfah)

Serves 8–12

> *Make dough by using two* raṭls *of excellent clean very fine semolina, then after moistening it with hot water, knead it extremely well. Cover it until it cools. Then pour water over the dough and it is washed in the same manner as you prepare* talbīnah[3] *for clothes, until the dough dissolves and it becomes soft. Then squeeze the liquid through a tightly woven cloth until nothing remains except the bare grains, then leave in a receptacle similar to bread. Pour into it a sufficient measurement of water until its texture is between lightness and toughness. Place a mirror used for it [for* kunāfah*] on a charcoal fire with no flame. When it is heated, it is brushed with a clean cloth soaked in fresh oil. Pour enough of the dough on it [the mirror] as much as it can hold. Leave it on for a little time until it becomes very thin bread. Then remove and put it on a platter. Pour on the mirror from the remaining dough and cook it in the same manner as thin bread one after another until it is all finished, [making sure] to brush the mirror with the oiled cloth for each one. Remove [the cooked bread/sheets] with a knife so that its edges will not stick to it that which will spoil it. Then melt the amount of one-quarter* raṭl *of butter or clarified butter over the fire with the measurement of two* raṭls *of honey until it is blended. If desired, a little pepper can be added. Then arrange the thin breads evenly and pour on them the melted butter and honey while it is hot. Clarified butter is better than butter. He who wishes to keep them aside and reserve them, then cut the thin breads with scissors as thin as possible. When ready to use, put a new pot on the fire with enough honey. When it boils and the foam subsides add the cut thin bread to it and cook them in it until fully absorbed. When it is almost cooked, it should be moistened with* tharīdah *or clarified butter or oil. When it is ready, it should be removed from the fire and from the pot*

and stored until it is needed. It can be eaten cold or hot. At the time that it is ready to be used, sprinkle sugar or cinnamon on it and eat, God willing.

—al-Tujībī, *Faḍālah al-Khiwān fī Ṭayyibāt al-Ṭaʿām wa al-Alwān*

Kunāfah is a paper-thin pastry made of batter dried very slowly on a tray or mirror made of steel or iron. The cooked sheets may be left as they are, or they may be cut into very thin strips like noodles (*rishtā*), or threads of dough as thin as or even thinner than vermicelli. In its vermicelli form, *kunāfah* is today used to make a very popular cheese-filled baked pastry that is enjoyed for breakfast or dessert. It can also be stuffed with various types of nuts, usually walnuts or pistachios. If you are familiar with Greek cuisine, you know this stringy form of the pastry as kataifi. Al-Tujībī's process for making *kunāfah* dough is too tedious for most of us even to try, and we have opted to use filo dough instead of working the dough out from scratch. We remain impressed, however, by what we saw on one of our visits to Syria a few years ago. There, in a village south of Damascus, we witnessed women preparing the noodle-type of *kunāfah* dough by dropping the batter through a sieve onto metal sheets. They made it look so easy.

You will need the filo sheet form of *kunāfah* dough for the recipe below.

The source recipe offers two methods for making this sweet: to stack the layers of cooked thin dough and pour the honey syrup over the top, or to break up the cooked dough and pour the honey syrup into it. We found the results too dry with the first method and too soggy with the second, so we have combined the two to create a crunchy, satisfying dessert.

1/2 pound filo dough
4 tbsp. cornstarch dissolved in 1/2 cup milk
4 1/2 cups milk
2/3 cup + 4 tbsp fruit (caster) sugar
1/8 tsp. salt
1 1/2 cups honey
1/2 cup unsalted butter, melted
1 1/2 tsp. cinnamon

Preheat oven to 350°F.

Cut each filo sheet into pieces, about 2 x 2 inches. Place on a greased baking pan and bake until light golden brown, turning them over once to ensure both sides have browned. Distribute evenly onto a large serving platter.

Mix remaining milk, 2/3 cup fruit (caster) sugar, and salt in a saucepan and bring to a boil over medium heat. Stirring constantly with a wooden spoon, add cornstarch paste and cook until thickened, about 15 minutes. Remove from heat and allow to cool in the saucepan. Chill, if desired.

While the milk sauce is cooling, mix the honey and butter in a saucepan over medium heat, stirring occasionally. Bring to a soft rolling boil and remove from heat.

Spoon the thickened milk sauce evenly over the filo pieces, and pour the honey-butter syrup evenly over them.

Mix the remaining 4 tbsp. sugar and cinnamon and sprinkle evenly over the *kunāfah*. Serve immediately.

Seven-Layer Ricotta Cake

(*Qayjāṭah*: Layered Cheese Pastry, Made in al-Andalus, and Called "Seven Bellies")

Serves 8–12

> *Take moist, fresh cheese and knead it in the hands. Then take a deep-wide-bellied clay tajine and in the bottom of it put a thin flatbread, made like* kunāfah*. Put the cheese over this, and then another crepe, and repeat this until there remains a third to a quarter of the pan.*
>
> *Pour fresh oil over it, place it in the oven, and leave it a little; then take it out, moisten it with a little fresh milk, and return it to the oven, and take it out and moisten with fresh milk and return to the oven thus until the milk and the oil disappear. Leave it until its surface is browned to the color of musk; then take it out and pour skimmed honey cleaned of its foam, or rose syrup, over it. There are those who sprinkle it with ground sugar and spices, and others who leave it be.*
>
> *—Anonymous Andalusian Cookbook (Kitāb al-Ṭabikh fī al-Maghrib wa al-Andalus fī ʿAṣr al-Muwaḥḥidīn, li-muʿallif majhūl), page 150, translated by Charles Perry*

In al-Tujībī this cheese cake is called *al-Qayḥāṭah* (83) or possibly *al-Qayjāṭīyah* (290). According to Waines, the dish was also known throughout al-Andalus as the "Seven Stomachs" (*Sabʿah Buṭūn*), although we wonder whether the Andalusian name isn't better rendered as "Seven Interiors," alluding to the seven layers of the cake.

Waines points out that preparation of this sweet dish entailed three different visits to the communal oven: first for baking the thin sheets of bread and cheese; then after the milk was added; and finally after honey or spiced sugar was added ("Culinary Culture" 731). Thank goodness, things are much simpler today.

This is a very light dessert in layered cake form with a delicious filling of ricotta and honey. It should be eaten immediately once prepared.

---

1 cup honey
1/4 cup butter
1 1/2 lb. ricotta cheese
1 pound filo dough (22 sheets)
1/4 cup olive oil
1/4 cup milk

Preheat oven to 350° F.

Place the honey and butter in a saucepan and bring to a boil. Keep warm over very low heat.

Divide the ricotta into 7 parts.

Spread filo dough flat. To prevent dough from drying, cover with plastic wrap until ready to use.

To prepare the first layer of the *Qayjāṭah*, place 5 sheets of the filo dough into a greased 13 x 9 baking dish, brushing each sheet lightly with oil. Spread one portion of the ricotta evenly over the layer. Repeat the process six times, using only 2 sheets of filo for each subsequent layer. Top the final seventh layer with remaining 5 sheets of filo, again brushing each sheet with oil.

With a sharp knife, carefully cut the *Qayjāṭah* into approximate 1 1/2-inch squares. Pour the remaining oil evenly over the *Qayjāṭah* and bake for 15 minutes.

Remove from oven and sprinkle 2 tbsp. milk evenly over the top of the *Qayjāṭah*. Bake 10 minutes more, remove from oven, and sprinkle with remaining milk. Return to oven and cook another 5 minutes.

Remove *Qayjāṭah* from oven and pour honey mixture evenly over the top. Let sit for about 5 minutes, then serve while warm.

Almond Fingers

(*Lawzīnaj*)

About 54–66 pieces, depending on number of filo sheets in package

> *As for the moist (Lawzīnaj), take a* raṭl *of sugar and finely pulverize. Take one third of a* raṭl *of peeled almonds and finely pound them and mix with the sugar. Knead with rosewater. Take thin dough like the dough of* Sanbūsak. *If it is thinner then it is better, the most suitable being that of the* Kunāfah. *Roll out the loaf from this dough and put the kneaded sugar and almonds in it and then roll up and cut into small pieces. Layer them in a serving platter. Refine fresh sesame-oil as much as is needed and put it over them. Then cover them with syrup dissolved with rosewater. Sprinkle over them finely pounded sugar and pistachios and then use.*
>
> —Ibn al-ʿAdīm, *Kitāb al-Wuṣlah ilà al-Ḥabīb fī Waṣf al-Ṭayyibāt wa al-Ṭīb*

Caliph Hārūn al-Rashīd and his wife Zubaydah summoned the Qāḍī, or chief judge, of Baghdad to enter a judgment in a dispute: which confectionery was better, *Lawzīnaj* or *Fālūdhaj*? When dishes filled with each sweet were brought forward, the Qāḍī ate from one and then the other, worrying that he might offend either party. Finally, the caliph asked the judge to announce his verdict. "I have never come across such debate between two opposing parties," he declared, refusing to render a decision. "Every time I was ready to find in favor of one, the other presented his argument. I became confused between the two." The caliph laughed, gave the judge 100 dinars, and let him go (Ibn Khallikān II 316–317). Perhaps this story contributed to the later eleventh-century designation of *Lawzīnaj* as *Qāḍī Quḍāah al-Ḥalwayāt* (judge of all judges of sweets) (al-Rāghib al-Aṣbahānī II 619).

There are actually two versions of *Lawzīnaj*: one, as in the recipe below, is an almond paste wrapped in a thin dough; the other is an almond paste candy, so delicate, easy to swallow, and tasty that some have suggested that our word "lozenge" is derived from it.

2 cups ground almonds
1 1/4 cups superfine sugar
2 tsp. rosewater
1 lb. butter, melted
1 pound package filo dough
1 egg, beaten
vegetable or light sesame oil for frying

*Sugar Syrup (*Qaṭr*) recipe (see page 133), using rosewater, cooled*
1 cup ground pistachios
1/2 cup confectioner's sugar

To make the filling, mix the almonds, sugar, rosewater, and 1 tbsp. butter. Set aside.

Separate the filo sheets and place on a flat working surface. Cut each sheet into three equal strips. Cover with a slightly dampened towel.

Take one strip of filo and lightly brush all the edges with the melted butter. Place a heaping teaspoon of filling near the bottom edge and spread slightly, not touching the edges of the filo. Fold over the sides of the filo, approximately 1/4 inch. Roll upward, tucking in the sides creating a log shape. Brush the egg on the seam to seal it well. Place the roll, seam side up, on a lightly floured surface and let stand until all the rolls are completed.

Heat the oil over medium heat and deep fry the *Lawzīnaj* for a few minutes until golden. Remove with a slotted spoon, place on paper towels to absorb any excess oil, and transfer to a tray until cooled.

Dip the *Lawzīnaj* into the *Qaṭr* and place pastries on a serving tray, next to each other but not touching.

Sprinkle the pistachios over the *Lawzīnaj*. Once cooled, sprinkle with the confectioner's sugar.

Fried Dough Bites

(*Luqam al-Qāḍī*: Judge's Morsels)

About 3 dozen balls

> *This type is made from firm dough. When it ferments, take it in the size of a hazelnut and fry it in sesame oil. Then, dip in syrup. Sprinkle over them finely pounded sugar.*
>
> —al-Baghdādī, *Kitāb al-Ṭabīkh*

The recipe for *Luqam al-Qāḍī* has remained unchanged since the medieval period. These are basically bite-sized balls of fried dough dipped in syrup. In some Arab countries, this sweet ball is called *Luqmah* (plural: *Luqam* or *Luqmāt*), in others, *ʿAwāmī* (plural: *ʿAwaymāt*). Easy to make and delicious, they are one of the most popular desserts in the Arab world, sometimes lightly spiced with saffron and cardamom.[4]

The following recipe is taken from Habeeb Salloum's *Classic Vegetarian Cooking from the Middle East and North Africa* under the heading "Deep-Fried Sweet Balls—*Awamee*."

1 tablespoon sugar
1 package dry yeast (1/4 oz.)
2 1/4 cups lukewarm water
2 cups flour
4 tablespoons cornstarch
1/2 teaspoon salt
*Sugar Syrup (*Qaṭr*) recipe (see page 133)*
2 cups cooking oil
superfine sugar

Dissolve the sugar and yeast in 1/4 cup lukewarm water, cover, and allow to stand in a warm place until yeast begins to froth, about 10 minutes.

Combine the flour, cornstarch, and salt in a mixing bowl, make a well, then pour in the yeast, and mix well. Add 2 cups lukewarm water and stir until the mixture has the texture of pancake batter, adding more flour or water if necessary. Cover and set aside for 1 hour.

Heat the oil in a saucepan and drop the batter into the hot oil 1 tablespoon at a time, to form individual balls. Cook over medium heat until the balls turn golden, then remove with a slotted spoon and place on paper towels to drain. Dip the balls into the *Qaṭr* and arrange on a serving platter. Sprinkle each with sugar.

These balls taste best when served the same day they are prepared.

Crunchy Beaded Honey Squares

(*Barad*: Hail)

Approximately 18 3-inch square pieces

> *Its procedure is to take excellent white flour, knead it thinly and leave it until it ferments. Then set up a big pot on the fire and put sesame oil in it. When it boils, spoon the dough out with a plaited scoop, stirring them quickly in the sesame oil in order that each piece of dough that has been*

dropped in the sesame oil becomes hard. Whenever piece after piece is cooked, scoop them out with another plaited scoop until the sesame oil dries from them. Take the necessary amount of honey dissolving it in rosewater. Place it on the fire until it boils and it reaches the right consistency. Remove it from the fire and beat while it is in the pot until it whitens. Then throw the Barad *in it then put on a thin greased tile, collecting it together in the shape of the mold. Then cut into pieces and serve it.*

—al-Baghdādī, *Kitāb al-Ṭabīkh*

Barad, the Arabic term for "hail," are little beads of deep-fried crispy dough, mixed with honey and pressed into a pan. The preparation is tedious and time-consuming—and well worth the effort. The dessert is very sweet but extremely light, and we guarantee there will be no leftovers. It is excellent served with mint tea.

1 tbsp. sugar
1 package dry yeast (1/4 oz.)
2 3/4 cups lukewarm water
2 cups flour or extra fine semolina
light sesame oil for frying
2 cups honey
3 tsp. rosewater

Dissolve the sugar and yeast in 1/4 cup lukewarm water, cover, and allow to stand in a warm place until the yeast begins to froth, about 10 minutes.

In another bowl, mix the flour and the remaining 2 1/2 cups lukewarm water until smooth. Add yeast and stir in until well blended. Cover and let stand for 1 1/2 hours.

Place about 2 inches oil in a frying pan over medium heat. Pour the batter through a slotted ladle or spoon or any type of instrument that has small holes in it, allowing the batter to drip through, forming small balls in the oil. Fry until golden and drain on paper towels. Allow the *Barad* to cool completely.

Mix the honey and rosewater in a deep saucepan and cook over medium heat, stirring constantly until bubbles begin to form. Lower heat, stir, and simmer for 5 minutes more.

Allow to cool, then beat until its consistency is similar to whipped butter and it turns a golden yellow.

Mix the whipped honey with the fried dough beads, and transfer to a buttered 10 x 15 baking pan. Press down evenly by hand, with waxed paper, or with a buttered spatula. Chill for at least an hour, then cut into serving pieces.

Crispy Lattice Fritters

(*Zalābiyah Mushabbakah Wāthiqīyah*: al-Wāthiq's Lattice-Shaped Fried Dough)

Serves 6

Take half a raṭl *of good quality flour and knead with yeast to make a soft dough. Cover and let it rise overnight. On the following day, take the same weight, half a* raṭl *of starch then knead it with the starter. Then mix the two and knead all together with water bit by bit until it becomes thin similar to Qaṭā'if batter. Add a little baking borax to it. You should have an already prepared nut bowl for the batter. It is a nut bowl made from a coconut, its rounded top cut off, leaving it like a cup. Then pierce the other end, its width the thickness of a probe. Then allow the batter to sit for a bit. Then take a flat-bottomed iron or copper frying pan. Pour enough fat into it to cover the* Zalābiyah. *Light the fire under it until it boils. Then ladle some of the pre-made batter into the prepared coconut shell holding it in the left hand while using your finger to block the hole until it is full. Then with your right hand grasp its rim allowing the batter to run through the hole into the frying pan, all the while as you guide it in a circular motion with your hand forming the lattice shape (in the form) that you like, either circular, meatball-shaped or square.*

You will see that the batter has risen properly if when dropped into the oil in the frying pan, it will form into circles looking like light hollow bracelets. Then throw them into honey that you have already boiled, skimmed of its froth and aromatized, leaving them to soak up the honey. Then remove them and place them on a sweets platter. If they are good, serve them. The mark of their excellence is that when they are in the mouth of the one eating them, they are brittle and dry and break up and melt in the mouth. If they turn out soft like leather, then they are not good. Or this could be due to the batter not rising enough or because the yeast was bad or the honey was too thin due to it not being boiled enough or from the period of time in the year when it is cold or there is too much moisture. If there was not enough yeast, wait until it ferments. If the yeast was bad then treat it with baking borax. If the honey still has moisture in it, return it to the fire and let it boil as much as is needed. If it is during winter and the rains, then make the Zalābiyah *in warm and dry rooms of a house and light more of a fire. It should be made during the days of the northern and western winds. The yeast-dough should be close to the fire covered from the cold. Avoid making it wherever the southern winds blow. This is all the best insight in making them, God willing.*

—al-Warrāq, Abū Muḥammad al-Muẓaffar ibn Naṣr ibn Sayyār, *Kitāb al-Ṭabīkh wa Iṣlāḥ al-Aghdhiyah al-Ma'kūlāt wa Ṭayyibah al-Aṭ'imah al-Maṣnū'āt*

Zalābiyah Mushabbakah are elegant, light, crispy, yet syrupy fritters that continue to be enjoyed throughout the Arab world. The process of drawing the batter into a design by quick hand movements creates a fritter that is lattice-shaped (*mushabbak*).

In this recipe, we have substituted an egg white for baking borax, which is called for in the original recipe but is not readily available. Either ingredient helps give the fritters their crispy texture.

Zalābiyah Mushabbakah are fun to make because the cook becomes quite the artist in creating each one.

Honey Syrup ('Asal*) recipe (see page 134)*
1 tbsp. sugar
1 cup lukewarm water
1 package dry yeast (1/4 oz.)
1 cup flour
3/4 cup cornstarch
1/8 tsp. salt
1 egg white, beaten until stiff
oil for frying

Prepare *'Asal* recipe and keep warm.

Dissolve the sugar and yeast in 1/4 cup lukewarm water, cover, and allow to stand in a warm place until the yeast begins to froth, about 10 minutes.

Place the flour, cornstarch, and salt in a deep bowl and mix well. Form a well and add the yeast, remaining water, and egg white. Beat with an electric mixer for one minute to make a smooth batter.

Cover the bowl and let sit for 1 hour to allow the batter to rise. After it has risen, stir.

Heat the oil in a deep saucepan over medium heat.

Place a finger under the small opening of a funnel and spoon 3 tablespoons batter into the top. Holding the funnel over the saucepan, dribble the batter into the oil by quickly moving the funnel back and forth to create a lattice-shaped form. Fry on both sides until golden.

Remove the *Mushabbak* from the oil with tongs, gently shaking off any excess oil, and immerse in the syrup, making sure to cover both sides. Place on a serving platter.

Fried Stuffed Pancakes

(*al-Qaṭāʾif al-Maḥshī*: Stuffed Pancakes)

Makes 22–24 pieces

Qaṭāʾif Dough (*ʿAjīn al-Qaṭāʾif*)

Take two sifted Baghdadi raṭls *of* samīdh.[5] *Also take one quarter Baghdadi* raṭl *of yeast dough [starter] made from* ḥawwārà[6] *or* samīdh *flour. Dissolve it [with water] and remove any lumps. Throw in salt, being the weight of three dirhams and a dirham of baking borax, both having been crushed and sifted. Sprinkle it over the* [samīdh] *flour and knead well with water until it becomes smooth and without lumps to the degree that if it is ladled out and poured onto the marble slab it will spread. You should mark the dough with a measuring device for flour. If it has risen in the amount of a finger-width or less, then it has fermented. Heat a clean marble slab over a fire and when it is heated, using a ladle, pour onto it the amount you wish, either large or small. When it is done, remove it. If you find the bottom of the pancake too brown, wipe the marble slab with a moist cloth and lower the heat. Every time five pancakes are done, wipe the slab with a cloth. When all the pancakes are done, cover them with a clean, damp cloth for about an hour then stuff them with whatever you wish, God willing.*

—al-Warrāq, Abū Muḥammad al-Muẓaffar ibn Naṣr ibn Sayyār, *Kitāb al-Ṭabīkh wa Iṣlāḥ al-Aghdhiyah al-Maʾkūlāt wa Ṭayyibah al-Aṭʿimah al-Maṣnūʿāt*

Filling (*al-Maḥshi*)

Take sugar and the same amount of either peeled almonds or pistachios. Pound everything and mix together. Sprinkle rosewater perfumed with camphor and musk enough for the mixture and knead. Then roll up in the Qaṭā'if. *After that, fry them in sesame oil and arrange them in dishes and when they are ready to be eaten, drench them in syrup or bees' honey that has been dissolved in rosewater.*

—Kanz al-Fawā'id fī Tanwīʿ al-Mawā'id

Qaṭā'if are best described as pancakes, usually stuffed with a nut-sugar mixture, folded in a half-moon shape, either fried or baked, then drenched in syrup. The name is derived from Arabic *qaṭīfah*, or velvet, and seems to refer to the plush texture of the sweetmeat.

Today's *Qaṭā'if* filling is basically the same as that used in the Middle Ages: almonds, walnuts, pistachios, pine nuts, or a mixture of all mirror the medieval versions; cheese stuffings are also now popular, but below we stick with tradition.

---

*Sugar Syrup (*Qaṭr*) recipe (see page 133)*

For the batter:

1 tbsp. sugar
1 package dry yeast (1/4 oz.)
1 1/2 cups lukewarm water
1 1/3 cups + 1 tbsp. flour

For the filling:

1/2 cup ground almonds
1/2 cup ground walnuts
1/2 cup ground pistachios
1/4 cup sugar
2 tsp. rosewater
light sesame oil for deep-frying
sugar

Dissolve the sugar and yeast in 1/4 cup lukewarm water, cover, and allow to stand in a warm place until the yeast begins to froth, about 10 minutes.

Place 1 1/3 cups flour in a deep large mixing bowl; add the yeast and add 1 1/4 cups lukewarm water slowly, beating with an electric mixer until batter is creamy and lump-free. Cover with plastic wrap and let sit for 2 hours. The batter will have risen and be bubbly.

While the dough is resting, prepare the filling. Mix the nuts, sugar, remaining 1 tablespoon flour, and the rosewater, and set aside.

Stir the batter well.

Brush a little sesame oil on the surface of a large frying pan or a pancake griddle over medium heat. When the oil in the pan begins to sizzle (or steam, if you are using a griddle) pour out about 2 tbsp. of the batter, spreading it quickly but gently into a rounded shape. Cook until the underside is slightly browned and little holes begin to appear on the batter surface. Place the pancake on waxed paper, cooked side down, and repeat until you have used up all the batter.

Place one full teaspoon of the filling in the middle of each pancake. Pull up one side of the pancake and fold over, pressing firmly along the edge to form a half-moon shape. Press the edges down securely.

In a saucepan, heat 4 inches oil over medium heat, place the stuffed *Qaṭāʾif* in the oil, and deep-fry until golden brown, turning over once to ensure both sides are browned. Place the fried *Qaṭāʾif* on paper towels to drain, then immerse in the *Qaṭr* for a minute. Dip in sugar and place on a serving platter.

Serve either warm or cooled.

Sweet Cheese Fritters

(*Mujabbanah al-Miqlah*: That Made of Cheese and Fried)

Makes 25

> *Moisten the semolina in cold water during the summer and hot water in winter. Then knead it like the* Isfunj *dough and allow to sit. Then take soft cheese—if it is moist wash it in water and rub it with the palm of the hand in the kneading bowl until it becomes like marrow. If it is dry and salty, cut it in pieces and leave it in water until it becomes moist and not salty. When it is moist, wash it in water and also rub it with the palm of the hand until it becomes like marrow. Then test it. If it is not salty enough, add salt. If it is too dry then moisten it with milk or hot water, that is, if there is no milk then with a measure of one-quarter of the dough and a little aniseed, mint water and fresh coriander water. Then knead it all until it holds firmly together in one (piece). Then put a tin frying pan on the fire with a lot of oil. When the oil is hot, then the one making it should wash his hands with*

water and cut off a piece of the dough and open with it his left hand and take a piece of the cheese with his right and put it in the middle of the piece of dough and squeeze it with his left hand until the roll of the dough comes out (between) his thumb and his index finger. Then he breaks off the excess of the dough and spreads the Mujabbanah *(roll) above his thumb with the back of his right hand and makes one puncture in the middle of it. Then he puts them in the frying pan, one at a time until it is filled. He turns them over with an iron hook until they are cooked and browned. If you see one has risen to the top of the oil, put another one on top of it until it is done and all are evenly cooked. Then take them out and put them in a vessel and leave them there a while. Then move them to a bowl and moisten them with fresh clarified butter and liquefied honey. Sprinkle on them sugar and cinnamon and eat them in good health, Almighty God willing.*

—al-Tujībī, *Faḍālah al-Khiwān fī Ṭayyibāt al-Ṭa'ām wa al-Alwān*

Mujabbanah is a pastry associated with the Arabs of al-Andalus. We learn in the *Anonymous Andalusian Cookbook* that it was made in Toledo, Seville, Córdoba, and Jerez and in the *Maghrib*, and we know that it gained popularity all over Spain through the centuries: the Arabic term *al-Mujabbanah*, meaning "made of cheese," moved into Spanish, where it survives as the sweet cheese ball called *almojabana*.

The *Anonymous Andalusian Cookbook* recommends using both sheep and cow cheese, noting that if made with sheep cheese alone, the pastry will fall apart, and with cow cheese alone it will come out as one solid mass of the wrong consistency. In our version of this puffy fritter, we combine ricotta and cream cheese, and results seem quite fine.

---

1 tbsp. sugar
1 package dry yeast (1/4 oz.)
1/4 cup lukewarm water
3 cups flour
1/2 tsp. salt
1/2 cup warm milk
2 tbsp. butter, melted
1 tbsp. olive oil
8 oz. cream cheese softened at room temperature
1 lb. ricotta cheese
1/2 cup sugar

1 1/4 tsp. cinnamon
light olive or vegetable oil for deep frying

Dissolve the sugar and yeast in water, cover, and allow to stand in a warm place until the yeast begins to froth, about 10 minutes.

While the yeast is rising, combine the flour and salt in a mixing bowl and make a well in the middle. Add the yeast, milk, and butter. Knead into a dough, adding more flour or milk if necessary; do not allow the dough to become sticky. Shape into a ball and brush the outside with olive oil. Place in a bowl and cover. Allow to rest in a warm spot for 2 hours, or until doubled in size.

In the meantime, prepare the filling by mixing the cream cheese and ricotta with a fork. Refrigerate until the dough has risen. Punch it down lightly and form into 25 balls, keeping the balls covered with a towel as they are formed.

Roll balls into 3 1/2-inch rounds. Cover with a towel. Place 1 tbsp. filling in the center of each round. Wetting the fingertips slightly, pull up the dough evenly to cover the filling and pinch together tightly and twist to form a small stem. Place the finished balls on a baking sheet and cover with a towel.

Mix the sugar and cinnamon and set aside.

Heat the oil over medium heat and deep-fry the balls until golden. Drain on paper towels. While still warm, sprinkle the *Mujabbanah* with the sugar/cinnamon mixture.

Honey-Dipped Almond-Stuffed Rings

(*al-Qāhirīyah al-Khāṣṣ*: the Distinguished Qāhirīyah)

Makes 30 rings

> *Take a* raṭl *of sugar and a quarter* raṭl *of almonds and a quarter* raṭl *of a brand of good flour. Pound the sugar fine and put it through a sieve and then return what remains coarse to the mortar and pound again and put through the sieve until it becomes like wheat semolina. Then take the almonds, put them in hot water and peel them from their skin. Take out the coarse [ones] and pound and also put through a sieve. Then mix everything together and knead with an amount of four* ūqīyahs *of sesame oil. Then, after this, knead it also with water, rubbing it until it becomes like*

Kaʿk *dough. Then add water to it and knead. Then after that, make into* Qāhirīyah *rings like* Kaʿk *rings. Then after that sprinkle flour on a wooden board and put those rings on it. Leave them in the air. If they are made in the afternoon, leave them until they dry until the next morning. The next day take a pot and put the amount of a* raṭl *and a half of fresh yeast in it and beat it well by hand in the same manner as beating* Zalābiyah *batter. Then add to it the amount of two dirhams of natron and beat. Then put in it two egg whites without yolks and beat everything until it becomes similar again to the batter of* Zalābiyah. *At the beginning with the sugar add to it as much as you want of musk, rosewater and camphor when kneading. Then place the pot on your right-hand side and set the tajine on the fire and put in it a lot of sesame oil so that the rings can rise in it. Then bring the oil to a boil. Also take fresh honey and put it in a pot on your left-hand side. Then take those rings that have already dried, one by one with an iron hook and dip it into the yeast-batter that is in the pot and remove them then put them in the tajine. Do the same with all the others as was done with the first until they are all coated. They will be removed one by one and immersed in that pot that has the honey. Then fry them and put them in the honey until they are done. Then place them in a serving dish. Sprinkle on them some musk and rosewater in the amount you want. Then also pound pistachios and sprinkle over them. This is how the* Qāhirīyah *is prepared, so understand that.*

—Kanz al-Fawāʾid fī Tanwīʿ al-Mawāʾid

This sweet biscuit may have been named after the Abbasid caliph al-Qāhir bi-Allāh (r. 932-934) or may have taken its name from its city of origin, Cairo (*al-Qāhirah*). In the Arab East, *Qāhirīyāt* were referred to in the singular form *Qāhirīyah*.

Plan ahead before undertaking this recipe. It is an overnight, multi-step affair.

---

3 tbsp. flour

For the cookie:

2 cups confectioner's sugar
1 cup ground almonds
1 cup flour
1/4 cup light sesame oil
1/4 cup plus 1 tsp. lukewarm water

For the batter:

1 tbsp. sugar
1 package dry yeast (1/4 oz.)
1 cup lukewarm water
1 cup flour
1 tbsp. rosewater
1/2 tsp. cinnamon
1/4 tsp. nutmeg
1/2 tsp. ginger
1 tbsp. baking soda
1/8 tsp. salt
2 egg whites

For the syrup:

2 cups honey
light sesame oil for deep frying
1/2 cup ground pistachios mixed with 1/2 tsp. rosewater and 1/4 tsp. cinnamon

Sprinkle 3 tbsp. flour onto a tray and set aside.

To make the cookie, mix the confectioner's sugar, almonds, 1 cup flour, and sesame oil. Gradually add the water and knead into a dough. Make into 30 balls and form each ball into a 4-inch rope. On a flat surface, take each rope and bend to form a ring, pinching the ends closed. Place on the floured tray. Refrigerate overnight uncovered.

To make the batter, dissolve the sugar and yeast in 1/4 cup lukewarm water, cover and let stand in a warm place until the yeast froths, about 10 minutes.

Combine the flour, rosewater, cinnamon, nutmeg, ginger, baking soda, and salt in a deep bowl and mix well. Form a well and add the yeast mixture, remaining 3/4 cup lukewarm water, and the egg whites. Beat with an electric mixer for one minute to make a smooth batter. Cover and let sit for 1 hour, allowing the batter to rise.

For the syrup, heat the honey in a saucepan over medium heat, stirring until it comes to a boil. Reduce the heat to low to keep the honey warm, stirring occasionally.

Preparing the *Qāhirīyāt*:

Heat 4 inches of oil in a saucepan over medium heat.

Stir the risen batter and completely dip each of the rings into it. Carefully inserting the tip of a thin-bladed knife into the hole, lift each ring gently out of the batter, and place in the heated oil until golden on both sides. Remove with a slotted spoon, shaking off any excess oil, place in the warm honey for 1 minute, and place on a serving platter.

Sprinkle the prepared pistachios evenly over the *Qāhirīyāt*.

Braided Fried Dough with Spices

(*Ḍafā'ir*: Braids)

Makes 20 braids

> *Take what you will of white flour or of semolina, which is better in these things. Moisten it with hot water after sifting, and knead well, after adding some fine flour, leavening, and salt. Moisten it again and again until it has middling consistency. Then break into it, for each* raṭl *of semolina, five eggs and a dirham of saffron, and beat all this very well, and put the dough in a dish, cover it and leave it to rise, and the way to tell when this is done is what was mentioned before [it holds an indentation]. When it has risen, clean a frying pan and fill it with fresh oil, then put it on the fire. When it starts to boil, make braids of the leavened dough like hair-braids, of a handspan or less in size. Coat them with oil and throw them in the oil and fry them until they brown. When their cooking is done, arrange them on an earthenware plate and pour over them skimmed honey spiced with pepper, cinnamon, Chinese cinnamon, and lavender. Sprinkle it with ground sugar and present it, God willing. This same way you make* Isfunj, *except that the dough for the* Isfunj *will be rather light. Leave out the saffron, make it into balls and fry them in that shape, God willing. And if you wish stuffed Ḍafāir or* Isfunj, *stuff them with a filling of almonds and sugar, as indicated for making* Qāhiriyāt.
>
> *—Anonymous Andalusian Cookbook (Kitāb al-Ṭabikh fī al-Maghrib wa al-Andalus fī ʿAṣr al-Muwaḥḥidīn, li-muʿallif majhūl), page 154, translated by Charles Perry*

With the Arab conquests and expansion of the empire came luxury and refinement in all aspects of life. The rudimentary fried dough, dipped in honey or sugar syrup, evolved into ever more complicated and time-consuming sweets, of which *Ḍafā'ir* is an example. Because the dough needs to be formed into ropes that are then braided, *Ḍafā'ir* take time and patience to prepare.

We found that the pepper called for in the medieval recipe gives too spicy a taste to this sweet, and lavender is just a little too strong. We, therefore, have replaced them in the syrup with cloves and nutmeg—but we encourage you to experiment.

---

1 cup honey
4 tbsp. butter, salted or unsalted
1 tsp. orange blossom water or rosewater
1/8 tsp. ground cloves
1/4 tsp. cinnamon
1/4 tsp. nutmeg
1 tbsp. sugar
1 package dry yeast (1/4 oz.)
1 1/2 cups fine semolina
1 1/2 cups flour
1/2 tsp. salt
2 eggs, beaten
1/8 tsp. crushed saffron mixed with 1/4 cup warm water
vegetable oil for deep-frying
sugar for decorating

To make the syrup, mix the honey, 2 tbsp. butter, orange blossom or rosewater, cloves, cinnamon, and nutmeg in a saucepan and bring to a boil over medium heat. Reduce heat to low and keep warm.

Mix the sugar and yeast into 1/4 cup lukewarm water and add the yeast, cover, and allow to stand in a warm place until the yeast froths, about 10 minutes.

Combine the semolina, flour, and salt in a bowl. Add the remaining butter, breaking it into the mixture by hand until crumbly. Make a well and add the yeast and eggs. Work into a dough by slowly adding the water-saffron mixture. Form into a ball and cover, allowing it to rise in a warm place for 1 1/2 hours. Punch down the dough, cover, and let sit for another 30 minutes.

Break off a ball of dough of 2 tablespoons in size. Roll the dough back and forth on a flat surface to make a 6-inch rope about 1/4 inch in diameter. Make two more ropes of equal size and braid the three together, pinching the ends to ensure they do not come apart. Repeat with the remaining dough.

Heat 4 inches of oil in a saucepan over medium heat. Deep-fry the *Ḍafā'ir*, three or four at a time, until golden, and place on paper towels to drain any excess oil.

Dip each piece in the syrup for about 1 minute. Remove and sprinkle with the sugar. Serve at room temperature.

Aromatic Nut-Stuffed Half-Moons

(*Ādhān*: Ears)

Makes about 24 pieces

> *Knead white flour with water and oil without leaven, then roll out little thin rounds, like the rounds of* aqrūn,[7] *and let them be as big as the palm of a hand or bigger. Fold in two, and match edge with edge, and open the mouth, and fry, after inserting thick sticks into them so that the open end does not seal. And when they are fried, make a filling of pistachios or almonds and sugar and knead with rosewater, and stuff the "ears" with them. Whoever wishes to aromatize the stuffing may. Then set on a plate and sprinkle with rosewater and then moisten with stiffly thickened rosewater syrup. And sprinkle with sugar, galingale, cloves, and ground cinnamon and use.*
>
> *—Anonymous Andalusian Cookbook (Kitāb al-Ṭabikh fī al-Maghrib wa al-Andalus fī ʿAṣr al-Muwaḥḥidīn, li-muʿallif majhūl), page 154, translated by Charles Perry*

Translated as "ears" because of their shape, *Ādhān* are stuffed with a paste of almonds, pistachios or walnuts, sugar, and rosewater. Even though preparation of the dough, filling, and syrup is quite simple, it is time-consuming to shape the ears and a bit challenging to make sure the edges remain closed before they are fried. We recommend that you purchase a long wooden dowel, 1/4 inch in diameter, and cut it into 6-inch pieces to prepare the *Ādhān*. The other option is to use cannoli tubes.

Just as today, almonds ground, pulverized, or whole were characteristic of almost all Arab sweets in al-Andalus.

---

*Sugar Syrup (*Qaṭr*) recipe (see page 133)*

For the dough:

3 cups flour
3/4 cup olive oil

1/2 cup water
special cooking utensil: 6-inch wooden dowel, 1/4-in. diameter or cannoli tubes
vegetable oil for deep frying

For the filling:
1 cup ground almonds, pistachios, or walnuts
2/3 cup sugar
1 tbsp. rosewater

For the topping:
1 tsp. cinnamon and 1/4 tsp. ground cloves, mixed

Place the flour in a mixing bowl, make a well, and add the olive oil and water, mixing well, adding more water or flour if necessary to make a dough. Turn the dough onto a flat surface and knead for about 5 minutes until smooth. Form into a ball, place in a bowl, cover with plastic wrap, and let sit for 1 hour.

Form the dough into 24 balls, each the size of a walnut. Roll each ball into a round, about 5 inches in diameter. Lay the dowel on the center of the round and fold over one end of the dough to form a half-moon shape. Pinch along the edge where the two sides meet to ensure it seals well, then turn the pinched edge over slightly and pinch again.

Heat the oil over medium heat and deep-fry the "ears" until golden. Remove with a slotted spoon and carefully remove the wooden sticks. Place on paper towels. To make the filling, mix the nuts, sugar, and rosewater into a crumbly texture. Carefully push this into each "ear" through both openings, gently pushing the stuffing in with the handle of a regular spoon or fork.

Dip each "ear" in the *Qaṭr* and place on a serving platter. Sprinkle with the cinnamon and clove topping.

Almond-Sealed Stuffed Cigars

(*Qanānīṭ al-Maḥshūwah*: Stuffed Pipes)

Makes about 30

> *Knead well fine white flour mixed with water only and with no yeast. Then wrap the dough around tubes made of reed cane until covered and then roll the tubes on a surface by hand until the dough is smoothed out. Then cut the dough in small tubes separating each one from the other. Leave them to*

dry on the reed cane as they are. Then put honey in a pot, continue to a boil over a fire and mix with it good shelled ground walnuts and whatever can be used of the known spices. If anything of the tube dough breaks, then grind the broken parts and mix them with that until all is thickened in the honey. Then remove the tubular dough gently from the cane tube. Fry in a earthenware pot in good oil until browned. Then stuff them with the aforementioned filling. On each end of the tube, put a peeled almond. Sprinkle over them cinnamon and sugar. Enjoy them with the power of Almighty God.

—al-Tujībī, *Faḍālah al-Khiwān fī Ṭayyibāt al-Ṭaʿām wa al-Alwān*

Qanānīṭ translates as canes, cylinders, or tubes; in this recipe they are filled with a mixture of nuts, sugar, and spices. In the *Anonymous Andalusian*, there is a similar recipe, but with saffron-colored tubes. In the East, on the other hand, al-Warrāq describes a recipe for fried, then baked *Ḥalāqīm* (windpipes), a tubular pastry colored with red, yellow, green, and blue food dyes and stuffed with mixed nuts and sugar. They are then dipped in a thick sugar syrup to seal the tips, whereas the two recipes from al-Andalus call for sealing the ends with a nut.

Qanānīṭ bear a resemblance to Sicilian cannoli, and we suggest substituting modern cannoli tubes for the reeds called for in the original preparation.

3 cups flour
1 1/2 cups water
1/2 inch cannoli tubes
vegetable oil for deep-frying
6 cups ground walnuts
1 1/2 tsp. cinnamon
1/2 tsp. nutmeg
1 tsp. ground ginger
1/2 tsp. ground cloves
1/4 cup orange blossom water
3 cups honey
60 blanched whole almonds (to seal the ends)
3 tbsp. sugar and 1 tbsp. cinnamon (garnish)

Gradually stir the water into the flour and mix to form a dough, adding a few drops of water if necessary. Knead well for 5 minutes. Form into 30 balls and cover with plastic for 1/2 hour.

Roll each ball into a very thin round and place a cannoli tube along the edge of the dough. Lift the dough over the top of the tube and roll, pinching edges of the dough tightly with slightly dampened fingertips to seal over the tube. In a saucepan, heat the oil over a medium-high heat. Deep-fry the *Qanānīṭ* until golden. Remove and place on paper towels. Once the dough is cool enough to handle, remove the tube carefully. Grind any broken shells in a coffee grinder.

Mix the walnuts, ground *Qanānīṭ* pieces, cinnamon, nutmeg, ginger, cloves, and orange blossom water.

Boil the honey in a saucepan for 1 minute, stirring constantly. Add the walnut mixture and stir for 1 minute. Remove from heat and allow to cool.

Carefully spoon the walnut filling in through both open ends of the *Qanānīṭ* forms, stuffing them well. Insert an almond at each end. Place the *Qanānīṭ* on a serving platter and sprinkle with sugar and cinnamon mixture.

Fried Nut Turnovers

(*Sanbūsak Ismuhu Fāḍil*: *Sanbūsak* Which is Called Outstanding)

Makes 25 pieces

> For each raṭl *of flour, three* ūqīyahs *of butter: knead and rub well. Then soak four* ūqīyahs *of starch and mix in with the dough also rubbing very well. Spread it out thinly and cut in thin slices. Make for it a filling of pistachio meats and sugar and make* Sanbūsak. *Put the sesame oil on the fire. When it is heated, throw in the* Sanbūsak *until they are absorbed (by the oil). Do not leave them too long. Remove them and immerse them in honey that has not been boiled but (rather) heated. Then take them out. Honey with musk has been prepared for them: It is to take three* ūqīyahs *of honey and an* ūqīyah *of sesame oil. Put it on the fire, a gentle fire, and stir until it is musky and dress the* Sanbūsak *with it. Do not boil it but thicken it over a low fire. Whenever it boils, the honey darkens.*

> —Ibn al-ʿAdīm, *Kitāb al-Wuṣlah ilà al-Ḥabīb fī Waṣf al-Ṭayyibāt wa al-Ṭīb*

When served as an appetizer or part of the main meal in the medieval Arab kitchen, the small turnover pasties known as *Sanbūsak* were usually filled with minced meat, spices, and nuts such as Fried Lamb Turnovers (Two Ways) (see page 85). But there was also the dessert variety that used the same dough stuffed with a sweeter mixture of nuts and sugar.

These crunchy sweet pastries are filling, but a delight on any dessert table.

For the dough:

4 cups flour
1 tsp. salt
1 cup butter, at room temperature
2 tbsp. cornstarch dissolved in 1 cup cold water

For the filling:

1 1/2 cups ground almonds or pistachios or a mixture of both
1 cup sugar

For the syrup:

4 cups honey
2 tsp. light sesame oil
4 tsp. rosewater
1/2 tsp. cinnamon
light sesame oil for deep-frying

Mix the flour and salt in a bowl. Rub the butter by hand into the flour. Make a well and pour in the dissolved starch. Knead for 5 minutes, adding more flour or water as necessary. Allow to sit covered for 1 hour.

Mix the ground nuts and sugar to make the filling. Set aside.

Blend the honey and 2 tsp. sesame oil in a saucepan. Over low heat, stir in the rosewater and cinnamon. Keep warm over very low heat, stirring occasionally.

On a working surface lightly sprinkled with cornstarch, roll out the dough to 1/8-inch thickness. Cut into 4-inch squares. Roll each square out again to retain the size in case of shrinkage.

Place one heaping teaspoon of filling in the center of each square, fold over diagonally forming a triangle, and then pinch on the two sides to seal the *Sanbūsak*. Fold over those pinched sides again and pinch to reinforce them.

Heat 4 inches of the oil in a saucepan over a medium-low heat. Carefully place the *Sanbūsak* in the oil without crowding them and deep-fry until golden brown, turning them once. Remove with a slotted spoon, immerse in the honey syrup, and place on a serving platter. Cool before serving.

Beverages

Hot Sweet Rosewater Drink

(*Sharāb Jullāb*: A Beverage Made of Rosewater Syrup)

Serves 6–8

> *Take five* raṭls *of aromatic rosewater, and two and a half of sugar, cook all this until it takes the consistency of syrup. Drink two* ūqīyahs *of this with three of hot water. Its benefits: in phlegmatic fever; it fortifies the stomach and the liver, profits at the onset of dropsy, purifies and lightens the body, and in this it is most extraordinary, God willing.*
>
> *—Anonymous Andalusian Cookbook (Kitāb al-Ṭabikh fī al-Maghrib wa al-Andalus fī ʿAṣr al-Muwaḥḥidīn, li-muʿallif majhūl), page 14, translated by Charles Perry*

The term *jullāb* refers to rosewater syrup. It was a key ingredient in many sweets and some entrées, and was used for medicinal purposes. Once mixed with ice or cold water, *jullāb*, from which modern English "julep" is derived, became known as *Sharbah*, source of the modern English "sherbet."

The following recipe is for a hot beverage made with *jullāb* and is quite similar to *Qahwah Bayḍah* (white coffee), a drink made with rosewater and served in the eastern Arab world today that is a great substitute for coffee.

1 cup rosewater
1/2 cup sugar

Bring the rosewater and sugar to a boil over medium heat, stirring a few times. Lower heat to medium-low and simmer for 15 minutes, stirring occasionally. Remove from heat.

Mix 1 tsp. syrup with boiling water in a demitasse cup and serve.

The syrup can be stored in a covered glass jar and refrigerated for up to three weeks.

Lemonade

(*Māʾ al-Laymūn li-al-Sharāb*: Lemon Water for Drinking)

Serves 4–6

> *Squeeze out juice from lemons, after having washed them, over a piece of sugar. Place in a glass container. It is used for drinks.*
>
> *—Kanz al-Fawāʾid fī Tanwīʿ al-Mawāʾid*

Just as we find few things more refreshing on a hot summer day than lemonade, a syrup of lemon is recommended in various medieval sources for quenching thirst. So too in the modern Arab kitchen, where for a special touch, orange blossom water or rosewater is sometimes added to a preparation very much like the one below. One tablespoon of either of these flavored waters should suffice for the full recipe.

6 lemons, washed thoroughly
1 cup sugar
6 cups ice water

In a mixing bowl, squeeze the lemons over sugar and blend well with a wooden spoon until sugar absorbs the juice.

Place in a glass container, cover, and refrigerate.

To make the drink, mix the lemon paste with 6 cups of ice water and serve.

Aromatic Honey and Grape Juice Drink for Wintertime

(*Sharāb Ākhar Yustaʿmalu fī al-Shitāʾ*: Another Beverage Used in the Winter)

Serves 6

> *Take ten* raṭls *of bees' honey and the same of water and the same amount of both of white grape juice. Boil all together then add to it some spikenard and cloves. When it has finished boiling put it in a green-glazed earthenware jar and it is beneficial to use.*
>
> —al-Warrāq, Abū Muḥammad al-Muẓaffar ibn Naṣr ibn Sayyār, *Kitāb al-Ṭabīkh wa Iṣlāḥ al-Aghdhiyah al-Maʾkūlāt wa Ṭayyibah al-Aṭʿimah al-Maṣnūʿāt*

In the medieval Arabic culinary sources there are many recipes for drinks based on fruits such as apples, grapes, quince, pomegranates, plums, or peaches, mixed with honey or sugar and spices such as ginger and cinnamon. Many of these recipes were actually for syrups that could be preserved until needed, often to alleviate the symptoms of specific ailments. When a beverage was required for medicinal purposes, all that had to be added was water. One of the most popular of these drinks was made of grapes, either the black variety, which were compared to the beauties of Abyssinia, or the white, to those of Byzantium (Ibn ʿAbd Rabbih VI 285).

A hot beverage of honeyed grape juice, this drink is, as its name indicates, ideal for a cold winter day.

We have replaced the spikenard with lime zest mainly because it is a difficult ingredient to find and expensive. As it turns out, our choice of lime zest was an ideal one.

1 cup honey
1 cup water
2 cups white grape juice
1 tsp. lime zest
1/2 tsp. ground cloves

Place the honey, water, and grape juice in a saucepan and bring to a boil over high heat. Remove immediately from the heat to avoid boiling over.

Stir in the remaining ingredients. Bring to a boil again and once more remove immediately from the heat.

Pour into a teapot and serve while hot.

Zesty Mint Drink

(*Sharāb Naʿnāʿ*: Syrup of Mint)

Serves 4–6

> *Take mint and basil, citron and cloves, a handful of each, and cook all this in enough water to cover, until its substance comes out, and add the clear part of it to a* raṭl *of sugar. The [spice] bag: an* ūqīyah *of flower of cloves. And cook all this until a syrup is made. Its benefits: it frees bodies that suffer from phlegm, and cuts phlegmatic urine, fortifies the liver and the stomach and cheers it a great deal; in this it is admirable.*
>
> *—Anonymous Andalusian Cookbook (Kitāb al-Ṭabikh fī al-Maghrib wa al-Andalus fī ʿAṣr al-Muwaḥḥidīn, li-muʿallif majhūl), page 15, translated by Charles Perry*

Cultivated since the dawn of history in the Middle East and Far East, mint has long been highly valued for its refreshing scent and pleasant taste as well as for its perceived medicinal value.

In the ancient and medieval worlds, mint was employed to repress the curdling of milk in women's breasts, to stop bad breath, hiccoughing, and vomiting, as an aid during pregnancy, to facilitate digestion, and as a relief for difficult menstruation, sore gums, stomach disorders, and gonorrhea. All these attributes were, no doubt, known to the culinary doctors of Baghdad.

Today, in the Middle East and North Africa, mint leaves are used in every course, from appetizers to desserts and drinks, especially tea. Sweetened hot mint tea soothes the digestive tract after a heavy meal. It is not surprising to hear a host advising a guest who has eaten to the limit to drink a cup of hot mint tea. The host would say *"Ishrub! Bi-haḍḍam!"* (Drink! It will help you digest!).

Though called a mint drink, this beverage has the added flavor of fresh basil and lemon. We find it quite refreshing.

1 cup fresh mint leaves
1/2 cup fresh basil leaves
1 tbsp. grated lemon rind
1/2 tsp. cloves
6 cups water
1/2 cup sugar

Place all the ingredients, except the sugar, in a saucepan. Bring to a boil, cover, lower heat to low, and cook for 35 minutes, stirring occasionally.

Strain the contents and return the clear liquid to the saucepan. Stir in the sugar, cover, and simmer over low heat for 15 minutes, stirring occasionally.

Pour into a pitcher and refrigerate until ready to serve.

Hot Aromatic Honeyed Milk

(*Sharāb min Albān al-Baqar*: A Beverage Made from Cow's Milk)

Serves 6

> *Take twenty* raṭls *of cows' milk and put it in a vessel. Add to it ten* raṭls *of bees' honey, refined and skimmed of its froth. Put it in a large copper pot and boil [adding] the weight of five dirhams of spikenard and the weight of three musk pieces and five dirhams of mastic. Once it comes to a strong boil remove it and sprinkle in it three dirhams of saffron. Allow to sit until cool then use it. It is excellent.*
>
> —al-Warrāq, Abū Muḥammad al-Muẓaffar ibn Naṣr ibn Sayyār, *Kitāb al-Ṭabīkh wa Iṣlāḥ al-Aghdhiyah al-Maʾkūlāt wa Ṭayyibah al-Aṭʿimah al-Maṣnūʿāt*

In affluent Baghdad, where cuisine, imagination, and creativity merged, milk could develop into a drink such as *Sharāb min Albān*, rich and aromatic, yet unusual for its curious texture.

When the milk and honey come to a boil, the milk appears to curdle, and the finished drink has almost a chewy texture. We recommend this to the adventurous. It is sweet and flavorful and, quite understandably, in the words of al-Warrāq, "excellent."

2 cups milk
1 cup honey
1 tsp. lime zest
1 cardamom seed
1/2 tsp. crushed mastic
1/8 tsp. saffron

Stir the milk and the honey in a saucepan over medium-low heat until the mixture comes to a boil. Add the lime zest, cardamom, and mastic and bring to a boil again, stirring constantly, for 5 minutes.

Remove the cardamom seed and transfer the milk-honey mixture to a pitcher. Sprinkle with the saffron, and allow to cool before serving.

Pomegranate Seed Smoothie

(*Ḥabb Rummān*: Pomegranate Seed Beverage)

Serves 4–6

> *Pomegranate seeds, two portions pounded finely. Put one portion of white sugar and mint leaves in the mortar to make it sweet. Sprinkle on it rosewater and pound. Make it fragrant with three pieces of ambergris and it is used.*
>
> —Ibn al-ʿAdīm, *Kitāb al-Wuṣlah ilà al-Ḥabīb fī Waṣf al-Ṭayyibāt wa al-Ṭīb*

In the eastern region of the Islamic empire, and specifically in Baghdad, pomegranates were classified in three groups, *aḥmar* (red), *aswad* (black), and *ḥilū* (sweet). The sour variety was used for cooking, while the sweet type garnished dishes such as *Bawārid* or was simply eaten as a snack.

Sultan Nūr al-Dīn of Damascus enjoyed the fruit. Knowing his pomegranate orchards were replete with ripe fruit, he commanded that some be brought to him. When it was discovered that, after six months on duty, Abū Yaʿqūb Yūsuf, the orchard guard, had not picked a ripe and sweet one, he was reprimanded. How could anyone eat the inedible sour ones? Abū Yaʿqūb responded with sheer honesty that he had been hired to guard the pomegranates, not to eat them (Ibn Baṭṭūṭah 63).

Ambergris, one of the ingredients called for in this recipe, was an expensive aromatic, well suited for the noble courtly class and giving a touch of extravagance to any dish or beverage to which it was added. The regal aura of this pomegranate-seed drink remains, despite our having replaced the difficult-to-find ambergris with a few drops of almond extract.

This beverage is not the typical thinned-out fruit juice drink. There is a texture to it: the white of the seeds that remain allows for a crunch in the thick liquid. It is an unusual combination of tart pomegranate and sweetness. Some may prefer sipping it with a spoon.

4 cups pomegranate seeds
1 cup sugar

4 tbsp. fresh mint leaves
2 tsp. rosewater
1/2 tsp. almond extract

Place all the ingredients in a blender and process until smooth. Pour into a pitcher and refrigerate until ready to serve. Stir before pouring into serving glasses.

Sour Apple Syrup

(*Sharāb al-Tuffāḥ*: Apple Beverage)

Number of servings depends on amount of syrup used per glass

> *Take pure rosewater syrup and green apples. Pound them [the apples] and take out their juice. Add them to the rosewater syrup while it is over the fire. For every* raṭl *of rosewater syrup, four* ūqīyahs *of apple juice; quince beverage is made the same way. Remove from the heat after it has reached its [proper] consistency.*
>
> *—Kanz al-Fawā'id fī Tanwīʿ al-Mawā'id*

Although called a beverage, this is actually an apple-based syrup that can either be stored for future use or used immediately by diluting it in water to make a drink. Sometimes these fruit-based syrups were served with crushed ice, no matter the season.

3 apples (Granny Smith or any other tart type)
2 cups sugar
1/4 cup water
1/8 cup rosewater

Process the apples in a juicer, discarding the pulp.

Make a *jullāb* by mixing the sugar and water in a saucepan. Bring to a boil, lower the heat to medium-low, and simmer for 12 minutes.

Stir in the rosewater and simmer for a further 3 minutes.

Stir in the apple juice and simmer for one minute more. Remove from heat.

Stir one tsp. syrup into a 6-ounce glass of boiling water and serve.

Cold Apricot Drink for Breaking a Fast

(*Mishmish Lawzī*: Sweet-Kerneled Apricot)

Serves 4–6

> *Wash sweet-kerneled apricots. Add nenuphar water, rue water, and a little rosewater. Squeeze sour pomegranate over (the mixture). Throw mint into it and sweeten with sugar, enough to sweeten the apricots. This is the ultimate of taste, excellence and benefit.*
>
> —Ibn al-ʿAdīm, *Kitāb al-Wuṣlah ilà al-Ḥabīb fī Waṣf al-Ṭayyibāt wa al-Ṭīb*

During Ramadan a nectar is made by soaking sheets of dried apricot paste in water and then boiling them, with more water and some sugar added. It is the most popular drink for breaking the fast.

The apricot drink below is somewhat more elaborate. We have replaced the nenuphar called for in the original recipe with either almond extract or honey. Rue, although available in certain specialty stores, can be replaced with fresh lemon juice.

This is a good drink to start off a meal.

1 cup dried apricots, soaked for 1 hour in 2 cups boiling hot water
4 cups water
1 tsp. almond extract or 1 tbsp. honey
1 tsp. fresh rue leaves or 1 tbsp. fresh lemon juice
1 tsp. rosewater
1/2 tsp. pomegranate syrup
1 tbsp. fresh mint leaves
2 tbsp. sugar

Place the apricots with their water in a saucepan. Add the remaining water and bring to a boil. Reduce the heat to low and cover.

Cook for 1 1/2 hours or until the apricots are very soft, stirring occasionally. Remove from the heat and cool.

Transfer the contents of the saucepan into a blender, add the remaining ingredients, and process until the mixture is smooth. Refrigerate and serve cold.

Sample Menus for Special Occasions

A Dinner During Ramadan

(Breaking the Fast)

Appetizers

Mishmish Lawzī (Sweet-Kerneled Apricot)

A Bāridah of Abū Jaʿfar al-Barmakī (Cold Roasted Chicken with Lime and Cucumber)

Zaytūn Akhḍar Marṣūṣ (Green Olive Spread)

Soup

Nawʿ al-Ḥummuṣ al-Yābis (Tart Chickpea Soup)

Entrées

al-Maghmūm (Zesty Almond and Chicken Pie)

Aruzz Mufalfal (Browned Lamb with Saffron-Cinnamon Rice)

Murūzīyah (Lamb and Prune Tajine)

Silq bi-Laban (Garlicky Yogurt and Chard)

Dessert

Kul wa Ushkur! (Fried Dough with Pistachios and Rosewater)

Beverage

Sharāb min Albān al-Baqar (Hot Aromatic Honeyed Milk)

A Dinner During Lent

Appetizers

al-Bādhinjān (Tangy Eggplant Stir-Fry)

Bāqillà bi Khall (Fava Bean Salad)

Soup

Marqah Ḥabb al-Rummān wa al-Aruzz al-Maqlū

(Aromatic Soup with Rice and Pomegranate Seeds)

Entrées

ʿUjjah Min Ghayr Bayḍ (Spiced Chickpea Patties)

Muzawwarah Mulūkhīyah (Sautéed Aphrodisiac Greens)

Ṭabāhajah min al-Rūbiyān (Ginger-Fried Shrimp for Lent)

Dessert

Khushkanānaj Gharīb (Caliph's Favorite Shortbread)

Beverage

Māʾ al-Laymūn li-al-Sharāb (Lemonade)

A Dinner During Passover

Appetizers

Baṣal (Mukhallal) (Pickled Onions)

Al-Jazar (Honeyed Carrots in Rosewater)

Soup

Māʾ al-Bāqillà (Spiced Lamb and Fava Bean Soup)

Entrées

Aruzz Mufalfal (Browned Lamb with Saffron-Cinnamon Rice)

Basbāsīyah (Poached and Baked Fish with Fennel

al-Tafāyā al-Bayḍāʾ (Savory Meatballs and Cubed Lamb with Coriander)

Dessert

*Hays** (Muhammad's Wedding Cookies)

Beverage

Sharāb Naʿnāʿ (Zesty Mint Drink)

**replace bread crumbs with ground matzo*

A Dinner for Christmas

Appetizers

al-Bāqillà (Fava Beans with Yogurt and Garlic)

Ḥummuṣ Kasā (Hummus with Ground Nuts)

Tatbīl al-Qanbīṭ (Cauliflower with Tahine-Walnut Sauce)

Soup

Marqah Ḥabb al-Rummān wa al-Aruzz al-Maqlū

(Aromatic Soup with Rice and Pomegranate Seeds)

Entrées

Sanbūsaj (also called *Sanbūsak*) (Fried Lamb Turnovers (Two Ways))

Shawī (Spiced Lamb with Walnuts)

Shushbarak (commonly now known as *Shīsh Barak*)

al-Sikbāj (Stuffed Dumplings in Yogurt)

Ṭabīkh Ḥabb Rummān (Chicken Stew with Pomegranate Juice and Pumpkin)

Desserts

Kunāfah (Honey-Cream Crunch)

al-Qaṭā'if al-Maḥshi (Fried Stuffed Pancakes)

Beverages

Ḥabb Rummān (Pomegranate Seed Beverage)

Sharāb Ākhar Yustaʿmalu fī al-Shitā'

(Aromatic Honey and Grape Juice Drink for Wintertime)

A Dinner Feast Such as That Held in the Caliph's Court

Appetizers

Bāridah min Bāqilà Ibn Abū Nūḥ al-Kātib (Spicy Chard and Fava Bean Dip)
Bādhinjān Maḥshī li-Ibn al-Mahdī (Seared Eggplant with Walnuts)
Bāridah Mujarrabah (Roasted Chicken with Almonds and Pomegranate Seeds)

Soups

Khulāṭ Baysānī (Cold Yogurt and Cucumber Soup)
Shūrbā Khaḍrā' (Meatball and Chickpea Soup)

Entrées

Luḥūm al-Ḍa'in Yuṭbakh bi al-Isfarāj (Asparagus Wrapped in Lamb)
Būrānīyah (The Caliph's Wife's Eggplant and Lamb Stir-Fry)
Dīkabrīkāt or Dhājibrijah of Ibrāhīm ibn al-Mahdī
(Lamb and Vegetables with Spiced Onion Sauce)
Sukhtūr (also Called *Kībā*)(Hearty Stuffed Tripe with Lamb, Chickpeas, and Rice)
Fustuqīyah (Pistachio-Stuffed Roasted Chicken)
al-Samak al-Sikbāj (Summertime Fried Fish)

Desserts

Ḍafā'ir (Crunchy Beaded Honey Squares)
Lawzīnaj (Almond Fingers)
Luqam al-Qāḍī (Fried Dough Bites)
Qanānīṭ al-Maḥshūwah (Almond-Sealed Stuffed Cigars)

Beverages

Ḥabb Rummān (Pomegranate Seed Smoothie)
Mishmish Lawzī (Cold Apricot Drink for Breaking a Fast)
Sharāb Jullāb (Hot Sweet Rosewater Drink)

Regal Recipes for Stuffed Meats

Regal dining also included complicated and seemingly fantastical culinary creations as compared to today's kitchen standards. These dishes could take a full day or more to prepare, thanks to a large kitchen staff that included cooks and their assistants.

In the case of stuffed meats or poultry, there are, of course, the almost-straightforward preparations for stuffings such as al-Tujībī's Couscous with Lamb (#4 (89)) or even the elaborate but workable recipe from al-Warrāq: a recipe for a large stomach in which a suckling kid stuffed with a chicken serves as the stuffing (226).

Over time the culture of food demanded even more embellished dishes and even more ingenuity, creativity and presentation to reflect the nature of the time—a period of opulence and of haute cuisine. By the thirteenth century we know that Almohad rival Caliph Abū al-ʿAlāʾ Idrīs al-Maʾmūn (r. ca. 1227–1232) enjoyed a roast lamb stuffed with a roast goose stuffed with a roast hen stuffed with a roast pigeon stuffed with a roast starling stuffed with a roasted or fried bird. Intricate, complex, and requiring multi-tasking for the cook and his staff, this type of dish would not only satisfy appetites but be a source of culinary experience and entertainment. If only the guests of al-Mustakfī had been hosted by this Almohad—imagine the verses that would have been composed about such a dish.

Even more lavish is a recipe from al-Tujībī for a ram's stomach used as the receptacle for a filling made up of stuffed chicken, stuffed pigeons, mergaz (sausages), meatballs, meat patties, and egg yolks. Once presented at the table, the stomach would be sliced and served. Imagine the presentation! Slices of stuffing upon stuffing all in one piece. How better to display the opulence of a dining table than with this impractically complicated dish?

Although we have included a far simpler recipe for stuffed stomach in the Entrées chapter, we include here stuffings that would be appropriate for al-Tujībī's *al-Kirsh.*

Fī ʿAml al-Kirsh al-Maḥshūwah

(*Preparing Stuffed Stomach*)

Serves 6–8

Take a fatty ram's stomach and boil it in hot water. Scrape it with a knife until it becomes white and clean out everything from in it. Leave it in one piece without piercing it. Cut the top part off of it. Then take good meat and pound it extremely well as much as possible. Then take a tender chicken and stuff it as was presented in the second chapter of the third section of this book. Likewise, take two young pigeons that have also been stuffed. Take mergaz, meatballs, Asfarīyah *[see below] and curdled egg yolks. Then take young ram's meat such as the breast and the tail and anything that resembles them and cut it up in medium-sized pieces and put it in a new pot and put over (the chopped meat), water, salt, oil, black pepper, dried coriander and a little chopped onion. Put the pot over the fire to cook. Then take tender moist cabbage and pick off (the outer leaves). Take the cores and put them in the pot with the meat. Then take the chickens and the young birds and put them in a pot. Put over them water, salt, oil, black pepper, dried coriander and a little pounded onion and put the pot on the fire to cook. Then take a small pot and put in it the mergaz and the meatballs and put over them a little water and oil and put it on the fire to cook. Leave it on the fire until the water dries. Then fry them gently in the remaining oil in the small pot. Then remove it from the fire. Then look at the pot of meat. If you find the meat is done, put fresh coriander juice over it then remove it (from the fire); likewise, with the chicken and young birds. Then, take the meat that was pounded at the beginning and put with it salt, black pepper, cinnamon, ginger and a little mastic, spikenard and cloves diluting them in a little water and put over the meat. Then take ten eggs and a little bit of bread crumbs and mix with the meat and spices. Then take the stomach and put in it some of the meat and egg mixture, then from the cooked meat, the cabbage and the chard, then one young bird, then chicken, the second young bird, then the meat and greens. Add a lot of blanched almonds and pine nuts, then the egg yolks, the mergaz, the meatballs and the* Asfarīyah, *after having fried them, and divide up evenly stuffing from one end to the other. Then take the remainder of the stuffing and put in it the clear broth of the meat and the broth of the chicken and young birds and put this in the stomach. Then tie the stomach up with a strong string and put it in a big tajine. Put the rest of the broth and (some) water over it to cover it. Put it over the fire to cook. Once you see that it is done, remove it. Remove the water from the tajine and remove any remaining fat and put it back in the tajine after cleaning it. Then return the stomach to the oven until it browns, after having put a little* murrī naqīʿ *on it. When it browns take it out of the oven then put it in a large dish and slice it. Sprinkle cinnamon over it and eat in good health, God Almighty willing.*

—al-Tujībī, *Faḍālah al-Khiwān fī Ṭayyibāt al-Ṭaʿām wa al-Alwān*

Lawn Ākhir

(Another Preparation for Stuffing Chicken)

Take a big-sized young chicken and slaughter it and prepare it as was done previously. Swell it (with air) at its neck until the skin pulls free from the meat. Then cut it from its neck to the end of its breast. Separate the skin from its thigh and leg, rump and sides. Gently remove the meat but keep the bones intact. Then take another chicken or a big-sized young chicken that is (tender) like dough and clean out its sinews. Then put salt, black pepper, cinnamon, a small piece of mastic, dried coriander over and crack open over it six eggs or about that amount and knead everything by hand until blended and stuff the cavity of the chicken with it. With the stuffing put a pickled lime and five olives. Then put the meat (mixture) on the thighs and legs, the breast and the rump. Carefully put the skin back. Sew it up and sew the neck up. Put it in a wide-mouth pot. Put water, salt, oil, black pepper, dried coriander and a little chopped onion on it and then put it over the fire to cook. It should be turned gently so that it cooks. When it is completely cooked, take it out of the pot and put it in a big tajine and colour it with saffron. Put with it a little of the strained broth and put it back in the oven. Put with it whatever it (still) needs. Keep turning the chicken until it is browned on all sides. When it is browned, take it out and put it in a large serving platter and put with it whatever broth remains in the tajine. Decorate it with sliced eggs and the flowers of mint. Eat in good health, God Almighty willing.

—al-Tujībī, *Faḍālah al-Khiwān fī Ṭayyibāt al-Ṭaʿām wa al-Alwān*

Lawn Ākhir Mashriqī

(Another Eastern Way)

Take a chicken as described before and prepare it as previously presented. Then take its gizzards, after having washed them, and chop them up in small pieces. Put good oil, black pepper, dried coriander, chopped greens, salt, a little chopped onion, finely chopped blanched almonds and three eggs on them. Beat them all together and stuff the chicken cavity with it. Sew it up, put it on a spit and grill it over a gentle fire after this. When it has cooked and browned, take vinegar, murrī, *dried coriander, caraway, fresh coriander juice and thyme and mix them all together. Then take the chicken off the spit and place it in a large serving dish. If desired, put the broth over it, and if not, leave it as is. Dip the bread and meat in it and eat in good health, God Almighty willing.*

—al-Tujībī, *Faḍālah al-Khiwān fī Ṭayyibāt al-Ṭaʿām wa al-Alwān*

Lawn Ākhir Mashriqī

(Another Eastern Way)

Take a chicken as described before and prepare it as previously presented. Then take its gizzards and cut them into small pieces and put over them spices and eggs and stuff the chicken and sew it up. Then take the gizzards of a goose and put them in a pot and add to them salt, murrī, *vinegar, black pepper, caraway and dried coriander and put in the pot the chicken. Put the pot in the oven and add what is missing. Turn the chicken over time to time. Taste the broth and if you find it to be tasty, this is good otherwise add whatever is missing, being careful that it does not burn. Once it is cooked and browned, take it out and place it in a serving platter and put over it its broth and eat in good health, God Almighty willing.*

—al-Tujībī, *Faḍālah al-Khiwān fī Ṭayyibāt al-Ṭaʿām wa al-Alwān*

Asfarīyah

Take the type of meat previously mentioned and clean it from its sinews and pound it on a wooden surface with an iron cane used for pounding meat. Once you have finished pounding it and removed the sinews, put it in a bowl and put over it a measure of salt, black pepper, cinnamon, a little mastic, spikenard, cloves, and egg whites. Then knead all of this until it becomes like marrow. If it is not pounded enough then pound it in a mortar made of wood along with its spices and egg whites. Then take a frying pan and brush it with oil and heat it a little. When it is heated somewhat over the fire, then take the meat and put it in the frying pan and spread it out with your hand and spread oil over it. Gently remove the patty that you have made and it should be smooth and thin. Then put it on a slab and cut it with a knife lengthwise. Then put it in a large clay dish to spruce up the food (on the table) when it is presented in the dish. God Almighty willing. Then present the Asfarīyah *with sliced eggs.*

—al-Tujībī, *Faḍālah al-Khiwān fī Ṭayyibāt al-Ṭaʿām wa al-Alwān*

Measurements

MEASUREMENTS IN MEDIEVAL ARABIC RECIPES

1 *raṭl*	= 12 *ūqīyah* (406.25 grams (14.33 oz.) in the eastern Arab world and al-Andalus)
1 *ūqīyah*	= 10 *dirhams* (in the eastern Arab world, 33.85 grams (1.19 oz.); in al-Andalus, 39 grams (1.38 oz.))
1 *dirham*	= 6 *dāniq* (in the eastern Arab world, approximately 3 grams (.11 oz.); in al-Andalus, 3.9 grams (.14 oz.))
1 *dāniq*	= 1/6 *dirham* (1/2 gram (.02 oz))
1 *dīnār*	= also called *mithqāl* (in the eastern Arab world, 4.25 to 4.5 grams (.15 to .16 oz.); in al-Andalus, 5.7 grams (.20 oz.))
1 *thumn*	= 1/8 *qadaḥ* (11.75 deciliters: 1.18 liters (.31 U.S. gal.) also meaning the eighth part of any measurement)
1 *qadaḥ*	= 0.94 liters (.25 U.S. gal.) (in al-Andalus, the *qadaḥ* was a liquid measurement of 32 liters (8.5 gal.))
1 *kayl*	= a dry measure, used generally for measuring grain. It is also the name of the vessel used for measuring dry ingredients, in particular grains.

There are other measurements, but the above are the standard used for the source recipes used in this study. These measurements are based upon A. J. Arberry's "A Baghdad Cookery Book" (*Medieval Arab Cookery* 36), Friedman's notes to *The Anonymous Andalusian Cookbook of the Thirteenth Century* (181–182), Perry's measurements in "The Description of Familiar Foods" (287), and Nasrallah's detailed weights and measures in *Annals* (800). For further details concerning measurements used in the Muslim world, see Walther Hinz, *Islamische Masse und Gewichte* (Leiden: Brill, 1955).

METRIC CONVERSION CHART

Standard		Metric
Volume		
1/4 teaspoon	=	1 milliliter
1/2 teaspoon	=	2 milliliters
1 teaspoon	=	5 milliliters
1/2 tablespoon	=	14 milliliters
1 tablespoon	=	28 milliliters
1/4 cup	=	60 milliliters
1/2 cup	=	120 milliliters
1 cup	=	230 milliliters
1 1/4 cups	=	300 milliliters
1 1/2 cups	=	360 milliliters
2 cups	=	460 milliliters
2 1/2 cups	=	600 milliliters
3 cups	=	700 milliliters
4 cups (1 quart)	=	.95 liter
1.06 quarts	=	1 liter
4 quarts (1 gallon)	=	3.8 liters
Weight		
1/4 ounce	=	7 grams
1/2 ounce	=	14 grams
1 ounce	=	28 grams
1 1/4 ounces	=	35 grams
1 1/2 ounces	=	40 grams
2 1/2 ounces	=	70 grams

4 ounces	=	112 grams
5 ounces	=	140 grams
8 ounces	=	228 grams
10 ounces	=	280 grams
15 ounces	=	425 grams
16 ounces (1 pound)	=	454 grams

Length

13 x 9 x 2 inches	=	33 x 23 x 2.5 centimeters
8 x 8 inches	=	20 x 20 centimeters

Oven Temperature

300°F	=	150°C
325°F	=	163°C
350°F	=	175°C
375°F	=	190°C
400°F	=	205°C
425°F	=	218°C
425°F	=	218°C
450°F	=	232°C

Tools and Ingredients

We have attempted, when redacting the recipes, to be as faithful as possible to the original. In some cases, however, we decided to use modern kitchen utensils such as a food processor, blender, and electric mixer/beater. There are also some instances when we decided to replace specific herbs such as elecampane and lavender, and some spices in particular recipes such as musk and camphor, with similar tastes for the sake of availability. Also, certain instructions specify rosewater, but in some instances, we changed this to orange blossom water for the sake of variety.

The following is a glossary of some of the terms used in medieval Arabic cookbooks. They are listed here for clarification purposes:

Alyah (sheep tail fat): This is the rendered fat from the tail of the sheep. It is heavy with a strong taste and is called for in many of the medieval Arabic recipes. These recipes will usually instruct that this fat be melted and the liquid retained for use in a dish. We have replaced the fat with butter, oil, or shortening, depending on the other ingredients.

Aṭrāf al-ṭīb (mixture of spices): Under the Abbasids, culinary creations included new types of appetizers, relishes, hors d'oeuvres, and pickled delicacies. Various seasonings and aromatic spices added new flavors to new dishes. Spices and fresh or dried herbs were added individually or prepackaged as an "all inclusive spice mixture," commonly called *aṭrāf al-ṭīb, abāzīr, afāwīh,* and *afwāh al-ṭīb,* or even more specifically labeled as *al-afāwīh al-arbaʿah* (the four spices), including spikenard, cloves, cassia, and nutmeg (al-Warrāq 313).

Loosely translated as "parts of scents," it is actually a mixture of spices. Ibn al-ʿAdīm lists the combination of these spices to be spikenard, betel, laurel leaf, nutmeg, mace, cardamom, cloves, rose hips, common ash, long pepper, ginger and pepper. A second type of mixture includes only cardamom and cloves.

In the modern Middle East, *bahārāt* is the common term for the premixed spices available in groceries and spice markets, made of black pepper, allspice, cinnamon, and nutmeg. Its mixture differs from the Tunisian *bahārāt* spice mixture, comprised of cinnamon, dried rose petals, and black pepper, or that of the Arabian Gulf, under the same name but including red crushed pepper or cayenne, cumin, cinnamon, dried lime, cloves, black pepper, cardamom, nutmeg, coriander, and saffron.

The Gulf countries also have another blend with almost the same mixture of spices, *ibzār*.

You can still find *aṭrāf al-ṭīb* in the souks of Damascus and Aleppo, containing variations of the original medieval spices. These are available as well in North America, prepackaged, in any grocery store selling Middle East products.

There may be a connection between this complex mixture of spices and that of the Moroccan spice mixture known as *rā's al-ḥanūt* (see entry below).

For the purpose of our redacted recipes, we have chosen to use the packaged *aṭrāf al-ṭīb* used in Middle Eastern stores. The contemporary version includes (Syrian style) allspice, cloves, cinnamon, nutmeg, ginger, rose hips, and cardamom. Any combination of other prepackaged *aṭrāf al-ṭīb* will work as well.

Chickpeas: In recipes calling for cooked chickpeas, either precooked canned chickpeas or dried chickpeas, soaked and cooked, can be used interchangeably.

To use dried chickpeas for a recipe, soak the chickpeas overnight by covering them with water to about 4 inches above them. A half-teaspoon of baking soda can be added to the water to speed the softening process and cut the cooking time in half. Drain the chickpeas and place them in a large saucepan. Cover with fresh cold water to about 4 inches above the chickpeas. Cover and bring to a boil. Cook over medium-low heat for 1 1/2 to 2 hours or until tender but not mushy, skimming off any foam. Drain, then use. These can be stored covered in a container in the refrigerator for up to three days .

To split chickpeas: the easiest method is to lay a tea towel on a counter and spread the drained uncooked chickpeas evenly on it. Cover with another tea towel. Using a rolling pin, gently roll over the entire towel back and forth a few times in order to separate the skin from the chickpeas. Uncover and remove the chickpeas and discard the skin. If some chickpeas have not been separated from their skin, then repeat the process, or with the forefinger and thumb, pop the chickpeas out of their skin.

Couscousière: A *couscousière* is a large double boiler perforated on the bottom of the upper pot, thus allowing its contents to steam. This is generally used for cooking couscous. *Couscousières* can be purchased in specialty kitchenware shops or online.

Dibs: A condensed, thick syrup prepared from carobs, dates, pomegranates, grapes, or sumac by boiling the natural fruit until it has thickened. Prepared *dibs* can be purchased at any Middle Eastern grocery outlet.

Filo dough: Also called phyllo, strudel, and, in the Arab East, *baqlāwah* dough, filo is unleavened paper-thin sheets of dough used for many Arab pastries. It is usually sold in 1 lb. packages in the freezer section of supermarkets. To thaw, refrigerate 12–24 hours before use; never thaw at room temperature. When working with filo, the trick is to work quickly with the sheets. If a recipe calls for the use of a sheet, one at a time, make sure to cover the sheets not in use with a piece of plastic over which is laid a lightly dampened tea towel. Filo dries very quickly.

We chose filo dough as a replacement for the medieval Arab *kunāfah* called for in a number of the sweets recipes. The medieval method to prepare the *kunāfah* batter involved pouring it onto heated mirrors made of warmed sheet metal. These dried paper-thin pieces were also cut into very thin noodles (*rishtā*) to be used for various dishes, especially for sweets. The decision to use filo dough, then, was simply a time saver and to avoid the long procedure of preparing sheets of *kunāfah*. Another option is to replace the filo with Moroccan *ouarka* (*warqah*).

Garlic: It is best to use a wooden, brass, or porcelain mortar and pestle when the recipe calls for pounded or crushed garlic. Since ancient times, the mortar and pestle have been used to crush coffee, garlic cloves, and herbs and spices. We prefer the wooden type that is available at any Middle Eastern outlet.

Kāmakh: A fermented condiment; a sour-salty relish paste made with various ingredients, placed on the tables as a condiment or used as a spread on bread. The most popular *Kāmakh* was known as *Kāmakh al-Aḥmar* (Red *Kāmakh*) made by mixing fermented barley, milk, and salt. Perry describes its taste and smell as being similar to a pungent salty blue cheese ("Cooking" 18, 21). *Kāmakh al-Aḥmar* is used as a base to make other kinds of *Kāmakh* such as *Kāmakh* of cloves, of cassia, caraway seeds, roses, aromatic spices and plants, capers, and thyme (al-Warrāq 98–99). Other types of *Kāmakh* include one called White *Kāmakh* (al-Warrāq 99), presumably familiar to cooks since no recipe for it appears to be given. Another variety called *Kāmakh Rījāl* takes approximately three months from start to finish in preparation time and the sitting period (al-Baghdādī 68–69).

Kebab: In the medieval cooking sources, kebabs are meatballs made of finely ground meat, usually the size of hazelnuts.

Lentils: There are three basic types of lentils: brown, green, and red. The brown variety is readily available in any grocery. While the green is sometimes available, the red is found in food stores specializing in international ingredients. Remember, however, that red lentils cook faster than the brown and green varieties. Make sure to rinse lentils with cold water before using.

Mastic: Mastic has a sweet, aromatic, licorice-like flavor and is popular throughout the Middle East. It is used as a flavoring and as a binding agent in a variety of desserts, breads, chewing gum, and some savory dishes. Mastic can be purchased in Middle Eastern and Mediterranean grocery stores.

Murrī: A cereal-based fermented salty sauce used as a condiment, also named *mā' al-kāmakh* (al-Warrāq 14). Perry prefers to equate its taste to soy sauce and the fish *murrī* to that of fish sauce (*Anonymous Andalusian* 75).

There is a strong possibility that *murrī* may have a connection with the Mesopotamian *siqqu* (Nasrallah, *Annals* 580) and with the Roman *garum*, fish sauce, or the Greek *garos*, another fish-based seasoning (Perry, "Description" 282). Most of the recipes where salt would seem to be needed do not give salt as an ingredient if *murrī* is being used (*Anonymous Andalusian* Preface 4).

To make *murrī*, the first step is to make the *fūdhaj* or rotted barley (Perry, *Baghdad Cookery* 107, 115) (also *būdaj* that Nasrallah translates as "rotted bread or dough" made of wheat or barley; *Annals* 201, 575); in al-Tujībī referred to as *būdhaq* (262); also referred to as *qamn* (al-Warrāq 97)). This is the main ingredient for making fermented condiments such as *murrī* and *kawāmikh* (pl. of *kāmakh*, see entry above). Al-Warrāq (97) and al-Tujībī (262) provide the details on how to make it. The *Kanz* describes the process as well but does not give a name for the final product (63–64).

Al-Baghdādī (Perry, *Baghdad Cookery* 107), al-Tujībī (262–270) and the *Kanz* (63–65) have detailed recipes, especially al-Tujībī, on how to make *murrī* using the base ingredient *fūdhaj* (*būdhaq*). This would be mixed with flour, salt, and water and placed in containers that would be stored for weeks, allowing the contents to rot in order for bacteria and yeast to form. This would make the basic *murrī* that would then be flavored with spices.

Generally, specialists in the field of medieval Arab cookery suggest that soy sauce be used in place of *murrī*, advising that because of *murrī*'s salty, sour taste, this would be a good substitute, and we followed their advice. The problem we encountered, however, with using soy sauce was that the dishes all seemed to taste the same regardless whether we reduced the amount or added to it. The soy sauce taste was always there.

On the other hand, we had heard of miso, a Japanese seasoning produced by fermenting barley, rice, or soy beans with salt and mold. We decided to try the barley-based red miso, which provided the salty, tart taste the original *murrī* would have offered. It served as a good flavor enhancer and seemed to be not as strong as soy sauce.

Everything is dependent on the cook's taste. After all, "the customs and the tastes are different, and if one sort of person detests, hates, and avoids it, it may be that another may prefer, enjoy, and be inclined toward it" (*Anonymous Andalusian* 6–7).

Thus, there is no written rule that states that miso should be the only replacement for *murrī*. We urge the reader to go ahead and try soy sauce, miso, or even, as Perry suggests, to replace the *murrī* with Worcestershire sauce. Of course the best option would be to re-create al-Tujībī's *al-Murrī al-Naqīʿ* (262–264) or any of the other recipes he gives for *murrī* (264–270).

Rā's al-ḥanūt: This mixture of spices used in Morocco, Algeria, and Tunisia translates as "top or head of the shop," so named because owners of spice shops all have their own exclusive aromatic blend of spices. The celebrated spice of Morocco and the country's most used condiment, *rā's al-ḥanūt* can include from at least 10 to over 20 spices along with aromatic herbs and leaves; the spice mixture is not always the same. The most commonly used are cardamom, cinnamon, clove, coriander, cumin, ginger, mustard, nutmeg, turmeric, and various types of pepper. However, also included, at times, are such enhancers as lavender, rosebuds, and Spanish fly. For Moroccans this is the ultimate of all spices. It is often equated with *aṭrāf al-ṭīb* (see entry above).

Roasted chicken: Many of the source recipes include prepared "roasted chicken" as an ingredient. This, typically, would mean roasting a chicken that has been rubbed with oil, salt, and pepper. However, according to personal preference more spices can be added, such as cinnamon, ginger, garlic powder, and allspice. The other option is to purchase a pre-roasted chicken.

Salt (as an ingredient): In many of the recipes, salt is not listed, even though expected, as an ingredient. This is because the fermented condiments such as *murrī* and *kāmakh* provide the saltiness to the dish. If salt is a requirement, as in dishes including meats or pulses, the cookbooks recommend that it be added to the pot once these ingredients have been cooked (*Kanz* 8). In the case of vegetables and pulses, such as eggplant, gourds, and chickpeas, the *Kanz*, for instance, directs placing them in water and salt for a good amount of time before cooking. (8). In addition, it is recommended that meat be washed in warm salted water before cooking to cleanse it of any blood or impurities (al-Baghdādī 8).

Sesame oil: (Arabic: *shīraj* or *shayraj*) Mediterranean sesame oil is pressed from raw seeds, while Chinese sesame oil is pressed from toasted seeds, resulting in a stronger flavored, darker oil. For the medieval Arabic recipes, we recommend that the light sesame oil be purchased, as the dark is far too strong in its flavor.

Sumac: The crushed dried berries of the Mediterranean sumac tree, used widely in Middle Eastern cuisine, sumac is a condiment with a lemony and tangy flavor and as a seasoning gives a tart taste to dishes. Sumac is found in Middle Eastern supermarkets and grocery stores, from spice or gourmet emporiums.

Tahini: This is the byproduct of hulled and crushed sesame seeds and is considered the mayonnaise of the Middle East. For the Arabs, it is used almost daily in various dishes, providing a nutty flavor. It is a thick paste that should be stirred with a wooden spoon before use. It is also referred to as sesame seed paste and can be purchased in either the light or dark variety from any Middle Eastern grocery store and even at some of the larger supermarkets. It can be stored in the pantry and has a long shelf life.

Tajine: A North African cooking dish made of heavy clay. It has a flat, circular bottom and low sides, with a cone-shaped cover that is used as a lid during the cooking process. Once the dish is cooked, the cover is removed and the bottom is used as the serving dish. Dishes prepared in tajines are cooked at low temperatures.

Yogurt: It is important to stir the ingredients constantly with a wooden spoon when preparing any dish being cooked with yogurt. The old Arab cooking tradition, handed down through generations, is that with yogurt one should stir always in one direction.

Notes

Introduction

1. For example, the tenth-century Ibn Waḥshīyah's *al-Filāḥah al-Nabaṭīyah* (*Nabatean Agriculture*), the eleventh-century Ibn Ḥajjāj al-Ishbīlī's *al-Muqniʿ fī al-Filāḥah* (*The Handbook of Agriculture*), the twelfth-century Ibn al-ʿAwwām al-Ishbīlī's encyclopaedic *Kitāb al-Filāḥah* (*Book of Agriculture*), and from the same century, Ibn Baṣṣāl's *Kitāb al-Filāḥah* (*Book of Agriculture*).
2. Almost half a century later, Ibn ʿAbd Rabbīh, in the western Arab land of al-Andalus, would choose to report the same, yet with the Umayyad caliph Hishām (724–743) as protagonist (Ibn ʿAbd Rabbīh VI 182).

Appetizers

1. The manuscript used for this recipe is that edited by Dāwūd al-Jalabī (1934). However, Perry includes caraway and cinnamon in his translation of al-Baghdādi's text, based on the *Kitāb al-Ṭabīkh* ms. located in Istanbul.
2. Perry's recipe is called *bādhinjān muḥassah*, based on his reading of an al-Warrāq ms. He translates it as "puréed."
3. *al-shaḥm* in the edited Arabic text; *al-saljam* according to the Helsinki text (al-Warrāq 71 n55)

Soups

1. This instruction is in the Helsinki manuscript copy (al-Warrāq 288 n6-6).

Chapter 3. Entrées

1. Qur'an 7:57. A similar story appears in the *Muḥāḍarāt*. However, that incident involves Caliph Muʿāwiyah and a Bedouin (II 630).

2. *Sitt al-Shanʿ* is a dish using colcosia, listed in Ibn al-ʿAdīm's chapter on "'Dried' Dishes and Fried Dishes, Patties, Etc.'" See *al-Wuṣlah ilà al-Ḥabīb*, page 569.
3. In the Helsinki copy of the manuscript: *baql al-ramān* [sic], seasonal vegetables or vegetables available by the season (*baql al-zamān*) such as leeks, carrots, eggplant, or gourds (al-Warrāq 150 n11–11)
4. The Öhrnberg and Mroueh edited volume of al-Warrāq has the term *baṣal* (onions) used to make the filling sour. Nasrallah corrects this ingredient to *maṣl* (yogurt whey), based on the Istanbul manuscript, which makes more sense since whey is a souring agent (Nasrallah 191).
5. The Arabic term used is *rakhbīn*, which Nasrallah translates as dried buttermilk (191).
6. Our thanks to Nawal Nasrallah for clarifying the Arabic term that appears at the end of this source recipe. In the Öhrnberg-Moureh edition, the Arabic reads "*b-d-r-h*" but Nasrallah states that the Istanbul copy of the al-Warrāq manuscript rectifies this term. Instead, it should read "*yudraju*" or "*tudraju*," meaning "to roll up."
7. *murrī naqīʿ* is a type of macerated *murrī* special to the cuisine al-Andalus and to North Africa. The "Description" contains a detailed recipe for it (400–401).
8. Persian milk is yogurt. Perry believes it to have been made from either sheep or goat milk ("Description" 285).

Chapter 4. Desserts

1. Sugar, honey, or *dibs* with beaten egg whites; a confection made with sugar, honey, or, nougat-like if beaten with egg whites or a nutty-brittle candy.
2. See "Description" 416, 422.
3. *talbīnah*: when wheat is soaked in water until it softens and the wheat then releases its starch into the water (Charles Perry, "Preparation of Khubaiz [Little Bread] That Is Made in Niebla," in *An Anonymous Cookbook of the Thirteenth Century*); a thick paste.
4. The following recipe is taken from Habeeb Salloum's *Classic Vegetarian Cooking from the Middle East and North Africa* under the heading "Deep-Fried Sweet Balls—*Awamee*."
5. Also spelled *samīd*; the purest and finest variety of white wheat flour. It is high in starch content, free of bran, and low in gluten, used to make sweets (*Annals* 573).
6. Another type of fine wheat flour, bran-free and lower in starch, but higher in gluten, used to make bread (*Annals* 561, 573). Dozy explains this to be the best type of flour.
7. A sweet made of round flat dough.

Bibliography

Primary Sources

al-ʿAskarī, Abu Hilāl. *al-Awāʾil*. Ed. Muḥammad al-Miṣrī and Walīd Qassāb. 2 vols. Damascus: Wizārah al-Thaqāfah wa al-Irshād al-Qawmī, 1975.

——. *Jamharāt al-Amthāl*. Ed. Aḥmad ʿAbd al-Salām. 2 vols. Beirut: Dār al-Kutub al-ʿIlmīyah, 1988.

al-Baghdādī, Muḥammad ibn al-Ḥasan ibn Muḥammad ibn al-Karīm al-Kātib. *Kitāb al-Ṭabīkh*. Ed. Dāwūd al-Jalabī (Chelabi). Mosul: Maṭbaʿah Umm al-Rabīʿayn, 1934.

al-Ibshīhī, Shihāb al-Dīn Muḥammad ibn Aḥmad. "al-Mustaṭraf fī Kull Fann Mustaẓraf." *al-Warrāq*. Electronic Village in Abu Dhabi, 2000–2010. Web, 4 January 2011. 181.

al-Iṣfahānī, Abū al-Faraj ʿAlī. *Kitāb al-Aghānī*. 25 vols. Beirut: Dār al-Thaqāfah, 1983.

al-Jāḥiẓ, ʿAmr ibn Baḥr. *al-Bukhalāʾ*. Ed. Ṭāhā al-Ḥājirī. Cairo: Dār al-Maʿārif, 1967.

——. *Kitāb al-Ḥayawān*. Ed. ʿAbd al-Salām Muḥammad Hārūn. 7 vols. Cairo: Maktabah Muṣṭafà al-Bābī al-Ḥalabī, 1938.

——. *Kitāb al-Tāj fī Akhlāq al-Mulūk*. Ed. Aḥmad Zāk Bāshā. Cairo: Al-Amīrīyah, 1914.

——. *Rasāʾil al-Jāḥiẓ*. Ed. ʿAbd al-Salām Muḥammad Hārūn. 4 vols. Cairo: Maktabah al-Khanjà, 1964–1965.

al-Jahshiyārī, Abī ʿAbd Allāh Muḥammad ibn ʿAbdūs. *Kitāb al-Wuzarāʾ wa al-Kuttāb*. Ed. Hans von Mžik. Leipzig: Otto Harrassowitz, 1926.

al-Jarīrī., Abū al-Faraj Muʿāfà ibn Zakarīyā al-Nahrawānī *Al-Jalīs al-Ṣāliḥ al-Kāfī wa-al-Anīs al- Nāṣiḥ al-Shāfī*. Ed. Muḥammad Mursī al-Khawlī. 4 vols. Beirut: ʿĀlam al-Kutub, 1981.

al-Khaṭīb al-Baghdādī, Abū Bakr Aḥmad ibn ʿAlī. *Tārīkh Baghdād*. 14 vols. Beirut: Dār al-Kitāb al-ʿArabī, 1931.

al-Khushanī, Abī ʿAbd Allāh Muḥammad ibn Ḥārith ibn Asad al-Qarawī. *Quḍāt Qurṭubah*. Ed. Ibrāhīm al-Ibyārī. Beirut: Dār al-Kutub al-Islāmīyah; Dār al-Kitāb al-Lubnānī. Cairo: Dār al-Kitāb al-Miṣrī, 1982.

al-Kutubī, Muḥammad ibn Shākir. *Fawāt al-Wafayāt*. Ed. Iḥsān ʿAbbās. 5 vols. Beirut: Dār al-Thaqāfah, 1973.

al-Maqqarī, Aḥmad ibn Muḥammad. *Nafḥ al-Ṭīb*. 2 vols. Amsterdam: Oriental Press, 1967.

al-Maqrīzī, Taqī al-Dīn Aḥmad ibn ʿAlī. *Ittiʿāẓ al-Ḥunafāʾ bi-Akhbār al-Aʾimmah al-Fāṭimīyīn al-Khulafāʾ*. Ed. Muḥammad Ḥilmī Muḥammad Aḥmad. 3 vols. Cairo: al-Lajnah Iḥyāʾ al-Turāth al-Islāmī, 1996.

al-Masʿūdi. *Murūj al-Dhahab wa Maʾādin al-Jawhar* (*Les Prairies d'or*). Trans. and ed. C. Barbier de Meynard and Pavet de Courteille. 9 vols. Paris: L'Imprimerie Nationale, 1861–1917.

al-Muqaddasī, Shams al-Dīn Abū ʿAbd Allāh Muḥammad ibn Aḥmad ibn Abī Bakr. *Aḥsān al-Taqāsīm fī Maʿrifah al-Aqālīm*. Ed. M. J. de Goethe. Leiden: Brill, 1906.

al-Nuwayrī, Shihāb al-Dīn Aḥmad Ibn ʿAbd al-Wahhāb. *Nihāyah al-ʿArab fī Funūn al-Adab*. 18 vols. Cairo: al-Mu'assasah al-Miṣriyah al-ʿĀmmah li-al-Ta'līf wa al-Tarjamah wa al-Ṭibāʿah wa al-Nashr, 1964.

al-Qalqashandī, Aḥmad ibn ʿAlī. "Ṣubḥ al-Aʿshà." *al-Warrāq*. Electronic Village in Abu Dhabi. 2000-10. Web, 4 January 2011, 449, 248.

al-Rāghib al-Aṣbahānī, Abī al-Qāsim Ḥusayn ibn Muḥammad. *Muḥāḍarāt al-'Udabāʾ wa Muḥāwarāt al-Shuʿarāʾ wa al-Balaghāʾ*. 4 vols. Beirut: Dār Maktabah al-Ḥayāah, 1961.

al-Ṣābīʾ, Hilāl ibn al-Muḥassin. *Rusūm Dār al-Khilāfah*. Ed. Mīkhāʾīl ʿAwwād. Baghdad: Maṭbaʿah al-ʿĀnī, 1964.

al-Tanūkhī, al-Muḥassin ibn ʿAlī. *Nishwār al-Muḥāḍarah wa Akhbār al-Mudhākarah*. Ed. ʿAbbūd al-Shāljī. 8 vols. Beirut: n.p., 1971.

al-Thaʿālabī, Abū Manṣūr ʿAbd al-Malik ibn Muḥammad ibn Ismāʿīl. *Adāb al-Mulūk*. Ed. Jalīl al-ʿAṭīyah. Beirut: Dār al-Gharb al-Islāmī, 1990.

——. *Thimār al-Qulūb fī al-Muḍāf wa al-Mansūb*. Ed. Muḥammad Abū al-Faḍil Ibrāhīm. Cairo: Dār Nahḍah Miṣr li-al-Ṭabʿ wa al-Nashr, 1965.

al-Tujībī, Ibn Razīn. *Faḍālah al-Khiwān fī Ṭayyibāt al-Ṭaʿām wa al-Alwān*. Ed. Muḥammad B. A. Benchekroun. Beirut: Dār al-Gharb al-Islāmī, 1984.

al-Warrāq, Abū Muḥammad al-Muẓaffar ibn Naṣr ibn Sayyār, *Kitāb al-Ṭabīkh fī Iṣlāḥ al-Aghdhiyah al-Maʾkūlāt wa Ṭayyib al-Aṭʿimah al-Maṣnūʿāt*. Ed. Kaj Öhrnberg and Sahban Mroueh. Helsinki: Finnish Oriental Society, 1987.

al-Washshā', Ṭayyib Muḥammad ibn Isḥāq ibn Yaḥyà. *Kitāb al-Muwashshà*. Beirut: Dār Ṣādir, 1965.

Ibn ʿAbd Rabbih, Abī ʿUmar Aḥmad ibn Muḥammad Ibn ʿAbd Rabbih al-Andalusī, *Kitāb al-ʿIqd al-Farīd*. 7 vols. Cairo: Lijnah al-Taʾlīf wa al-Tarjimah wa al-Nashr, 1948–73.

Ibn Abī Usaybiʿah. *ʿUyūn al-Akhbār fī Ṭabaqāt al-Aṭibbāʾ*. Ed. Nizār Riḍā. Beirut: Dār Maktabah al-Ḥayāah, 1965.

Ibn al-ʿAdīm, Kamāl al-Dīn ʿUmar ibn Aḥmad. *Kitāb al-Wuṣlah ilà al-Ḥabīb fi Wasf al-Ṭayyibāt wa al-Ṭīb*. Ed. Sulaymān Maḥjūb and Durrīyah al-Khaṭīb. 2 vols. Aleppo: University of Aleppo, 1988.

Ibn Baṭṭūṭah, Abū ʿAbd Allāh Muḥammad ibn Ibrāhīm. *Riḥlah Ibn Baṭṭūṭah*. Beirut: Dār Ṣādir, 1964.

Ibn Diḥyah al-Kalbī. *Al-Muṭrib fī Ashʿār Ahl al-Maghrib*. Ed. Muṣṭafà ʿAwḍ al-Karīm. Khartoum: Maṭbaʿah Miṣr, 1954.

Ibn Ḥayyān. *al-Muqtabas fī Tārīkh al-Andalus (al-juz' al-khāmis)*. Ed. Gendrón P. Chalmeta, F. Corriente, and M. Subh. Madrid/Rabat: Instituto Hispano-Arabe de Culture, 1979.

Ibn ʿIdhārī al-Marrākushī. *Kitāb al-Bayān al-Mughrib fī Akhbār al-Andalus wa al-Maghrib*. Ed. Georges Séraphin Colin and Évariste Lévi-Provençal. 4 vols. Leiden: Brill, 1951.

Ibn Khallikān. *Wafayāt al-Aʿyān*. Ed. Iḥsān ʿAbbās. 8 vols. Beirut: Dār al-Thaqāfah, 1968.

Ibn al-Nadīm, Muḥammad ibn Isḥāq. *al-Fihrist*. Cairo: al-Maktabah al-Tijārīyah al-Kubrah, 1929.

Ibn Quṭaybah al-Dīnawarī, Abū Muḥammad ʿAbd Allāh ibn Muslim. *ʿUyūn al-Akhbār*. 4 vols. Cairo:

Al-Muʾassasah al-Miṣrīyah al-ʿĀmah li-al-Taʾlīf wa al-Ṭibāʿah wa al-Nashr, 1924. Reprint 1964.
Kanz al-Fawāʾid fī Tanwīʿ al-Mawāʾid. Ed. Manuela Marín and David Waines. Beirut: Franz Steiner Stuttgart, 1993.
Lisān al-ʿArab. Ibn Manẓūr, Muḥammad ibn Mukarram. 15 vols. Beirut: Dār Ṣādir, 1955–1956.
Yāqūt al-Ḥamawī, Shihāb al-Dīn ibn ʿAbd Allāh al-Rūmī. *Muʿjam al-Buldān*. Ed. Muḥammad Amīn al-Khānajī. 10 vols. Miṣr (Cairo): Maktabah al-ʿArab, 1906.
——. *Muʿjam al-Udabāʾ: Irshād al-Arīb ilà Maʿrifah al-Adīb*. Ed. Iḥsān ʿAbbās. 7 vols. Beirut: Dār al-Gharb al-Islāmī, 1993.

Secondary Sources

Adamson, Melitta. *Food in Medieval Times*. Westport, Conn.: Greenwood Press, 2004.
——. *Medieval Dietetics: Food and Drink in Regimen Sanitatis Literature from 800 to 1400*. Ed. Manfred Kuxdorf. German Studies in Canada. 5. Frankfurt/M: Peter Lang, 1995.
——, ed. *Regional Cuisines of Medieval Europe: A Book of Essays*. New York: Routledge, 2002.
al-Baghdādī, Muḥammad ibn al-Ḥasan ibn Muḥammad ibn al-Karīm al-Kātib. *"Kitāb al-Ṭabīkh: A Baghdad Cookery Book."* Trans. A. J. Arberry. In *Medieval Arab Cookery*. 19–89.
——. *Kitāb al-Ṭabīkh: A Baghdad Cookery Book: the Book of Dishes*. Trans. Charles Perry. Blackawton, Totnes: Prospect Books, 2005.
al-Ḥamadhāni, Aḥmad ibn al-Ḥusayn ibn Yaḥyà ibn Saʿīd ibn Bashar Abū al-Faḍl. *The Maqāmāt of Badīʿ al-Zamān al-Ḥamadhāni*. Trans. W. J. Prendergast. London: Curzon, 1973.
al-Ṭabarī. *The History of al-Ṭabarī (Tārīkh al-Rusūl wa al-Mulūk)*. 40 vols. Albany: State University of New York Press, 1951–89.
Anonymous Andalusian Cookbook: Kitāb al-Ṭabikh fī al-Maghrib wa al-Andalus fī ʿAṣr al-Muwaḥḥidīn, li-muʿallif majhūl. (The Book of Cooking in Maghreb and Andalus in the era of Almohads by an unknown author). Trans. Charles Perry.
Ashtor, E. "Essai sur l'alimentation des diverses classes sociales dans l'orient médiéval." *Annales: Histoire, Sciences Sociales* 23, 5 (September–October 1968): 1017–53.
Bottéro, Jean. "The Cuisine of Ancient Mesopotamia." *Biblical Archaeologist* 48, 1 (March 1985): 36–47.
——. *Textes culinaires mésopotamiens*. Winona Lake. Ind.: Eisenbrauns, 1995.
Cattan, Henry, ed. and trans. *The Garden of Joys: An Anthology of Oriental Anecdotes, Fables and Proverbs*. London: Namara Publications, 1979.
Chabbouh, Ibrahim. *The Cuisine of the Muslims*. London: al-Furqan Islamic Heritage Foundation, 2004.
Chabrán, Rafael. "Medieval Spain." In *Regional Cuisines of Medieval Europe*. 125–52.
Chejne, Anwar. *Muslim Spain: Its History and Culture*. Minneapolis: University of Minnesota Press, 1974.
Corriente, Federico. *A Dictionary of Andalusi Arabic*. Leiden: Koninklijke Brill, 1997.
Davidson, Alan. *The Oxford Companion to Food*. Oxford: Oxford University Press, 1999.
Del Rio, Mariano. "Las Torrijas." *Grupo Gastronómico Gaditano* 13, 3.
Dozy, Reinhart. *Spanish Islam: A History of the Muslims in Spain*. Trans. Francis Griffin Stokes. London: Frank Cass, 1972.
——. *Supplément aux Dictionnaires arabes*. 2 vols. Beirut: Librairie du Liban, 1991.
Eigeland, Tor. "Arabs, Almonds, Sugar and Toledo." *Aramco World* 47, 3 (May–June 1996): 32–39.

——. "The Cuisine of Al-Andalus." *Aramco World* 40, 5 (September–October 1989): 28–35.
Garbutt, Nina. "Ibn Jazlah: The Forgotten ʿAbbasid Gastronome." *Journal of the Economic and Social History of the Orient* 39, 1 (1996): 42–44.
Goitein, S. D. *A Mediterranean Society: The Jewish Communities of the World as Portrayed in the Documents of the Cairo Geniza.* 6 vols. Berkeley: University of California Press, 1967–1993.
Hassan, Fayza. "The Sweet and the Savoury." *Al-Ahram Weekly Online* 559, 8-14 November 2001.
Hillenbrand, Robert. "Medieval Córdoba as a Cultural Centre." In *Legacy of Muslim Spain*, ed. Salma Khadra Jayyusi. 2 vols. Leiden: Brill, 1994. 112–35.
Hitti, Philip K. *History of the Arabs: From the Earliest Times to the Present.* New York: Macmillan, 1961.
Ibn al-Mabrad (or Ibn al-Mubarrad). "*Kitāb al-Tibākhah:* A Fifteenth-Century Cookbook." Trans. Charles Perry. In *Medieval Arab Cookery*. 467–75.
Ibn Jazlah. *Minhāj al Bayān fī mā Yastaʿmiluhu al-Insān: A Systematic Exposition of What Is Used by Man.* Trans. Charles Perry. Unpublished manuscript, 2003.
Ibn Khaldun. *The Muqaddimah*. Trans. Franz Rosenthal. Princeton: Princeton University Press, 1967
Ibn Razin Tujibi. *Fudalat al-Khiwan fi Tayibat at-Tàam wa al alwan: Les délices de la table et les meilleurs genres des mets.* Trans. and ed. Mohamed Mezzine and Laila Benkirane. Fès: Fès-Saïs, 1997.
Jackson, Gabriel. *The Making of Medieval Spain.* London: Thames and Hudson, 1972.
"*Kitāb Waṣf al-Aṭʿimah al-Muʿtādah:* The Description of Familiar Foods." Trans. Charles Perry. In Medieval Arab Cookery. 273–465.
Lambert, Carole. "Medieval France: The South." In *Regional Cuisines of Medieval Europe*. 67–84.
Lane, E. W. *Arabic-English Lexicon.* 2 vols. 1863. Cambridge: Islamic Texts Society, 1984.
Lapidus, Ira Marvin. *A History of Islamic Societies.* Cambridge: Cambridge University Press, 2002.
Lebling, Robert W., Jr. "Flight of the Blackbird." *Saudi Aramco World* 54, 4 (July–August 2003): 24–33.
Lévi-Provençal, Évariste. *La Civilisation arabe en Espagne: Vue générale.* Cairo: Institut Français d'Archéologie Orientale, 1938.
Levy, Martin. *The Medical Formulary of Aqrābādhīn of al-Kindī: Translated with a Study of Its Materia Medica.* Madison: University of Wisconsin Press, 1966.
Littré, Émile. *Dictionnaire de la langue française: Supplément.* Paris: Hachette, 1877.
Lunde, Paul. "The Iceman Cameth." *Saudi Aramco World* 29, 5 (September–October 1978): 2–3.
Marín, Manuela. "Beyond Taste: The Complements of Colour and Smell in the Medieval Arab Culinary Tradition." In *Culinary Cultures of the Middle East*, ed. Sami Zubaida and Richard Tapper. London: Tauris, 1994.
Marks, Gil. *Encyclopedia of Jewish Food.* Hoboken, N.J.: Wiley, 2010.
Medieval Arab Cookery. See Rodinson
Nasrallah, Nawal. *Annals of the Caliphs' Kitchens: Ibn Sayyār al-Warrāq's Tenth-Century Baghdadi Cookbook.* English Translation with Introduction and Glossary. Leiden: Brill, 2007.
——. *Delights from the Garden of Eden: A Cookbook and a History of the Iraqi Cuisine*: Bloomington, Ind.: 1stBooks, 2003.
Nūr, ʿAdlī Ṭāhir. *Kalimāt ʿArabīyah fī al-Lughah al-Isbāniyah.* Cairo: Egyptian Universities Publishing House, 1971.
Perry, Charles. "Cooking with the Caliphs." *Saudi Aramco World* 57, 4 (July–August 2006): 14–23.
——. "Medieval Arab Fish." In *Medieval Arab Cookery*. 478–86.
——. "Notes on Persian Pasta." In *Medieval Arab Cookery*. 251–55.
——. "*Romania* and Other Arabic Words in Italian." In *Medieval Arab Cookery*. 165–82.

——. "The *Ṣalṣ* of the Infidels." In *Medieval Arab Cookery*. 499–502.
——."A Thousand and One 'Fritters': The Food of the Arabian Nights." In *Medieval Arab Cookery*. 487–96.
——. "What to Order in Ninth-Century Baghdad." In *Medieval Arab Cookery*. 217–23.
Plouvier, Liliane. "L'Europe se met à table." Paper for DG Éducation et Culture, Initiative Connect lancée par la Commission Européenne et le Parlement Européen, Brussels, 2000.
Regional Cuisines of Medieval Europe. See Adamson.
Roden, Claudia. *A Book of Middle Eastern Food*. New York: Penguin, 1972.
——. *Mediterranean Cookery*. London: BBC Books, 1989.
Rodinson, Maxime. "Ma'muniyya East and West." Trans. Barbara Inskip. In *Medieval Arab Cookery*. 183–97.
——. "Studies in Arabic Manuscripts Relating to Cookery: *Kitāb al-Wuṣlah ilà al-Ḥabīb*." Trans. Barbara Inskip. In *Medieval Arab Cookery*. 91–164.
——. "Venice and the Spice Trade." Trans. Paul James. In *Medieval Arab Cookery*. 199–215.
Rodinson, Maxime, A. J. Arberry, and Charles Perry, eds. and trans. *Medieval Arab Cookery, Essays and Translations*. Blackawton, Devon: Prospect Books, 2001.
Salloum, Habeeb. *Classic Vegetarian Cooking from the Middle East and North Africa*. Brooklyn, N.Y.: Interlink, 2000.
——. *Journeys Back to Arab Spain*. Toronto: Middle East Studies Centre, 1994.
——. "Medieval and Renaissance Italy: Sicily." In *Regional Cuisines of Medieval Europe*. 113–23.
Salloum, Habeeb and James Peters. *Arabic Contributions to the English Vocabulary*. Beirut: Librairie du Liban, 1996.
——. *From the Lands of Figs and Olives: Over 300 Delicious and Unusual Recipes from the Middle East and North Africa*. New York: Interlink, 1995.
Salloum, Habeeb and Muna Salloum. *Spanish Words of Arabic Origin*. Toronto: Work in progress.
Serbe, Diana. "Sicilian Cooking: The History and Development of Sicilian Cooking." inmamaskitchen.com. Accessed June 25, 2010.
Simeti, Mary Taylor. *Pomp and Sustenance*. New York: Knopf, 1990.
Tales from the Arabian Nights, Selected from the Book of A Thousand Nights and a Night. Trans. Sir Richard F. Burton. London: Bestseller Publications, 1985.
Toussaint-Samat, Maguelonne. *A History of Food*. Trans. Anthea Bell. New York: Barnes & Noble, 1992.
van Gelder, Geert Jon. *God's Banquet: Food in Classical Arabic Literature*. New York: Columbia University Press, 2000.
——. *Of Dishes and Discourse: Classical Arabic Literary Representations of Food*. Richmond, Surrey: Curzon, 2000.
Waines, David. "The Culinary Culture of al-Andalus." In *Legacy of Muslim Spain*, ed. Salma K. Jayyusi. 2 vols. Leiden: Brill, 1994. 725–38.
——. "Dietetics in Medieval Islamic Culture." *Medical History* 43 (1999): 228–40.
——. *In a Caliph's Kitchen*. London: Riad El-Rayyes Books, 1989.
——. "Luxury Foods in Medieval Islamic Societies." *World Archaeology* 34, 3 (2003): 571–80.
Watson, Andrew M. *Agricultural Innovation in the Early Islamic World*. Cambridge: Cambridge University Press, 1983.
Wright, Clifford A. *A Mediterranean Feast*. New York: William Morrow, 1999.
Yamani, Mai. "You Are What You Cook: Cuisine and Class in Mecca." In *Culinary Cultures of the*

Middle East, ed. Sami Zubaida and Richard Tupper. London: Tauris, 1994. 173–84.

Yule, Henry and A. C. Burnell, eds, *Hobson-Jobson: A Glossary of Colloquial Anglo-Indian Words and Phrases and of Kindred Terms, Etymological, Historical and Discursive.* London: Blackie and Son, 1903.

Zayyāt, Ḥabīb. "Fann al-Ṭabakh wā Iṣlāḥ al-Aṭʿimah." *Al-Mashriq* (Al-Machriq). Beirut: Imprimerie Catholique, 1947. 1–26.

Index

Acknowledgments

Without the written records of the great men and women of the past our knowledge of what was may only be that of what may have been. We acknowledge those who composed works of their time and established the base for future generations to know and understand.

To Kaj Öhrnberg for providing us with a copy of his and Sahban Mroueh's edited version of al-Wārraq's *Kitāb al-Ṭabīkh* and for his encouragement to write and cook on this subject we acknowledge him with thanks.

We wish to thank Nawal Nasrallah for her insight into and clarification of certain terms appearing in al-Warrāq's recipes and her encouragement; to Charles Perry for providing us with a copy of his unpublished translation of Ibn Jazlah's *Minhāj* and permission to use his translations; and to Clifford Wright for leading us to some sources that we needed for this study. All four are committed to widening the field of medieval Arab cookery.

To Freda Salloum for her advice on cooking procedures passed on generation to generation from her family and for her patience in reading and re-reading the manuscript; to Yusuf and Aida Botrie for their willingness to spend evenings discussing anecdotes from medieval Arab history; to Issam for his help in translating the more difficult passages of text; and to our numerous colleagues and family members who "smelled the aromas" of the kitchen and were more than eager to taste our redacted re-creations from the medieval Arabic texts.

Though a co-author, Habeeb Salloum has been an inspiration not just to his offspring and to theirs, but to all those who have dabbled in the field of Arab history and culture—he has ignited the spark of the pursuit of knowledge. His pride in the great works of the Arabs and all those who wrote in Arabic is a beacon of light in a world dim with the knowledge of the Arab past and their achievements.

Finally, it is to those great gourmands in Arab history to whom we acknowledge our greatest thanks for recording for posterity their edible pleasures of life for it seems that they hoped that future generations would enjoy the repasts of their eras whether it be then, or centuries later.